Python Forensics

Python Forensics
A Workbench for Inventing and Sharing Digital Forensic Technology

Chet Hosmer

Technical Editor: Gary C. Kessler

AMSTERDAM • BOSTON • HEIDELBERG • LONDON
NEW YORK • OXFORD • PARIS • SAN DIEGO
SAN FRANCISCO • SINGAPORE • SYDNEY • TOKYO

ELSEVIER

Syngress is an Imprint of Elsevier

SYNGRESS

Acquiring Editor: Steve Elliot
Editorial Project Manager: Benjamin Rearick
Project Manager: Priya Kumaraguruparan
Designer: Mark Rogers

Syngress is an imprint of Elsevier
225 Wyman Street, Waltham, MA 02451, USA

Notices
Knowledge and best practice in this field are constantly changing. As new research and
experience broaden our understanding, changes in research methods or professional practices,
may become necessary. Practitioners and researchers must always rely on their own
experience and knowledge in evaluating and using any information or methods described here
in. In using such information or methods they should be mindful of their own safety and the
safety of others, including parties for whom they have a professional responsibility.

To the fullest extent of the law, neither the Publisher nor the authors, contributors, or
editors, assume any liability for any injury and/or damage to persons or property as a matter of
products liability, negligence or otherwise, or from any use or operation of any methods,
products, instructions, or ideas contained in the material herein.

Library of Congress Cataloging-in-Publication Data
Application Submitted

British Library Cataloguing-in-Publication Data
A catalogue record for this book is available from the British Library

ISBN: 978-0-12-418676-7

For information on all Syngress publications,
visit our website at store.elsevier.com/syngress

Printed and bound in the United States of America
14 15 16 17 18   10 9 8 7 6 5 4 3 2 1

Working together
to grow libraries in
developing countries

www.elsevier.com • www.bookaid.org

*To my wife Janet, for your love, kindness, patience, and inspiration
that you give every day. I am the luckiest guy in the world.*

Acknowledgments

My sincere thanks go to:

Dr. Gary Kessler, the technical editor for this book. Gary, your insights, fresh perspective, deep technical understanding, and guidance added great value to the book. Your constant encouragement and friendship made the process enjoyable.

Ben Rearick and Steve Elliot at Elsevier, for your enthusiasm for this topic and all the guidance and support along the way. This spirit helped more than you can know.

The many teachers that I have had over the years in software development and forensics that have helped shape the content of this book. Ron Stevens, Tom Hurbanek, Mike Duren, Allen Guillen, Rhonda Caracappa, Russ Rogers, Jordon Jacobs, Tony Reyes, Amber Schroader, and Greg Kipper.

Joe Giordano, who had the vision in 1998 to create the first U.S. Air Force research contract to study forensic information warfare. This one contract was the catalyst for many new companies, novel innovations in the field, the establishment of the digital forensic research workshop (DFRWS), and the computer forensic research and development center at Utica College. You are a true pioneer.

Endorsements

"Not only does Hosmer provide an outstanding Python forensics guide for all levels of forensics analysis, but also he insightfully illustrates the foundation of a rich collaborative environment that significantly advances the forensic capabilities of the individual, organization, and forensic community as a whole. For analysts, investigators, managers, researchers, academics, and anyone else with an interest in digital forensics: this is a must read!"

Michael Duren (CISSP), Founder of Cyber Moxie

"With today's rapid changes in technology digital forensics tools and practices are being forced to change quickly just to remain partially effective; and the technical skills investigators relied on yesterday are quickly becoming obsolete. However, with new technology comes new tools and methods, and the Python language is in one of the best possible positions to be leveraged by investigators. *Python Forensics* is quite simply a book that is ahead of its time, and because of this, it is the perfect book for both the beginner and the experienced investigator. Chet Hosmer does a great job of helping the reader refresh older skills and create new ones by offering step-by-step instructions and intelligently framing the information for maximum understanding and contextual awareness. The skills you will learn from *Python Forensics* will help you develop a flexible and innovative toolkit that will be usable for years to come."

Greg Kipper, Senior Security Architect and Strategist at Verizon

"This book presents a refreshing, realistic view on the use of Python within modern, digital forensics; including valuable insight into the strengths and weaknesses of the language that every knowledgeable forensics investigator should understand."

Russ Rogers, President of Peak Security, Inc.

"This book is extremely useful for the forensic Python programmer also for those with little or no programming experience, and an excellent reference cookbook for the experienced programmer. The book considers issues relating to Daubert including testing and validation which is vital for the accreditation of forensic solutions."

Zeno Geradts, Senior Forensic Scientist and R&D coordinator at the Netherlands Forensic Institute

"As always, Chet Hosmer provides a comprehensive and groundbreaking evaluation of a contemporary platform applicable to digital forensics. Extremely well written and user friendly, the book provides a solid foundation for all levels of forensic Python programmers, and includes a much-needed discussion on empirical validation. Quite simply, the book is a must have for all who maintain a digital forensics library."

Dr. Marjie T. Britz, Clemson University

Contents

List of figures

About the Author

Chet Hosmer is a Founder and Chief Scientist at WetStone Technologies, Inc. Chet has been researching and developing technology and training surrounding forensics, digital investigation, and steganography for over two decades. He has made numerous appearances to discuss emerging cyber threats including National Public Radio's Kojo Nnamdi show, ABC's Primetime Thursday, NHK Japan, Crime Crime TechTV, and ABC News Australia. He has also been a frequent contributor to technical and news stories relating to cyber security and forensics and has been interviewed and quoted by IEEE, The New York Times, The Washington Post, Government Computer News, Salon.com, and Wired Magazine.

Chet also serves as a Visiting Professor at Utica College where he teaches in the Cybersecurity Graduate program. He is also an Adjunct Faculty member at Champlain College in the Masters of Science in Digital Forensic Science Program. Chet delivers keynote and plenary talks on various cyber security related topics around the world each year.

About the Technical Editor

Gary C. Kessler, Ph.D., CCE, CCFP, CISSP, is an Associate Professor of Homeland Security at Embry-Riddle Aeronautical University, a member of the North Florida Internet Crimes Against Children (ICAC) Task Force, and president and janitor of Gary Kessler Associates, a training and consulting company specializing in computer and network security and digital forensics.

Gary is also a part-time member of the Vermont ICAC. He is the coauthor of two professional texts and over 70 articles, a frequent speaker at regional, national, and international conferences, and past editor-in-chief of the Journal of Digital Forensics, Security and Law. More information about Gary can be found at his Web site, http://www.garykessler.net.

Foreword

On June 16, 2008 a user in the home of 2-year old Caylee Anthony *googled* for the term *fool proof suffocation*. A minute later, the same user logged onto the MySpace website with the profile of Casey Anthony. Tragically within months, the police found the decomposed remains of the young girl. Prosecutors charged Casey Anthony with first-degree murder and subsequently tried her 3 years later. The trial lasted 6 months and contained over 400 pieces of unique evidence. Sadly, the details of the computer search never made it to trial. The prosecutor's computer forensic examiner employed a tool to retrieve the browser history results. In use of that tool, the examiner only searched the Internet Explorer browser history and not that of the Firefox browser. The moral of the story is that we are only as good as our tools and our understanding how they work.

In contrast to the failure of the computer forensic examiner, let us consider the most feared military force—The Spartan Army. The strength of the Spartan army relied upon the professionalism of its soldiers. From a young age, the elite warriors learned only one occupation—to wage war. In that profession, they relied heavily on the quality of their weaponry and armor. Instead of weapons being issued to a warrior, it was the responsibility of every Spartan warrior to bring his own weapons and armor to war. Fathers passed these tools to their sons before entering battle. In the following pages, Chet Hosmer passes down modern tools and weapons. As a forensic investigator, your terrain may include a hard drive's unallocated space instead of the pass of Thermopylae. However, just like the Spartan elders, Chet will teach you to forge your own tools. Building your own weaponry is what separates a forensic examiner that makes the gross mistake of missing browser artifacts versus that of a professional examiner.

The following chapters cover a breadth of topics from hashing, keyword searching, metadata, natural language processing, network analysis, and utilizing cloud multiprocessing. Chet covers this range of exciting topics as he teaches you to build your own weapons in the Python programming language. A visiting professor in the Cyber Security Graduate Program at Utica College, Chet is both an educator and a practitioner. He has served as the principal investigator on over 40+ cyber security, digital forensic and information assurance research programs and received international recognition and awards for his work. Like the Spartan elder, his knowledge will hopefully translate to the growth of a new breed of professional. So please enjoy the following pages. And as Spartan wives used to tell their husbands upon entering battle, *come back with your shield or on it*.

TJ OConnor
SANS Red&Blue Team Cyber Guardian

Preface

Over the past 20 years I have had the privilege to work with some of the best, brightest, and dedicated forensic investigators throughout the world. These men and women work tirelessly to find the truth—usually working under less than ideal conditions and under the stress of real deadlines. Whether they are tracking down child predators, criminal organizations, terrorists, or just good old fashion criminals trying to steal your money, these investigators are under the gun and need the best of the best at their fingertips.

I communicate regularly with industry leaders developing the latest forensic products, while evolving their current software baseline to meet the needs of the broadest audience possible. I also communicate with customers trying to solve real-world problems that require immediate answers to hard questions, while the volume of data holding the answer gets larger by the second.

As a scientist and teacher, I see a thirst from students, law enforcement personnel, and information technology professionals who possess a burning desire, unique investigative skills, an understanding of the problem, and most importantly innovative ideas pertaining to the problems at hand. However, in many cases they lack the core computer science skills necessary to make a direct contribution to the cause.

The Python programming language along with the global environment that supports it offers a path for new innovation. Most importantly the language opens the door for broad inclusion and participation of free tools and technology that can revolutionize the collection, processing, analysis, and reasoning surrounding forensic evidence. This book provides a broad set of examples that are accessible by those with zero or little knowledge of programming, as well as those with solid developer skills that want to explore, jump start, and participate in the expanded use of Python in the forensic domain. I encourage you to participate, share your knowledge, apply your enthusiasm, and help us advance this cause.

INTENDED AUDIENCE

I have written the book to be accessible by anyone who has a desire to learn how to leverage the Python language to forensic and digital investigation problems. I always thought of this as an on-ramp and a beginning that I hope this will inspire you to create something great and share it with the world.

PREREQUISITES

Access to a computer, familiarity with an operating system (Windows, Linux, or Mac) and access to the Internet, coupled with a desire to learn.

READING THIS BOOK

The book is organized with the first two chapters focused on introductory material and setting up the free Python development environment. Chapters 3 through 11 focus on differing problems or challenges within digital investigation, and provide guided solutions along with reference implementations that focus on the core issues presented. I encourage you to use, expand, evolve, and improve the solutions provided. Finally, Chapter 12 looks back and then forward to consider the path ahead.

SUPPORTED PLATFORMS

All the examples in the book are written in Python 2.7.x in order to provide the greatest platform compatibility. The associated web site has solutions for both Python 2.7.x and 3.x whenever possible. As more third party libraries complete support for Python 3.x, all the examples will be available for 2.7.x and 3.x. Most of the examples have been tested on Windows, Linux, and Mac operating systems and will most likely work correctly on other environments that fully support at least Python 2.7.x

DOWNLOAD SOFTWARE

Those purchasing the book will also have access to the source code examples in the book (in both 2.7.x and 3.x—when possible) from the python-forensics.org web site.

COMMENTS, QUESTIONS, AND CONTRIBUTIONS

I encourage you to contribute in a positive way to this initiative. Your questions, comments, and contributions to the source code library at python-forensics.org will make this a resource available to all.

I challenge you all to share your ideas, knowledge, and experience.

Why Python Forensics?

1

CHAPTER CONTENTS

INTRODUCTION

The Python programming language and environment has proven to be easy to learn and use and is adaptable to virtually any domain or challenge problem. Companies like Google, Dropbox, Disney, Industrial Light and Magic, and YouTube just to mention a handful are using Python within their operations. Additionally, organizations like NASA's Jet Propulsion Lab; the National Weather Service; The Swedish Meteorological and Hydrological Institute (SMHI); and Lawrence Livermore National Laboratories rely on Python to build models, make predictions, run experiments, and control critical operational systems.

Before diving straight in, I am sure you would like a little more information about what I will be covering and how a programming environment like Python matches up with digital investigations. Also, you might be interested to know what you will be learning about, generally what the scope of this book is, and how you can apply the concepts and practical examples presented.

The primary purpose and scope of the book is to show you how Python can be used to address problems and challenges within the cybercrime and digital investigation domain. I will be doing this by using real examples and providing the full source code along with detailed explanations. Thus the book will become a set of reference implementations, a cookbook of sorts, and at the end of the day, will hopefully get you involved in developing your own Python forensic applications.

I will be presenting the material without any preconceived notion about your programming expertise (or lack thereof). I only expect that you have an interest in using the examples in the book, expanding on them, or developing derivatives that will fit your situation and challenge problems. On the other hand, this is *not* a how to programming book, many of those exist for Python along with a plethora of online resources.

So, let us get started by defining just some of the challenges we face in cybercrime and digital investigation. These challenges after all were the catalyst behind the book and have come from the past two decades of working on solutions to assist law enforcement; defense and corporate entities collect and analyze digital evidence.

CYBERCRIME INVESTIGATION CHALLENGES

Some of the challenge problems that we face in cybercrime investigation include:

The changing nature of investigations: Much of the work over the past two decades has focused on the postmortem acquisition, search, format, and display of information contained on various types of media. I can clearly remember the phone call I received almost two decades ago from Ron Stevens and Tom Hurbanek at the New York State Police. They were investigating a case that involved a Linux computer and were quite concerned about files and other data that might have been deleted that could be impeding the investigation. At that point no technology existed to extract deleted files or fragments that were buried away inside deleted Linux inodes, although several solutions existed for the Windows platform at the time. We worked together to develop algorithms that eventually became a tool named "extractor" that we provided free to law enforcement.

The move from simply extracting data, recovering deleted files, and scouring unallocated or slack space from computers has rapidly shifted just in the last couple of years. Today we focus most of our attention on smart mobile devices, dynamically changing memory, cloud applications, real-time network forensics, automotive data analysis, and weather-based forensics, just to mention a few. In addition, new work is addressing the association of direct digital forensic evidence with a broad range of instantly available electronic information. Whether this information comes from text messages, Facebook posts, tweets, Linkedin associations, metadata embedded in digital photographs or movies, GPS data that tracks our movements or the digital fingerprints left from every Web site we surf, all may be relevant and used in civil or criminal cases. The question is how do we connect these dots while maintaining forensic efficacy?

The widening gap between technology developers and investigators: Investigators, examiners, incident response personnel, auditors, compliance experts tend to come into this field with a background in social science, whereas technology developers tend to have backgrounds in computer science and engineering. Clearly, there are some excellent examples of crossovers in both directions, but the vocabulary, thought process, and approach to problem solving can be quite different. Our goal, as depicted in Figure 1.1, is to leverage Python forensic solutions to close that gap and create a collaborative nonthreatening environment whereby computer science and social science can come together.

The challenge is to develop a platform, vernacular environment where both social scientists and computer scientists can comfortably communicate and equally participate in the process of developing new forensic solutions. As you will see, the Python environment provides a level playing field, or common ground at least, where new innovations and thought can emerge. This has already shown to be true in other scientific fields like Space Flight, Meteorology, Hydrology, Simulation, Internet Technology advancement, and Experimentation. Python is already providing valuable contributions in these domains.

Cost and availability of new tools: With a couple of exceptions (for example, EnCase® App Central), most new innovations and capabilities that come through vendor channels take time to develop and can add significant cost to the investigator's toolkit. In the past, investigators carried with them just a handful of hardware and software tools that they used to extract and preserve digital evidence. Today, to address the wide range of situations they may encounter, 30-40 software products may be necessary just to perform acquisition and rudimentary analysis of the digital crime scene. Of course this is just the start of the investigative process and the number and variety of analytic tools continues to grow.

The true cost and cost of ownership of these technologies can be staggering, especially when you factor in education and training. The barrier to entry into the field can easily reach high five or even six figures. This is in a field where backlogs continue to grow at law enforcement agencies around the world. Backlogs are also growing within the corporate sector, which is dealing with human resource actions, corporate espionage, insider leaks, and massive amounts of regulatory requirements.

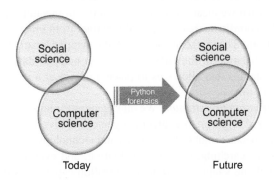

FIGURE 1.1

Narrowing the gap.

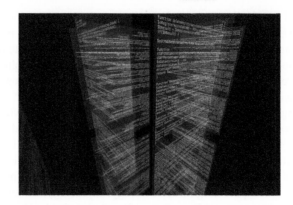

FIGURE 1.2

The future digital crime scene.

It is obvious that we need a better onramp and new ways for individuals that have both interest and aptitude, to participate and make entry into the digital investigative field easier and more streamlined. As we move forward in time, the digital crime scene will look more and more like the depiction in Figure 1.2.

Data vs. semantics: Due to constrained resources, new technologies and innovation we must move from simple data analysis and search to rapid semantic understanding and even situational awareness. Investigators need tools that can help them narrow in on targets or hotspots within an investigation, in order to better apply resources and more quickly identify important leads. This is especially true for investigations that are ongoing such as active fraud cases, denial of service attacks, sophisticated malicious code breaches, violent crimes such as murder, child abduction, rape, and aggravated assaults that have a digital component.

In addition, we must capture the knowledge and process of the most seasoned investigators before they leave the field. What is needed is a better way to capture that knowledge and experience, as most of the investigative analysis of digital evidence happens today between the ears of the investigator. To illustrate the difference, Figure 1.3 shows what we mean by data vs. semantics or meaning. The image on the left depicts a GPS coordinate that we typically extract from images, mobile devices, or online transactions. The image on the right is the mapped location—in other words the meaning or translation of the GPS location into mapped data. These GPS data also include timestamps that allows us to place a device at a particular location at a specific date and time.

The next-generation investigator: We must generate interest in this field of study to attract the best and brightest to a career in cybercrime investigation. In order to do so, this new breed needs to not only use tools and technology but also must play an important role in researching, defining, evaluating, and even developing some of these high demand and sophisticated next-generation capabilities (Figure 1.4).

Lack of a collaboration environment: Cybercriminals have the advantage of untethered collaboration, along with access to resources that assist in the execution

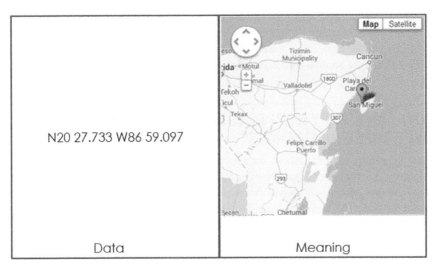

N20 27.733 W86 59.097

Data

Meaning

FIGURE 1.3

Data vs. semantics.

FIGURE 1.4

The next-generation cyber warrior.

of distributed attacks and sophisticated cybercrime activities. Investigators and developers of new methods and techniques need that same advantage. They require a platform for collaboration, joint development, and access to new innovations that could be directly applied to the situation at hand.

HOW CAN THE PYTHON PROGRAMMING ENVIRONMENT HELP MEET THESE CHALLENGES?

Creating an environment where social and computer scientists can collaborate and work together is challenging. Creating a platform to develop new technology-based solutions that address the broad range of digital investigation challenges outlined earlier in this chapter is difficult. Doing them both together is a real challenge, and whenever you take on a challenge like this it is important to consider the under-pinnings so that you create the best chance for success.

I personally have a few important considerations that have served me well over the years, so I will share them with you here.

1. Does the platform you are building on have broad industry support?
2. Is there an ample supply of technical data regarding the subject along with a large cadre of talent or subject matter experts?
3. Is the technology platform you are considering open or closed?
4. Where does the technology exist along its lifecycle (i.e., too early, too late or mature, and evolving)?
5. What is the cost or other barriers to entry? (especially if you are trying to attract a broad array of participants)
6. Finally, since we are trying to bridge the gap between social and computer science, is the environment well suited for cross-disciplinary collaboration?

Global support for Python

Python was created by Guido van Russom in the late 1980s with the fundamental premise that Python is programming for everyone. This has created a groundswell of support from a broad array of domain-specific researchers, the general software devel-opment community, and programmers with varying backgrounds and abilities. The Python language is both general purpose and produces easily readable code that can be understood by nonprogrammers. In addition, due to Python's intrinsic extensibility, copious amount of third-party libraries and modules exist. Numerous web sites provide tips, tricks, coding examples, and training for those needing a deeper dive into the lan-guage. It may surprise you that Python was ranked as the number 1 programming lan-guage in 2013 by codeeval.com (see Figure 1.5) edging out Java for the first time. A great place to start is at the official Python programming language web sites *python.org*.

Finally, sophisticated integrated software development environments exist that allow even the novice developer to innovate new ideas and design, and then build

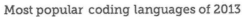

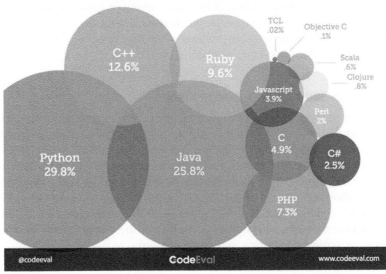

FIGURE 1.5

Programming language popularity according to codeview.com.

and test their inventions and prototypes. Python is an interpreted language; however, compilers are available as well, of course. As shown in Figure 1.6, developers have adopted the test-then code-then validate mindset.

By utilizing the Python Shell, experienced and novice users alike can experiment with the language, libraries, modules, and data structures before attempting to integrate them into a complete program or application. This promotes experimentation with the language, language constructs, objects, experimentation with performance considerations, and libraries, and allows users to explore and tradeoff approaches

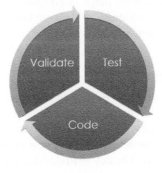

FIGURE 1.6

Test-then code-then validate.

prior to putting them into practice. Once confident with the use, characteristics and behaviors of the language, the integration into working programs tends to go more smoothly. In addition, this experimentation often leads to testing considerations that can then be applied to the working programs once they have been completed, thus completing the cycle of test-code-validate.

Open source and platform independence

Since Python is an open source environment, developers continue to create compatible versions that run across multiple platforms. Python implementations exist for today's most popular platforms including Windows, Linux, and Mac OS X as you would expect. However, the support for Python is much broader. Support for mobile device operating systems such as Android, iOS, and Windows 8 is also available. In addition, Python is supported on platforms that you might not expect such as AIX, AS/400, VMS, Solaris, PalmOS, OS/2, and HP-UX, just to mention a few. What this means for cybercrime investigators is portability of these applications for today's platforms, yesterday's platforms, and future platforms.

In March 2013, NVIDIA announced support for Python developers by opening the door to GPU-Accelerated Computing using NVIDIA CUDA, allowing for parallel processing capabilities, and advancing the performance of virtually any Python-developed application. This will deliver the ability to handle and process big data, perform advanced analytical operations, perform deductive and inductive reasoning, and meet future computational challenges. This versatility ensures that the investment made in creating new investigative solutions will be useable and sharable with colleagues that use different flavors of computing platforms.

Lifecycle positioning

Python today sits in the best position possible to be leveraged for investigative applications. The language is mature, hundreds of thousands of developers are experienced, a strong support organization is in place, extensible libraries are plentiful, applications are portable to a wide range of computing platforms, the source code is open and free, and new innovations to the core language are keeping pace with hardware and operating system advancements.

Cost and barriers to entry

One of the keys to Python's success is the lack of virtually any barrier to entry. The development environment is free, the language is platform independent, the code is as easy to read and write as English, and support is vast and worldwide. In my opinion, it should revolutionize the development of new cybercrime, forensic, and incident response-based solutions. The key is to develop outreach that will encourage, attract, and open the doors to social scientists, computer scientists, law enforcement organizations, forensic labs, standards bodies, incident response teams, academics, students, and virtually anyone with domain expertise within the broadest definition of cybercrime.

PYTHON AND THE DAUBERT EVIDENCE STANDARD

As many of us have encountered, the Daubert standard provides rules of evidence at the U.S. Federal level along with about one-third of the states that deal with the admissibility of expert testimony including scientific data. Digital data collected and analyzed with forensic software employed by an "expert" can be challenged by using, in laymen's terms, a Daubert motion to suppress or challenge the efficacy of the expert and/or the evidence produced by technology utilized.

In 2003, Brian Carrier [Carrier] published a paper that examined rules of evidence standards including Daubert, and compared and contrasted the open source and closed source forensic tools. One of his key conclusions was, "Using the guidelines of the Daubert tests, we have shown that open source tools may more clearly and comprehensively meet the guideline requirements than would closed source tools."

The results are not automatic of course, just because the source is open. Rather, specific steps must be followed regarding design, development, and validation.

1. Can the program or algorithm be explained? This explanation should be explained in words, not only in code.
2. Has enough information been provided such that thorough tests can be developed to test the program?
3. Have error rates been calculated and validated independently?
4. Has the program been studied and peer reviewed?
5. Has the program been generally accepted by the community?

The real question is how can Python-developed forensic programs meet these standards? Chapters 3–11 comprise the cookbook portion of the book and each example attempts to address the Daubert standard by including:

1. Definition of the Challenge Problem
2. Requirements Definition
3. Test Set Development
4. Design Alternative and Decisions
5. Algorithm Description (English readable)
6. Code Development and Walk-Through
7. Test and Validation Process
8. Error Rate Calculation
9. Community Involvement

This approach will provide two distinct advantages. First, the cookbook examples provided in the text will be useable out of the box and should meet or exceed the rules of evidence standards. Second, the process defined will assist both experienced and novice developers with an approach to developing digital investigation and forensic solutions. The cookbook examples then provide a model or reference implementations using Python that are designed as an educational and practical example.

ORGANIZATION OF THE BOOK

In order to support the broadest audience of potential contributors to new cybercrime investigative technologies, I have arranged the book to be accessible to those with little or no programming experience, as well as for those that want to dive directly into some of the more advanced cookbook solutions.

Chapter 2 will provide a walk-through for those wishing to setup a Python software environment for the first time. This step-by-step chapter will include environments for Linux and Windows platforms and will include considerations for Python 2.x and Python 3.x. I will also cover the installation and setup of high-quality third-party libraries that I will leverage throughout the book, along with integrated development environments that will make it easier to master Python and manage your projects.

Chapter 3 covers the development of a fundamental Python application that will outline one of the most common digital investigation applications—File Hashing. A broad set of one-way hash algorithms that are directly implemented within the core Python distributions will be covered. I will then show how this simple application can be transformed into a more sophisticated cyber security and investigation tool that could be applied immediately.

Each of the Chapters 4–11 tackles a unique cybercrime investigation challenge and delivers a Python cookbook solution that can be freely used, shared, and evolved, and includes opportunities for you to participate in the future expansion.

Chapter 12 takes a look at future opportunities for the application of Python within cybercrime investigation, a broader set of cyber security applications, and examines high-performance hardware acceleration and embedded solutions.

Finally, each chapter includes a summary of topics covered, challenge problems, and review questions making the book suitable for use in college and university academic environments.

CHAPTER REVIEW

In this chapter, we took a look at the challenges that are facing cybercrime investigators, incident response personnel, and forensic examiners that are dealing with a plethora of digital evidence from a multitude of sources. This chapter also discussed the computer science and social science gap that exists between the users of forensic/investigative technologies and the developers of the current solutions. We examined the key characteristics of the Python programming environment which make it well suited to address these challenges. These characteristics include the open source nature of the Python environment, the platform independent operational model, the global support and available technical data, and the current lifecycle positioning. Also, Python-developed solutions (provided they are done right) will meet or exceed the Daubert rules of evidence requirements. Finally, the organization of the book was discussed to give readers a better understanding of what to expect in upcoming chapters.

SUMMARY QUESTIONS

1. What are some of the key challenges that face forensic investigators today and what potential impacts could these challenges pose in the future?
2. From what has been presented or based on your own research or experience, what do you believe are the key benefits that Python could bring to forensic investigators?
3. What other organizations are using Python today for scientific endeavors and how is the use of Python impacting their work?
4. What other software languages or platforms can you think of that are open source, cross-platform, have global support, have a low barrier to entry, are easily understood, and could be used to collaborate among both computer scientists and social scientists?
5. What forensic or investigative applications can you think of that either do not currently exist or are too expensive for you to buy into?

Additional Resources

Open Source Digital Forensic Tools—The Legal Argument. Digital-Evidence.org, http://www.digital-evidence.org/papers/opensrc_legal.pdfhttp; 2003.

Python Programming Language—Official Website. Python.org, http://www.python.org.

Basu S. Perl vs Python: why the debate is meaningless. The ByeBaker Web site, http://bytebaker.com/2007/01/29/perl-vs-python-why-the-debate-is-meaningless/; 2007 [29.01.07].

Raymond E. Why Python? The Linux Journal 73, http://www.linuxjournal.com/article/3882; 2000 [30.04.03].

Setting up a Python Forensics Environment

CHAPTER CONTENTS

INTRODUCTION

A couple of decades ago, I was working for a large defense contractor and was part of a team that was developing a secure embedded device. My initial role was to setup a development environment for the team to use. This may seem like a pretty simple task. However, the embedded security hardware was completed and handed off to me, but the device itself did not include an operating system or supporting libraries—it was basically an open slate. Thus, the first painstaking task was to develop a boot loader that would allow me to load a program onto the device. Once that was completed, I needed to develop the ability to interface with the board and load additional software (the operating system, shared libraries, applications, etc.), that would bring the security hardware contained within the device online.

This interface software needed to include a debugger that would allow us to control the operating system and application software being developed by the team while it was running on the device. For example, the ability to start the program, stop the program, inspect variables, registers, etc., perform single steps, and set breakpoints in the code, all this was accomplished through a 19,200 baud RS232 interface.

You might be asking, what does this twentieth century example have to do with Python? The answer is simple, the requirements for a stable feature-rich development environment still exist in the twenty-first century, but now we have modern tools. Without the proper development environment, the chance of successfully developing high-quality, function-rich forensic or digital investigation software is quite low.

SETTING UP A PYTHON FORENSICS ENVIRONMENT

Many considerations exist before setting up an environment. I will explore some of the key areas that I myself consider when setting up an environment like this. Here are some important considerations:

1. What is the right environment for your situation? Are you a professional software developer; a novice developer with solid investigative skills and ideas that you would like to explore; do you work in a forensic lab or support an incident response team with new tools and methods; or maybe you might work in the IT Security group at a corporation and need better ways to collect and analyze what is happening on your network.
2. How do you choose the right third-party libraries and modules that enhance your program and allow you to focus on your application and not on reinventing the wheel?

3. What is the right integrated development environment (IDE) and what capabilities should be included in that environment?

   a. Code intelligence that provides automatic completion, built-in error indicators source browser, code indices, and fast symbol lookup.

   b. A robust graphical debugger that allows you to set breakpoints, single-step through code, view data, and examine variables.

   c. A powerful programmer's editor that has a complete understanding of the Python language rules, advanced search tools, bookmarking, and code highlighting.

   d. Cross-platform support such that you can choose your platform and environment, (i.e., Windows, Linux, or Mac), and select any Python version from 2.x to 3.x and Stackless Python.

Stackless Python is a relatively new concept, allowing Python programs to execute which are not limited by the size of C Stack. In many environments, the size of stack memory is limited in comparison to the amount of heap memory. Stackless Python utilizes the heap and not the stack which provides greater distributed processing possibilities. For example, this allows for thousands of independently running *tasklets* to be launched. Online multiuser gaming platforms use this to support thousands of simultaneous users. I am sure if you are thinking ahead you can imagine some interesting digital investigation and forensic applications for such an environment.

---

   e. A unit testing capability that enables you to thoroughly validate your code within common testing frameworks such as unittest, doctest, and nose.

   f. Built-in revision control for advanced projects along with direct integration with popular revision control systems such as Mercurial, Bazaar, Git, CVS, and Perforce. When building larger applications that contain many moving components managing the many revisions becomes important.

   This selection will ultimately determine if the tools and applications developed will meet the standards of quality that are essential ingredients for digital investigation and forensic applications.

It is important right up front to realize this book is about building forensic applications that must meet the Daubert standard, thus we are not just hacking out some code that will work most of the time, but rather code that should work all the time or fail gracefully. And most importantly, we need to develop code that will create admissible evidence.

THE RIGHT ENVIRONMENT

One of the initial choices you will have to make is the platform you intend to use for the development of Python forensic applications. As discussed in Chapter 1, Python and Python programs will execute on a variety of platforms including the latest desktop, mobile, and even legacy systems. However, that does not mean you need to develop your applications on one of those platforms. Instead you will most likely be developing your applications on a Windows, Linux, or Mac platform that supports the latest development tools.

One great thing about Python ... If you follow the rules, develop quality programs and make sure you consider cross-platform idiosyncrasies, no matter what platform you choose for development, the resulting Python programs you create should easily run on a variety of operating systems that have a properly installed Python system.

The Python Shell

The Python Shell delivers an object-oriented, high-level programming language that includes built-in data structures and an extensive Standard Library. Python employs a simple easy to use syntax that virtually anyone can learn, provides support for third-party modules and packages which encourages program code reuse and sharing, and is supported on virtually all major platforms and can be freely distributed. What that delivers to the digital investigator or forensic specialist is the ability to quickly develop programs that will augment or even replace current tools and then immediately share them with the community. One of the other benefits of the interpreted environment is the ability to experiment with the Standard Library, third-party modules, commands, functions, and packages without first developing a program. This allows you to ensure that the commands, functions, and modules you are planning to use provide the results and performance you are looking for. Since there are many options and sources for these functions with more arriving on the scene every day, the interpreter allows you to easily experiment before you commit to a final approach.

CHOOSING A PYTHON VERSION

As with any programming environment, many currently supported versions of Python are available. However, two basic standards of Python exist today in versions 2.x and 3.x. The change from Python 2.x to 3.x has caused some difficulties in portability, and programs and libraries written for 2.x require modification to work within 3.x.

Some of the core Python functions have changed mainly due to full support of Unicode in version 3.x. This not only affects programs but also affects previous modules that have been developed and have not yet been ported and or validated for Python 3.x. Based on this conundrum, I have decided to develop the examples supplied in this book to conform to the 2.x standard, giving us access to the broadest set of third-party modules and compatibility across more platforms. The source code in the book will be available online as well, whenever possible I will provide both a 2.x and 3.x version of the source.

In addition, the 2.x class of Python has been proven, validated, and deployed in a broad set of applications. Therefore, developing forensic or digital investigation applications using the 2.x version provides us with a solid underpinning and broadest deployment platform. Also, once 3.x becomes broadly embraced and the third-party libraries become available and certified, we will have all the information necessary to port and even enhance the applications in this book.

Now that we have selected a version to begin with, I will walk you through setting up Python on a Windows desktop.

INSTALLING PYTHON ON WINDOWS

If you Google "Python Installation" you will get a little over 7 million page hits, as of this writing. In my opinion, the best and safest place to obtain tested standard Python installations is at www.python.org, which is the Python Programming Language Official Web site [PYTHON], shown in Figure 2.1. At this page, I selected Python version 2.7.5.

Next, I navigate to the download page and select the appropriate version for my situation. In this case I am going to select:

Python 2.7.5 Windows x86 MSI installer 2.7.5 (sig)

This will download the Windows runtime environment (as shown in Figure 2.2). Also shown is the hash of the download file allowing you to validate the download.

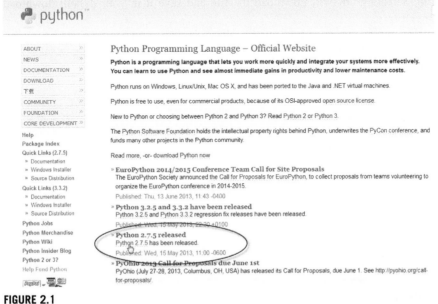

FIGURE 2.1

The Python Programming Language Official Web site.

This is a production release. Please report any bugs you encounter.

We currently support these formats for download:

- XZ compressed source tar ball (2.7.5) (sig)
- Gzipped source tar ball (2.7.5) (sig)
- Bzipped source tar ball (2.7.5) (sig)
- Windows x86 MSI Installer (2.7.5) (sig)
- Windows x86 MSI program database (2.7.5) (sig)
- Windows X86-64 MSI Installer (2.7.5) [1] (sig)
- Windows X86-64 program database (2.7.5) [1] (sig)
- Mac OS X 64-bit/32-bit x86-64/i386 Installer (2.7.5) for Mac OS X 10.6 and later [2] (sig). [You may need an updated Tcl/Tk install to run IDLE or use Tkinter, see note 2 for instructions.]
- Mac OS X 32-bit i386/PPC Installer (2.7.5) for Mac OS X 10.3 and later [2] (sig).

The source tarballs are signed with Benjamin Peterson's key (fingerprint: 12EF 3DC3 8047 DA38 2D18 A5B9 99CD EA9D A413 5B38). The Windows installer was signed by Martin von Löwis' public key, which has a key id of 7D9DC8D2. The Mac installers were signed with Ned Deily's key, which has a key id of 6F5E1540. The public keys are located on the download page.

MD5 checksums and sizes of the released files:

```
b4f01a1d0ba0b46b05c73b2ac909b1df  14492759  Python-2.7.5.tgz
€334b666b7ff2038c761d7b27ba699c1  12147710  Python-2.7.5.tar.bz2
5eea8462f69ab136bd32f9c4cd6272ab  10252148  Python-2.7.5.tar.xz
e632ba7c34b922e4485667e332096999  18236482  python-2.7.5-pdb.zip
55cc56948dcee3afb53f65d8bb425f20  17556546  python-2.7.5-amd64-pdb.zip
83f5d9ba639bd2e33d104df9ea969f31  16617472  python-2.7.5.amd64.msi
0006d6219160ce6abe711a71c835ebb0  16228352  python-2.7.5.msi
ead4f83ec7823325ae287295193644a7  20395084  python-2.7.5-macosx10.3.dmg
248ec7d77220ec6c770a23df3cb537bc  19979778  python-2.7.5-macosx10.6.dmg
```

[1] (1, 2) The binaries for AMD64 will also work on processors that implement the Intel 64 architecture (formerly EM64T), i.e. the architecture that Microsoft calls x64, and AMD called x86-64 before calling it AMD64. They will not work on Intel Itanium Processors (formerly IA-64).

[2] (1, 2) There is important information about IDLE, Tkinter, and Tcl/Tk on Mac OS X here.

FIGURE 2.2

Downloading the Windows installer.

As you would expect, selecting this link presents you with a Windows dialog box as shown in Figure 2.3, confirming that you wish to save the installation file. Selecting OK will download the file and save it in your default download directory.

Examining the contents of my download directory, you can see that I have actually downloaded both the latest 2.x and 3.x releases. I am now going to select and execute the 2.7.5 Installer (Figure 2.4).

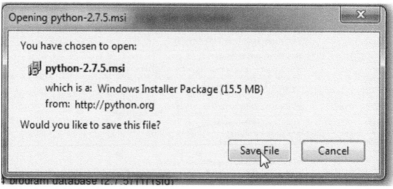

FIGURE 2.3

Windows download confirmation.

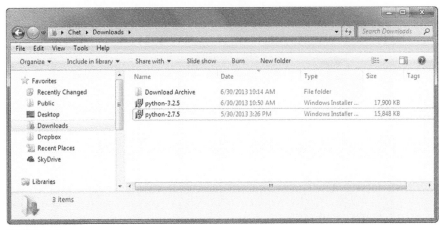

FIGURE 2.4

Executing the Python 2.7.5 Installer.

Upon execution, the Installer prompts you to determine whether Python should be installed for the current user or for all users on this machine. This is your choice of course, but if you choose to install this for every user make sure they are trusted and know the risks. The Python environment runs at a high privilege level and has access to operating system functions that not everyone should necessarily need (Figure 2.5).

Python allows you to select where the environment will be installed. The default location for Python 2.7.5 is *C:\Python27*, although you can specify another location (Figure 2.6). You should make a note of this so you can inspect and reference the directories and files stored there. This will be especially helpful later when you are looking for certain libraries, modules, tools, and documentation.

I have decided to customize my installation slightly. I want to ensure that the Python documentation is stored on my local hard drive so I can have access anytime. Also, I do not expect to need the TCL/TK Graphical User Interface (GUI) module, so I have selected this to only be installed when needed; this will reduce the size of the installation. If you have no restriction on disk storage, including this with your install is not an issue. We will be installing other easier to use GUI packages and modules later in the book (Figures 2.7 and 2.8).

Next, Windows will display the typical User Account Control (UAC) to help you stay in control of your computer by informing you when a program makes a change that requires administrator-level permission (Figure 2.9). Windows will also verify the digital signature of Python and display the name of the organization associated with the certificate used to sign the installer. Selecting Yes will install Python and allow the appropriate system changes to be made, provided that the user has administrative privilege. You might notice that this screenshot was taken with my iPhone because during UAC acknowledgment Windows locks out all other program access until either Yes or No is selected.

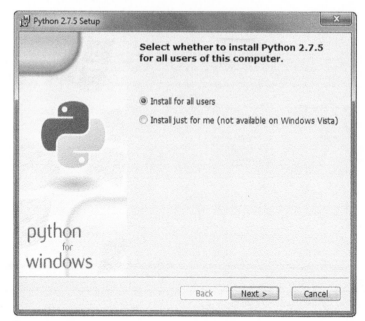

FIGURE 2.5

Python Installation user selection.

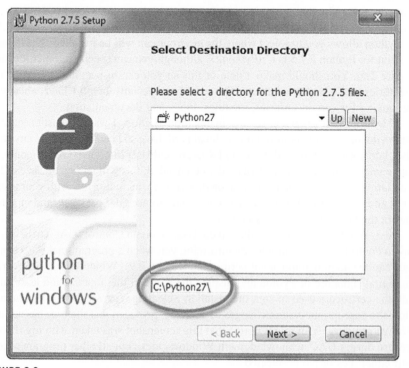

FIGURE 2.6

Python Installation directory.

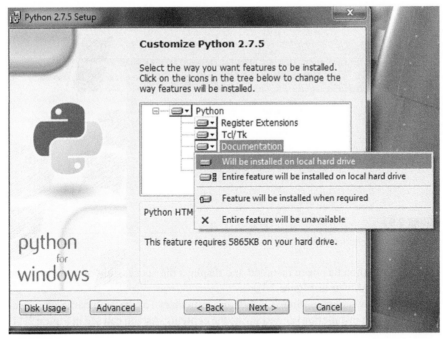

FIGURE 2.7

Python customization user manual.

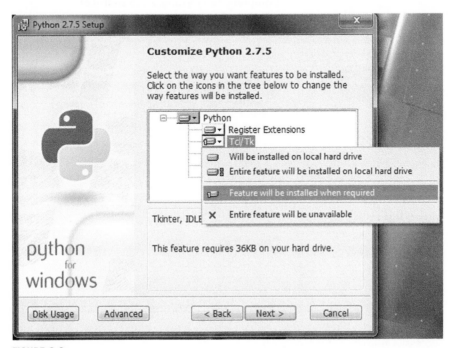

FIGURE 2.8

TCL/TK install when needed.

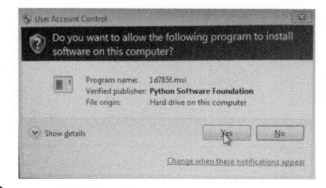

FIGURE 2.9

Windows user account control.

Finally, Python has been installed and displays the successful completion of the installation as shown in Figure 2.10.

We can now navigate to the *C:\Python27* directory (or the path name you specified for Python installation) and examine the contents. As you can see in Figure 2.11,

FIGURE 2.10

Successful installation of Python 2.7.5.

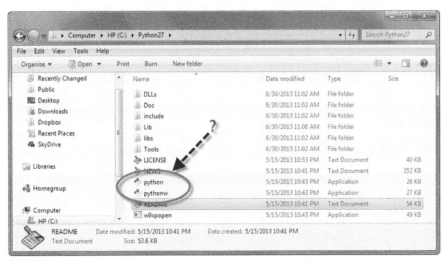

FIGURE 2.11

Python directory snapshot.

there are folders that contain Docs, Lib, DLL, and Tools along with key files License, News, and a Readme. Most importantly there are two application files *Python* and *pythonw*. These are the Python executable files.

To utilize the Python interactive interpreter you would double click on *Python*. If you have an existing Python program, and you do not want to display the interpreter window you would execute *pythonw* along with the associated Python file to execute (more on this later). For our immediate use, we will be using the *Python* application file. For easy access you can add this application to your Windows Taskbar and you will see the Python icon as highlighted in Figure 2.12.

By launching the Python Taskbar icon (clicking it), the Python Interactive window is displayed as shown in Figure 2.13. Your window will look a bit different from mine, as I have set mine up to be black on white to provide easier book publication. The title bar shows the directory the application was started from *C:\Python27*. The initial text lists the version of Python in this case Python 2.7.5, the date of the build and information regarding the processor, and Windows version in this case win32. The next line provides some helpful commands such as license, credits, help, and the copyright message. The next line starting with $>>>$ is the Python prompt awaiting instructions. The tradition here would be of course to test the installation by writing the standard programming language Hello World program, which only takes a single

FIGURE 2.12

Windows taskbar with Python icon.

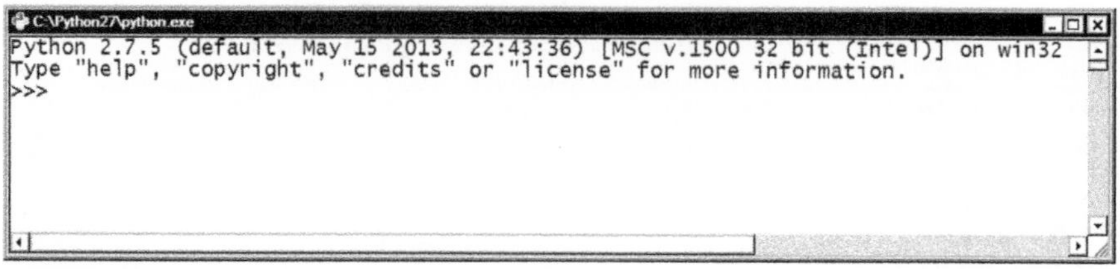

FIGURE 2.13

Python startup prompt and messages.

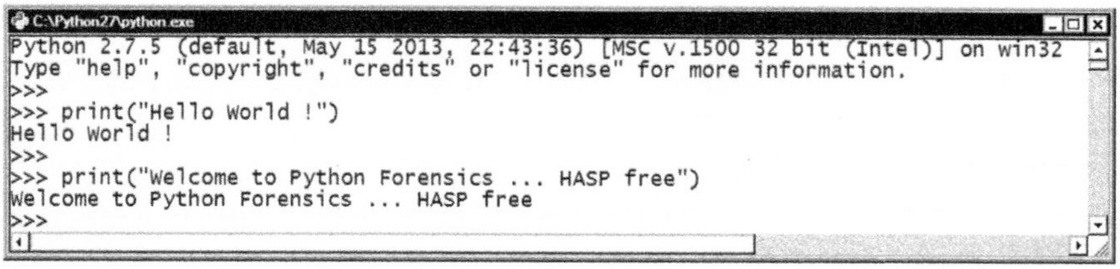

FIGURE 2.14

Python Hello World.

line in Python as shown in Figure 2.14. I added a second print statement as well, promoting the idea of open and free forensic software that can be developed in Python, without the need for a HASP.

For those unfamiliar with a HASP (Hardware Against Software Piracy) (sometimes referred to as a Dongle) this is a device that provides copy protection for certain software programs. Without the HASP inserted, the software will not operate, thus only allowing licensed users to utilize the software on a single machine or network.

Now that we have at least verified that the Python interpreter is running and accepting commands let us take a look at the commands, language structure, packages, and modules that are available.

PYTHON PACKAGES AND MODULES

Adding core functionality to an existing programming language is a standard part of software development. As new methods and innovations are made, developers supply these functional building blocks as modules or packages. Within the Python network, the majority of these modules and packages are free, with many including the full source code, allowing you to enhance the behavior of the supplied modules and to independently validate the code. Before we jump into adding third-party modules to Python, we need to understand what comes standard out of the box or more specifically what is included in the *Python Standard Library*. I think you will be pleasantly surprised at the breadth of capability delivered as part of the Standard Library along with the built-in language itself.

The Python Standard Library

Python's Standard Library [Standard Library] is quite extensive and offers a broad range of built-in capabilities. These built-in functions are written primarily in the C programming language for both speed and abstraction. Since the Standard Library layer is compatible across systems, interfacing with *platform-specific* APIs (application programming interfaces) are abstracted or normalized for the Python programmer.

One of the fundamental operations that investigators perform is the generation of one-way cryptographic hash values.

A one-way cryptographic hash is used to create a signature of an existing string of bytes regardless of length (typically referred to as a message digest). One-way hashes have four basic characteristics: (1) A function that easily calculates and generates a message digest. (2) Possessing the message digest value alone provides no clues as to the original message or file. (3) It is infeasible (or computational difficult) to change the contents of the message or file without changing the associated message digest. (4) It is infeasible to find two messages or files that differ in content, but produce the same message digest. It should be noted that attacks against known hash methods like MD5 and SHA-1 have been successful under certain controlled situations.

The Python Standard Library contains a built-in module named hashlib that can perform one-way cryptographic hashing. The following simple hashing example can be executed on virtually any Python platform (Windows, Linux, Mac, iOS, Windows 8 Phone, Android, etc.) and will produce the same result.

```
#
# Python forensics
# Simple program to generate the SHA-256
# one-way cryptographic hash of a given string

# Step 1
# Instruct the interpreter to import the
# Standard library module hashlib

import hashlib

# print a message to the user

print
print("Simple program to generate the SHA-256 Hash of the String 'Python
forensics'")
print
```

```
# define a string with the desired text
myString = "Python forensics"

# create an object named hash which is of type sha256
hash = hashlib.sha256()

# utilize the update method of the hash object to generate the
# SHA 256 hash of myString

hash.update(myString)

# obtain the generated hex values of the SHA256 Hash
# from the object
# by utilizing the hexdigest method

hexSHA256 = hash.hexdigest()

# print out the result and utilize the upper method
# to convert all the hex characters to upper case

print("SHA-256 Hash: " + hexSHA256.upper())
print

print("Processing completed")
```

This simple example demonstrates how easy it is to access and utilize the capabilities of the Python Standard Library, and how the same code runs on different platforms and generates the correct SHA256 hash value (see Figures 2.15 and 2.16).

In Chapter 3, we will spend considerable time and focus on the application of the one-way cryptographic hash algorithms for use in digital investigation and forensics.

In the next section, we will take a deeper dive into the Python Standard Library

```
C:\Windows\system32\cmd.exe

C:\Users\0\Desktop>python hashPrint.py
Simple program to generate the SHA-256 Hash of the String Python Forensics
SHA-256 Hash: 7A0BDF5725E0E032349871C8409522C0BF6971975C63F3F8041E2522148B9CF3
Processing completed
C:\Users\0\Desktop>
```

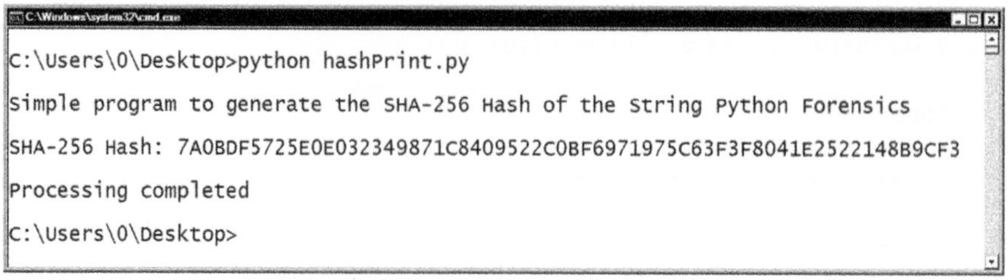

FIGURE 2.15

Windows execution of *hashPrint.py*.

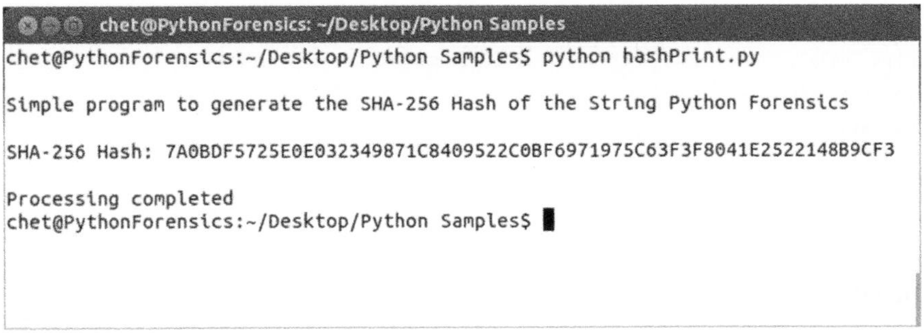

FIGURE 2.16

Ubuntu Linux execution of *hashPrint.py*.

WHAT IS INCLUDED IN THE STANDARD LIBRARY?

The Python Standard Library is broken down into broad categories: I will give you a brief summary description of the contents of each category with special attention on categories that I believe are unique or have forensic or digital investigation value. They are:

Built-in functions

Built-in functions, as the name implies, are always available to the Python programmer and provide fundamental capabilities that are additive to the language itself.

hex() **and** bin()

One of the capabilities that forensic investigators often encounter is the need to display variables in different bases; for example, from decimal (base 10), binary (base 2), and hexadecimal, or hex (base 16). These display capabilities are part of the built-in functions. The simple Python Shell session depicted in Figure 2.17 demonstrates their behavior. In this example, we set the variable a equal to the decimal

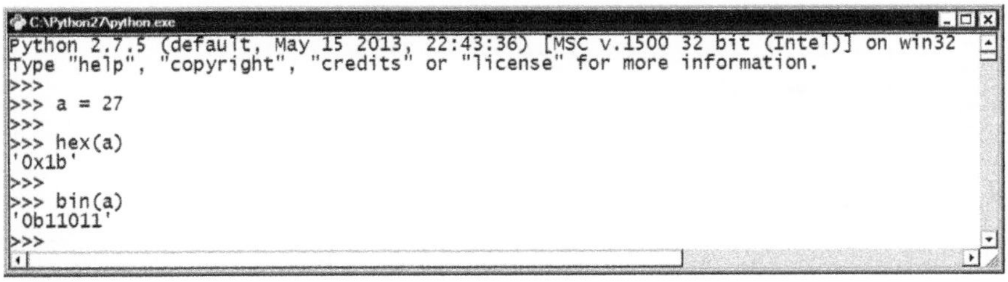

FIGURE 2.17

Python Shell session using hex() and bin().

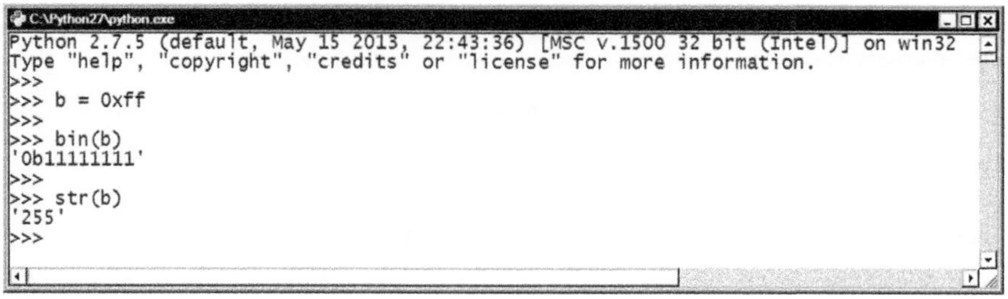

FIGURE 2.18

Python Shell session entering hex values.

number 27 (the default is a decimal number). We then execute the function `hex(a)`, it displays the value of `a` in hexadecimal form; note the use of *0x* prefix to denote hex. Utilizing the binary conversion function `bin(a)` renders the decimal value 27 as a binary string of 1 s and 0 s, or 11011; note the use of the *0b* prefix to denote binary.

As shown in Figure 2.18, you can perform the reverse by specifying a variable as a hex number and then displaying the variable in binary or decimal form. Note that the values stored in the variable `a` or `b` shown in these examples are simply integer values, the function `hex()`, `bin()`, and `str()` simply render the variables in hexadecimal, binary, or decimal notation. In other words the variable does not change, just the way we view it does.

range()

Another useful built-in function is `range()`. We often need to create a list of items, and this built-in function can assist us in automatically creating such a list. *Lists*, *Tuples*, and *Dictionaries* are quite powerful constructs in Python, and we will be using each of these to solve challenge problems throughout the book. For now I am just going to show you the basics.

I have executed a few examples using the Python Shell as shown in Figure 2.19. The first one creates a list of the first 20 integers starting at zero. The second provides

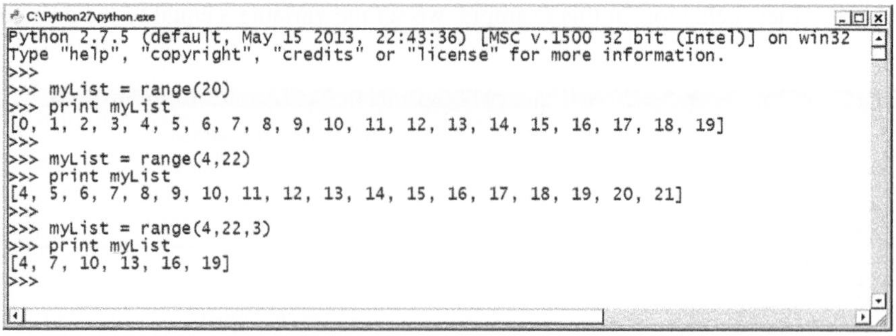

FIGURE 2.19

Python Shell creating lists using the `range()` built-in Standard Library function.

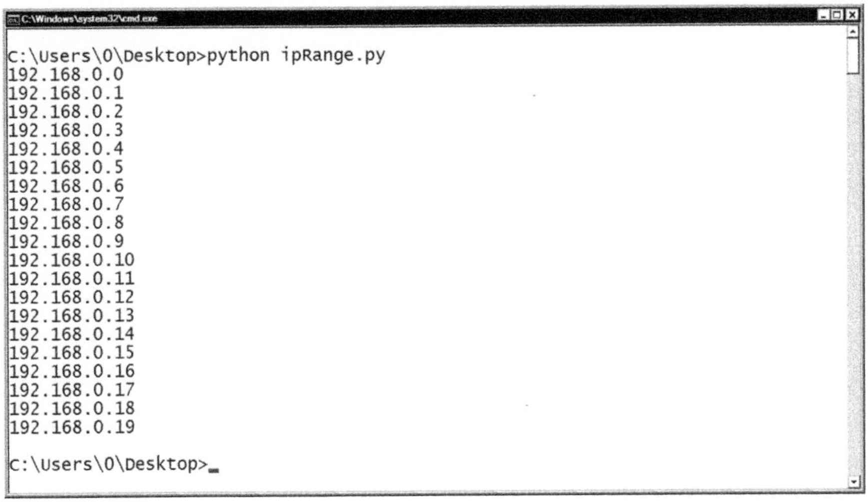

FIGURE 2.20

ipRange execution.

a list of integers starting at 4 and ending at 22 (notice this list stops at 22 and does not include it in the list). Finally, I create a list from 4 to 22 in steps of 3.

You will see later how using the range() function and *lists* can be helpful in automatically generating lists of useful values. For example, the program below generates a *list* that contains the first 20 host IP addresses for the class C address starting with 192.168.0. You can see the program output in Figure 2.20.

```
# define a variable to hold a string representing the base address
baseAddress = "192.168.0."
# next define a list of host addresses using the range
# standard library function (this will give us values of 1-19
hostAddresses = range(20)
# define a list that will hold the result ip strings
# this starts out as a simple empty list
ipRange = []
# loop through the host addresses since the list hostAddresses
# contains the integers from 0-19 and we can create
# a loop in Python that processes each of the list elements
# stored in hostAddresses, where i is the loop counter value
for i in hostAddresses:
# append the combined ip strings to the ipRange list
# because ipRange is a list object, the object has a set of
# attributes and methods. We are going to invoke the append method
# each time through the loop and concatenate the base address
# string with the string value of the integer
```

```
      ipRange.append(baseAddress+str(i))
#     |       |        |      |   |__ value of the host address
#     |       |        |      |__ function to convert int to str
#     |       |        |__ The string "192.168.0"
#     |       |__ The append method of the list ipRange
#     |__ The list object ipRange
#
# Once completed we want to print out the ip range list
# here we use the print function and instruct it to print out
# the ipRange list object, I wanted to print out each of the
# resulting ip address on a separate line, so I looped
# through the ipRange list object one entry at a time.
for ipAddr in ipRange:
      print ipAddr
```

Other built-in functions

The following is the complete list of *built-in functions* taken from the Python Standard Library documentation. You can get more information on each of the functions at the URL http://docs.python.org/2/library/functions.html

Built-in functions for Python version 2.x are given in Table 2.1.

I will be using a good number of these functions in Chapters 3–11, the Cookbook sections.

Table 2.1 Python 2.7 built-in functions

abs()	divmod()	input()	open()	staticmethod()
all()	enumerate()	int()	ord()	str()
any()	eval()	isinstance()	pow()	sum()
basestring()	execfile()	issubclass()	print()	super()
bin()	file()	iter()	property()	tuple()
bool()	filter()	len()	range()	type()
bytearray()	float()	list()	raw_input()	unichr()
callable()	format()	locals()	reduce()	unicode()
chr()	frozenset()	long()	reload()	vars()
classmethod()	getattr()	map()	repr()	xrange()
cmp()	globals()	max()	reversed()	zip()
compile()	hasattr()	memoryview()	round()	__import__()
complex()	hash()	min()	set()	apply()
delattr()	help()	next()	setattr()	buffer()
dict()	hex()	object()	slice()	coerce()
dir()	id()	oct()	sorted()	intern()

Built-in constants

There are several built-in constants within Python. Constants are different from variables in that constants, as the name implies, never change—while variables can take on ever changing values.

The two most important built-in constants within Python are True and False, which are Boolean values. Take a look at Figure 2.21, I have used the Python Shell to define two variables false = 0 and true = 1 (notice these are lower case). When I use the built-in Python function type() to identify the variable type, you notice that it returns the value of int (integer) for both true and false. However, when I use type() on True and False (the built-in constants) it returns type bool (Boolean).

By the same token you can create variables a = True and b = False (as shown in Figure 2.22) and check the type() and you see that they are of type bool. Do not get too dependent on this, however, as Python is NOT a *strongly typed language*. In a strongly typed language, a variable has a declared type that cannot change during the

```
C:\Python27\python.exe                                          _ |0| x|
Python 2.7.5 (default, May 15 2013, 22:43:36) [MSC v.1500 32 bit (Intel)] on win32
Type "help", "copyright", "credits" or "license" for more information.
>>>
>>> false = 0
>>> true = 1
>>>
>>> type(false)
<type 'int'>
>>> type(true)
<type 'int'>
>>>
>>> type(True)
<type 'bool'>
>>> type(False)
<type 'bool'>
>>>
>>>
```

FIGURE 2.21

Built-in True and False constants.

```
C:\Python27\python.exe                                          _ |0| x|
Python 2.7.5 (default, May 15 2013, 22:43:36) [MSC v.1500 32 bit (Intel)] on win32
Type "help", "copyright", "credits" or "license" for more information.
>>>
>>> a = True
>>> b = False
>>>
>>> type(a)
<type 'bool'>
>>>
>>> type(b)
<type 'bool'>
>>>
>>> a = range(100, 400, 2)
>>> type(a)
<type 'list'>
>>>
```

FIGURE 2.22

Python is not a strongly typed language.

life of the program. Python does not have this restriction; I could just as easily in the very next statement declare a = range(100, 400, 2) and change the type of variable a from a bool into a list. To a hard core developer in a strongly typed language such as Ada, C#, Java, or Pascal, this lack of structure would have them run for the hills, however, with the proper discipline in naming objects we can control most of the chaos.

When we develop our first real application in Chapter 3, I will cover some tips on how to develop forensically sound programs using a weakly typed language.

A strongly typed language must define the variable or object along with the specific type. This type must not change once declared and the compiler itself must enforce the typing rules, not the programmer. For example, if a variable is declared as an integer, it would be illegal to assign the value 3.14 to the variable.

Built-in types

Python has many built-in types that we can take advantage of in our forensic applications. For a detailed description of each of the standard built-in types, the most up-to-date information is available at: http://docs.python.org/2/library/stdtypes.html

The basic categories include:

Numeric Types: int, float, long and complex
Sequence Types: list, tuple, str, unicode, bytearray and buffer
Set Types: set and frozenset
Mapping Types: dict or dictionary
File Objects: file
Memory: MemoryView Type

We have already seen a few of these in action during the simple examples. We will be extensively leveraging some of the more advanced types throughout our example programs including: bytearray, lists, dictionaries, unicode, sets, frozensets, and the MemoryView Type. All of these have very unique forensic applications.

Some of the bitwise operations that are included in Python are vital to many forensic and examination operations. They are quite standard, but it is worth covering to give you a flavor of what is available. Bitwise operations are exclusive to integer data types of virtually any size. For the examples below the values of x and y are the integers.

x | y: bitwise *or* of the variables x and y
x ^y: bitwise *exclusive or* of variables x and y
x & y: bitwise *and* of variables x and y
x << n: variable x is *shifted* n bits left
x >> n: variable x is *shifted* n bits right
~x: the variable x bits are *inverted*

In Figure 2.23, I use the bitwise *exclusive or* operator ^ which is used in many one-way hash and cryptography operations. We start out by setting up our variables

```
C:\Python27\python.exe                                                    _ □ ×
Python 2.7.5 (default, May 15 2013, 22:43:36) [MSC v.1500 32 bit (Intel)] on win32
Type "help", "copyright", "credits" or "license" for more information.
>>>
>>> x=152
>>>
>>> y=103
>>>
>>> z=x^y
>>>
>>> print z
255
>>>
>>> print hex(z)
0xff
>>>
>>> print bin(z)
0b11111111
>>>
```

FIGURE 2.23

Apply an Exclusive OR (XOR)

x and y. We set x equal to 152 and y equal to 103—both decimal numbers. We then set z equal to the *exclusive or* of x and y. We can then print out the decimal, hex, and binary representations of the result.

As you can see *exclusive or* (XOR) differs from a simple OR operation. XOR requires that each bit of the two numbers be evaluated and a one is returned if and only if, only one of the bits is set to a one. For example:

> Binary 101
> Binary 001
> Produces:100

The least significant bit of each binary value is 1, therefore it does not meet the exclusivity test and the resulting value is 0.

Other more complex built-in types such as `memory view` types, `byte arrays`, `list`, `unicode`, and `dict` provide building blocks to tackle difficult data carving, search, indexing, and analytical analysis of the most complex digital evidence types available. I will be leveraging those extensively as we move into the example chapters.

Built-in exceptions

Most modern software languages support inline exception handling and Python is no different. Exception handling in most applications is important, but within forensic and digital investigation applications it is vital. When developing these applications it is important that you can demonstrate that you have handled all the possible situations. When developing an application we all tend to test our code using "happy mode testing." Ronda Caracappa, one of the best software quality people I have ever known, coined the phrase "happy mode testing" many years ago. This means that we test the normal flow of our programs with all the inputs, events, and third-party modules behaving exactly as we expect them to. The problem is they rarely, if ever do just that.

To facilitate exception handling, Python uses the `try/except` model. Here is an example: We setup our program to divide two numbers—in this case integer 27 divided by 0. If this were to happen while a program was running and we did not setup to catch such errors, the program would fault and crash. However, by using exception handling we can avoid trouble and handle the fault. In Chapter 3, our first real program, we will encounter several real-life conditions where exception handing is vital. And, with the help of Python's built-in exception handling, we can deal with the potential pitfalls with ease and use these exceptions to log any processing difficulties.

```
x = 27
y = 0
try:
    z = x / y
except:
    print("Divide by Zero")
```

Note this is a simple example of using the `try/except` method to catch execution-based exceptions, in a neat and tidy manner. Other examples dealing with operating system, file handling, and network exceptions will be demonstrated during the cookbook chapters.

File and directory access

The Python Standard Library provides a rich set of file and directory access services. These services not only provide the expected ability to open, read, and write files but they also include several very unique built-in capabilities; for example, common path name manipulations. Operating systems and platforms handle directory paths differently (i.e., Windows uses the *c:\users\...* notation while Unix environments utilize */etc/...* notation), and some operating environments support simple ASCII file and directory naming conventions, while others support full Unicode naming conventions. All file and directory access functions need to support these differences uniformly otherwise cross-platform operations would not be possible. In addition, built into the Python Standard Library file are directory compare functions, automatic creation of temporary directories and high-level file input handling which makes dealing with file systems easier for both novice and pros.

Data compression and archiving

Instead of having to use third-party libraries to perform standard compression and archiving functions like *zip* and *tar*, these functions are built-in. This includes not only compressing and decompressing archives but also includes extracting content information for *zip* files. During investigation, we often encounter encrypted *zip* files, and Python handles these as well (provided you either have the password or you can of course apply dictionary or brute force attack methods).

File formats

Also built into the Standard Library are modules to handle special file formats; for example, comma separated value (CSV) files, the Hypertext Markup Language (HTML), the eXtensible Markup Language (XML), and even the JavaScript Object Notation (JSON) format. We will be using these modules in later chapters to carve data from Web pages and other Internet content, and to create standardized XML output files for generating reports.

Cryptographic services

We will make extensive use of the hashlib cryptographic module to solve some basic problems that face digital investigators in Chapter 3. The hashlib module not only directly supports legacy one-way cryptographic hashing such as MD5 but also directly supports modern one-way hashing algorithms such as SHA-1, SHA256, and SHA512. The ease of integration and use of these libraries along with the optimized performance provides direct access to functions that are vital to digital investigation.

Operating system services

The operating systems (OS) services provide access to core OS functions that work across platforms. In Figure 2.24 I utilize the os *module* to list the contents of current working directory. The steps are pretty simple:

1. Import the os module
2. We use the os modules os.getcwd() method to retrieve the current working directory path, in other words the path we are currently on
3. We store that value in the variable myCWD

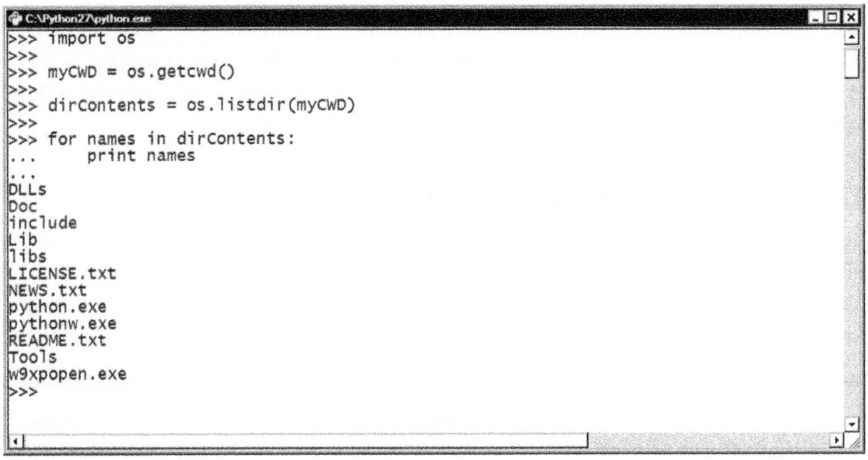

FIGURE 2.24

Example using the os module from the Standard Library.

4. We then use the `os.listdir()` method to obtain the names of the files and directories in the current working directory
5. Instead of just printing out `os.listdir()`, i.e., `print(os.listdir())` I decided to store the results into a new list named `dirContents`
6. I then use `dirContents` to print out each name on a separate line by processing through the list with a simple *for loop*

Having the files in a list enables us to process each of the files or directories based upon our needs.

Other operating system services such as stream-based `io`, `time`, `logging`, `parsing`, and `platform` modules all provide easy access to operating system services. Once again, on a cross-platform basis this is to easily handle Windows, Linux, Mac, and numerous legacy systems.

Standard Library summary

This has been just a quick introduction and tour of only a few of the Standard Library capabilities built directly into Python. There are many good references and complete books dedicated to this subject for those that want to delve further. However, there are also online resources available directly at Python.org, where you can find a plethora of tutorials, code examples, and support for every Standard Library data type, module, attribute, and method. My goal here was just to give you a taste of what you can do and how easy it is to use the Standard Library.

In the next section, I will introduce you to some of the third-party libraries that we will be using and what they bring to the party.

THIRD-PARTY PACKAGES AND MODULES

As I mentioned earlier, many third-party packages and modules are available and I will introduce each during the cookbook Chapters 3–11. However, I wanted to mention a couple here to give you an idea why third-party modules are available and the kind of capabilities that they bring to digital investigation.

The natural language toolkit [NLTK]

Today when performing investigations, e-discovery, or incident response, it is important to determine what was communicated via e-mail, text message, written documents, and other correspondence. We utilize crude tools and technologies today like simple keyword and phrase searching and *grep* to discover and parse these communications.

Grep, which is short for global regular expression print, allows users to search text for the occurrence of a defined regular expression. Regular expressions are composed of meta characters and usually a sequence of text characters that represent a given pattern, which allow the computer program to perform advanced or simple pattern matching.

The problem is these technologies do not consider language or semantics, thus it is easy to miss certain communications or maybe misunderstand them. The NLTK modules provide an infrastructure to create real Natural Language programs and build small or even large corpus.

A corpus is a collection of material which is most often written, but can be spoken material as well. The material is digitally organized in such a way that it lends itself to the study of linguistic structures which helps to understand meaning.

This gives us the ability to search, understand, and derive meaning. We will be using NLTK in one of our Cookbook examples to help produce specific applications to assist digital investigators. For example, we can use linguistics to help determine if specific documents were likely to have been written by a specific person.

Twisted matrix [TWISTED]

In a world where everything is connected, our ability to collect and examine evidence requires both a postmortem and a live investigation mindset. This implies that we must have a reliable network library that provides an asynchronous and event-based environment that is open source and written in Python. This includes TCP, UDP, Web Services, Mail Services, Authentication, Secure Shell support, and quite a bit more.

INTEGRATED DEVELOPMENT ENVIRONMENTS

As I mentioned at the outset of this chapter, one of the keys to success would be the establishment of an IDE that would provide value, instill confidence, and create efficiencies during the development process. In our case, we also want to ensure that the quality of what we create will exceed the standards of evidence. You have several options for an IDE—some of which are completely free—and some which have a nominal cost of entry. I will reveal my choice at the end of the section, but you can choose your own path, as in many ways this is like choosing between Nike® or Adidas® and is mostly defined by what you like and are comfortable with.

What are the options?

Actually, it may require a whole book to answer that question! Here is just a short list of the available options: IDLE, PyCharm, PyDev, WingIDE, and μDev. I will narrow my focus to just two—IDLE and WingIDE.

IDLE

IDLE specifically stands for Integrated Development Environment and the name was chosen by Guido Van Russom the creator of Python. IDLE is written in Python and has a nice set of features that can handle basic integrated development. It includes a Python Shell to experiment with commands; it highlights source code and provides cross-platform support. IDLE does support a debugger allowing users to set break-points and step through code (Figure 2.25). However, it was not developed as a professional development environment, but it does support users that are developing simple applications, and students that are learning the language. Best thing is that it is completely free. Please note, I am sure that there are many Python developers

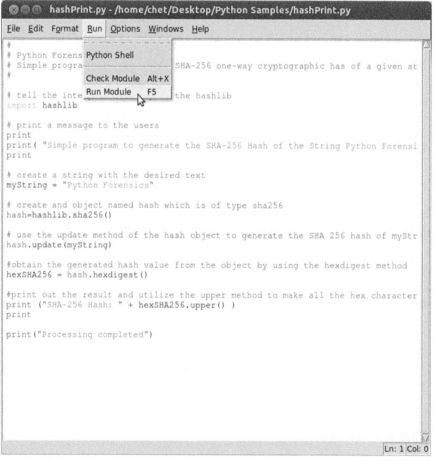

FIGURE 2.25

Python IDLE integrated development environment.

out there that use Python IDLE and will disagree with my statement about not considering it as a professional development environment, as I am sure many of you have developed quite sophisticated applications with IDLE and I accept that. But I think for developing digital investigation applications today, there are several other alternatives that have more advanced capabilities.

WingIDE

WingIDE on the other hand is not free (you can obtain a free version if you are a student or unpaid open source developer), but does have a rich feature set that will easily support the development of sophisticated Python Applications. WingIDE comes in three flavors based on your intended use:

1. Free for students and unpaid open source developers
2. WingIDE Personal—As the name implies, limits some features
3. WingIDE Professional—For those wanting all the features and support, for example, this version contains unit testing, direct interface with revision control systems, advanced debugging and breakpoint settings, and pyLint integration.

---

pyLint is a Python source code analyzer that helps to identify poor coding practices, points out potential bugs, and warns you about the likelihood of failure. It will also assign an overall grade for your code to help you to keep improving.

You can see the layout I have chosen for WingIDE in Figure 2.26. The IDE is configurable and resizable to allow you to customize the GUI. I have placed labels in each of the major sections in order to cover them here.

Section A: In this section, we find the current local and global variables associated with the current running program, since I have the program momentarily stopped at a breakpoint. As you can see, the text box at the top indicates that module *ipRange.py* is currently processing line 10. In the window it displays the variable `baseAddress` currently containing the string "192.168.0."

Section B: Displays the program output so far. The initial `print` statement has successfully printed the string "Generating ip Range." At the bottom of that window you can see several other options; the currently selected option is "Debug I/O." Another quite useful option is the "Python Shell." If this option is selected you can execute, learn, or experiment with any of the Python functions or even write a sequence of statements to try before you code (see Figure 2.27).

Section C: This window contains the project information. Due to the fact this is a very simple project only containing a single file, *ipRange.py*, that is all that is displayed in that window. As we build more complex applications this window will help you keep track of all the components of your program.

Section D: This window contains the source code of the current program, along with debug settings. Notice that line 10 contains a dot where the breakpoint was set and it is highlighted because the program reached that point and the breakpoint stopped execution.

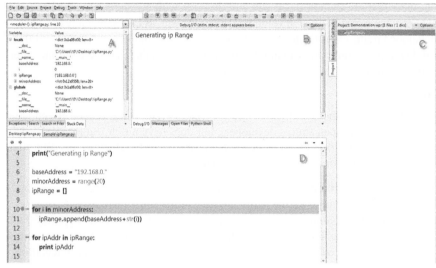

FIGURE 2.26

Snapshot of WingIDE 4.1 Personal.

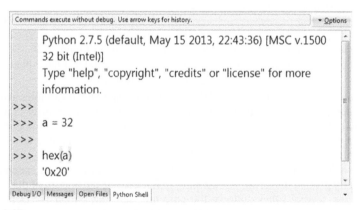

FIGURE 2.27

WingIDE Python Shell display.

Now that you have the general idea, let us actually step through this simple program with WingIDE and watch the changes happen. In Figure 2.28 we step over (I used the [F6] key to do this, you could also select the option under the debug menu) the code below and stop before executing the ipRange initialization.

```
baseAddress = "192.168.0."
minorAddress = range(20)
ipRange = []
```

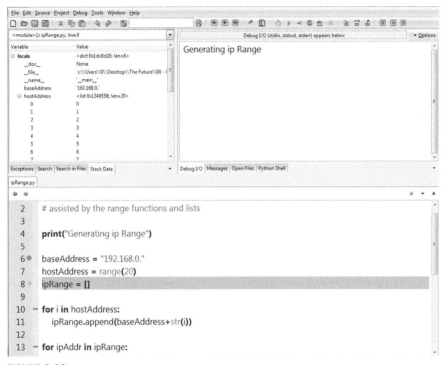

FIGURE 2.28

WingIDE in action.

At this point we can examine the variable section top left (in Figure 2.28) and we see that the variable `baseAddress` is equal to the string "192.168.0" and the variable `hostAddress` is a list with length 20 and has values 0-19 as expected. We name this variable `hostAddress` because in typical Class C address, the last dotted decimal digit typically identifies the host. We consider naming conventions for variables, functions, methods, and attributes as we get into the Cookbook chapters, but I am sure you can already see the pattern.

Next, I am going to step over the initialization of the `ipRange` (again using [F6]) and also step into the "for loop" stopping before we execute the first `ipRange.append` method. As you can see in Figure 2.29, the new variables `i` which equals 0, and is the first `hostAddress`, and `ipRange`, which is currently an empty list, have now appeared.

Now I am going to step through each of the for loop items, 20 iterations in this case and stop on the first print statement of the second loop. You notice in Figure 2.30 in the variable section, I have expanded the contents of the `ipRange` list and you see the completed `ipRange` strings that now contain the added host addresses. All that is left is to print out the `ipRange` array line by line.

This should give you a good overview of the capabilities of WingIDE and how to use it to set breakpoints, step through the code, and examine variables. I will be using this IDE throughout the rest of the book introducing advanced features as we go.

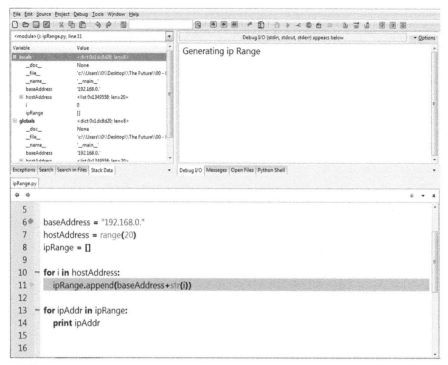

FIGURE 2.29

Using WingIDE to step through code.

One final feature that I use a great deal when writing code is auto-completion. In Figure 2.31, I want to see what other methods and attributes are associated with the list ipRange. We have seen what the append method does, but you might be wondering what else we can do. By simply adding a line of code, ipRange, and entering a dot (a period), a list box automatically appears and displays all the attributes and methods that are available for ipRange. Note that since ipRange is a *list*, these are actually the attributes and methods that can be generally applied to any list. The dropdown you see is only a partial list of methods and attributes. As you can see, I have scrolled down to the sort method which would allow me to sort the list. The parameters that I pass to the sort method will determine how the list will actually be sorted.

Up to this point we have focused on developing and debugging on a Windows platform. In the next section, we will walk through an Ubuntu Linux installation and quick session.

Python running on Ubuntu Linux

There are many investigation and forensic advantages to Linux-based tools. You can of course achieve greater performance, safely mount a wide range of media and image types, avoid the cost of the operating system, and have potentially greater flexibility. So let us setup Python running on Ubuntu. It really is easier than you might think.

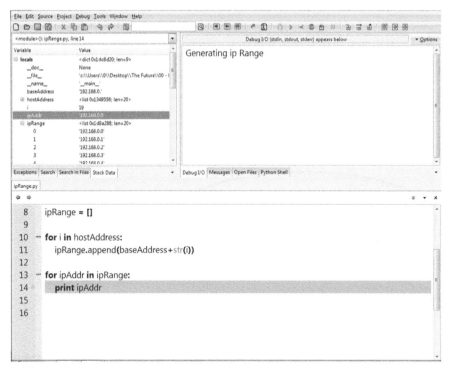

FIGURE 2.30

WingIDE examination of the completed list.

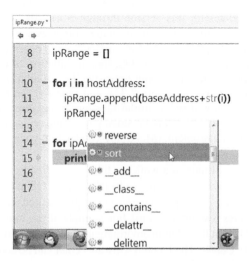

FIGURE 2.31

WingIDE auto complete feature.

FIGURE 2.32

Ubuntu download Web page 12.04 LTS.

As of this writing, I would make the following strong recommendation on Ubuntu installation and setup. In Figure 2.32 you see a screenshot from the Ubuntu download page (http://www.ubuntu.com/download/desktop). Version 12.x LTS of Ubuntu is your best bet. This version is available in either 32 or 64 bit and is verified to operate on a wide range of standard desktop PCs. I am choosing version 12.x LTS because this is the long-term support version of the OS. Ubuntu is promising to provide support and security updates for this version through April 2017, giving you a stable well-tested platform for digital investigation and forensics.

As far as installing and running Python on the Ubuntu operating system, version 2.7.3 is already installed as part of the OS, thus installation of the base product is done for you. If you are not sure about your specific installation, simply launch a terminal window (as shown in Figure 2.33), and type Python at the prompt. If it is installed properly you will see a similar message as the one shown.

If this does not produce the desired results, you should reinstall Ubuntu 12.x LTS and this should repair the problem. (Make sure you backup your data before attempting any reinstall.)

If you have not used Linux in a while, or this is your first time installing Ubuntu, you will find that the days of struggling to install a Linux OS are over. As the saying goes "it is as easy as pie." Once you have successfully installed the OS, the process of adding new capabilities is straightforward. For example, if you intend to install an IDE like WingIDE or IDLE in the Ubuntu environment, you can obtain the installers from the Ubuntu Software Center. The Ubuntu software center can be contacted by clicking on the taskbar item show in Figure 2.34, and searching for your desired application.

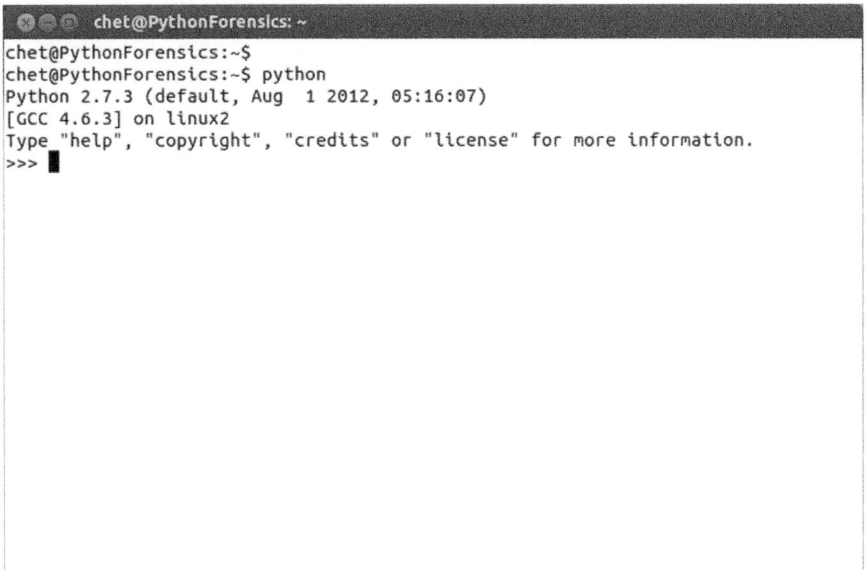

chet@PythonForensics: ~
chet@PythonForensics:~$
chet@PythonForensics:~$ python
Python 2.7.3 (default, Aug 1 2012, 05:16:07)
[GCC 4.6.3] on linux2
Type "help", "copyright", "credits" or "license" for more information.
>>>

FIGURE 2.33

Ubuntu terminal window Python command.

Ubuntu Software Center
All Software
Python integrated
Development Environment

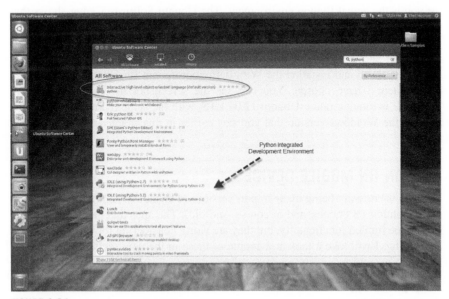

FIGURE 2.34

Ubuntu software center.

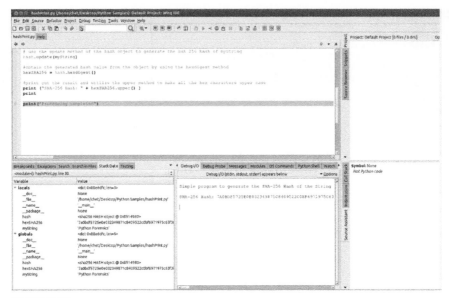

FIGURE 2.35

WingIDE running on Ubuntu 12.04 LTS.

As you see, I have searched for Python and the Software Center displays all the relevant applications and services for me. You notice the first item that I have circled for you is the actual Python environment. The Ubuntu Software Center shows that this application is already installed (notice the checkmark in front of the icon). Also, you see that two different versions of the IDLE IDE are also listed one supporting version 2.7 and the other supporting version 3.2.

I went ahead and installed the WingIDE environment for Ubuntu as this is the environment I have chosen. You can see the screenshot in Figure 2.35 where WingIDE is running under Ubuntu 12.04 LTS, with the same feature set and operation as the Windows version that you saw earlier in this chapter.

PYTHON ON MOBILE DEVICES

Progress is currently being made to port versions of Python to smart mobile devices (iOS, Windows 8 Phones, and of course Android). The apps that have been created have some limited functionality, but they are worth considering for experimentation or learning. I will take a look at a couple of these in the next section.

iOS Python app

Python for iOS is the version that I find most stable and supported for iPad. In Figure 2.36, you can see an image of the Python 2.7 Shell running on iOS, just

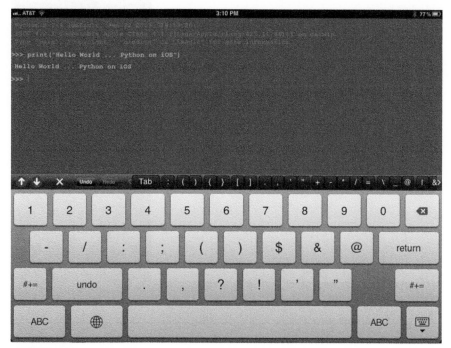

FIGURE 2.36

Python Shell running on iOS.

printing out the similar Hello World message. The Shell and editor have some great features that allow you to experiment with the Python language syntax and modules.

The capability is actually quite a bit better than this simple example. I imported one of the earlier examples that performs a SHA256 Hash of a string. At the top of the short program I added a couple of new methods, one contained in the Standard Library module *sys* and one in the Standard Library module *platform*. I imported the two modules and wrote the following code.

```
import sys
import platform
print("Platform: "+sys.platform)
print("Machine: "+platform.machine())
```

You can see the results of these new methods and the program in Figure 2.37. You notice that Platform is defined as Darwin and the Machine is identified as an iPad version 1. Correct in both cases. Darwin is the platform name specified by Apple for Mac OS X and of course the machine is my old and still faithful iPad 1.

For those interested in checking out this iOS application from the Apple App Store, Figure 2.38 is a screenshot from the Store with more details about Python for iOS.

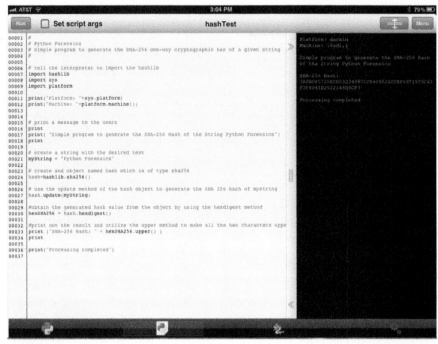

FIGURE 2.37

iOS implementation of HashPrint.

FIGURE 2.38

Apple App Store page regarding Python for iOS.

Windows 8 phone

Finally, we can take a look at the Microsoft Windows 8 OS on a Nokia Lumia Phone. Yes—Python on a Phone. I tried several applications from the Microsoft store before I found one that worked pretty well. *PyConsole* (short for Python Console), shown in the launcher menu in Figure 2.39, ran the sample *hashPrint.py* program unchanged.

As we progress through the book, we will come back to these devices and others to see how well the more advanced applications work on each of them.

When the app launches it brings up a simple Python Shell as shown in Figure 2.40. I typed in a simple Hello Mobile World message, and you can see that I ran the script. The result appears in the display windows at the bottom of the screen.

Turning to the simple SHA256 hashing example shown in Figure 2.41, we see the code and execution of the program producing the same results as the other platforms.

If you are interested in the Python Console Windows 8 Phone application, Figure 2.42 depicts a screenshot from the Windows Store.

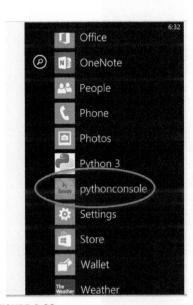

FIGURE 2.39

Windows 8 Phone screenshot of *PyConsole* launching

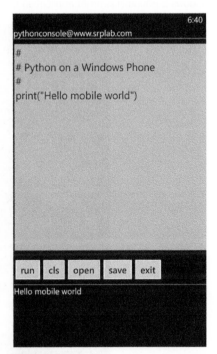

FIGURE 2.40

Python Console "Hello World" on a Windows 8 Phone.

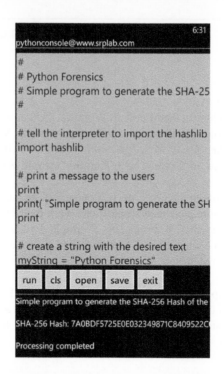

FIGURE 2.41

Windows 8 Phone HashPrint application execution.

FIGURE 2.42

Python Console Windows App Store page.

A VIRTUAL MACHINE

Today, we have virtual machines for everything from complete server infrastructures to specialized applications, standardized development environments, databases, client services, desktops, and more. For those who want a really quick start, I have created a Ubuntu Python Environment that will be available in conjunction with the publication of this book. The environment includes a standard Ubuntu install, all the packages, modules, and Cookbook applications from Chapters 3 to 11. I have also included any test data so you can start experimenting with the simplest or most advanced digital investigation or forensic applications found within. You can access the virtual machine by going to www.python-forensics.org.

CHAPTER REVIEW

In this chapter we took a very broad, and in some cases deep, look at setting up a Python environment in the Microsoft Windows and Linux environment. We reviewed where to download the latest Python environment from the official source and walked through the steps of installing a Windows Python environment. We also made specific recommendation on the Ubuntu version of choice that include Python version 2.x already installed as part of the OS. We looked at the key differences between Python 2.x and 3.x. We also pulled back the covers a bit on the Python Standard Library and dialed in on some of the key built-in functions, data types, and modules. We even developed a few example applications that exercised the Standard Library and showed how a program written in Python could run without modification on Windows, Linux, iOS, or on a Windows 8 phone. MacOS is also supported and Python 2.x comes with the standard install of the latest versions.

We examined two specific third-party packages that address Natural Language and network applications, respectively. We also examined some of the capabilities that we will need included in an IDE, and took a step-by-step look at the features of WingIDE and briefly covered the IDLE IDE. Finally, we experimented with the Python Shell on all the computing platforms mentioned here.

SUMMARY QUESTIONS

1. What do you think would be the best Python development environment based on the following circumstances?
   a. A student looking to experiment with Python forensics
   b. A developer that plans to build and distribute Python investigative solutions
   c. A laboratory that processes actual cases, but needs specialized tools and capabilities that do not exist within standard forensic tools

2. What are some of the key features you would be looking for in an IDE if you are creating and utilizing Python forensic applications on actual cases or during real investigations?
3. What version of Ubuntu Linux would you choose for your platform of choice and why?
4. How might you utilize mobile platforms like iOS, Android, or Windows 8 devices for investigative purposes when a fully functional Python environment is available for them?
5. What are some of the key considerations for choosing Python 2.x vs. 3.x today?
6. What third-party modules or package would assist in Natural Language Processing?
7. What third-party modules or packages would assist in creating asynchronous network applications?

LOOKING AHEAD

We are now going to transition into the Cookbook chapters of the book, where in each chapter we tackle a specific forensic or digital investigation challenge. We will define the challenge, specify requirements, design an approach, code a solution, and finally test and validate the solution.

As we go forward, I will be slowly introducing new language constructs, packages and modules, debugging methodologies, and good coding practices in each chapter. So, I hope by this time you have setup your Python IDE and are ready to get started.

Additional Resources

Python Programming Language—Official Website, Python.org. http://www.python.org.
The Python Standard Library. http://docs.python.org/2/library/.
The Natural Language Toolkit. nltk.org.
Twisted Network Programming for Python. http://twistedmatrix.com.

Our First Python Forensics App

CHAPTER CONTENTS

INTRODUCTION

In 1998, I authored a paper entitled "Using SmartCards and Digital Signatures to Preserve Electronic Evidence" (Hosmer, 1998). The purpose of the paper was to advance the early work of Gene Kim, creator of the original Tripwire technology (Kim, 1993) as a graduate student at Purdue. I was interested in advancing the model of using one-way hashing technologies to protect digital evidence, and specifically I was applying the use of digital signatures bound to a SmartCard that provided two-factor authenticity of the signing (Figure 3.1).

Years later I added trusted timestamps to the equation adding provenance, or proof of the exact "when" of the signing.

Two-factor authentication combines a secure physical device such as a SmartCard with a password that unlocks the capability of the card's. This yields "something held" and "something known." In order to perform applications like signing, you must be in possession of the SmartCard and you must know the pin or password that unlocks the cards function.

Thus, my interest in applying one-way hashing methods, digital signature algorithms, and other cryptographic technologies to the field of forensics has been a 15-year journey ... so far. The application of these technologies to evidence preservation, evidence identification, authentication, access control decisions and network protocols continues today. Thus I want to make sure that you have a firm understanding of the underlying technologies and the many applications for digital investigation, and of course the use of Python forensics.

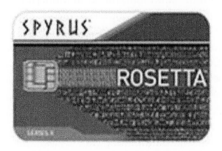

FIGURE 3.1

Cryptographic SmartCard.

Before I dive right in and start writing code, as promised I want to set up some ground rules for using the Python programming language in forensic applications.

NAMING CONVENTIONS AND OTHER CONSIDERATIONS

During the development of Python forensics applications, I will define the rules and naming conventions that are being used throughout the cookbook chapters in the book. Part of this is to compensate for Python's lack of the enforcement of strongly typed variables and true constants. More importantly it is to define a style that will make the programs more readable, and easier to follow, understand, and modify or enhance.

Therefore, here are the naming conventions I will be using.

Constants

Rule: Uppercase with underscore separation
   Example: HIGH_TEMPERATURE

Local variable name

Rule: Lowercase with bumpy caps (underscores are optional)
   Example: currentTemperature

Global variable name

Rule: Prefix *gl* lowercase with bumpy caps (underscores are optional)
   Note: Globals should be contained to a single module
   Example: gl_maximumRecordedTemperature

Functions name

Rule: Uppercase with bumpy caps (underscores optional) with active voice
   Example: ConvertFarenheitToCentigrade(...)

Object name

Rule: Prefix *ob_* lowercase with bumpy caps
   Example: ob_myTempRecorder

Module

Rule: An underscore followed by lowercase with bumpy caps
   Example: _tempRecorder

Class names

Rule: Prefix *class_* then bumpy caps and keep brief

Example: class_TempSystem

You will see many of these naming conventions in action during this chapter.

OUR FIRST APPLICATION "ONE-WAY FILE SYSTEM HASHING"

The objective for our first Python Forensic Application is as follows:

1. Build a useful application and tool for forensic investigators.
2. Develop several modules along the way that are *reusable* throughout the book and for future applications.
3. Develop a solid methodology for building Python forensic applications.
4. Begin to introduce more advanced features of the language.

Background

Before we can build an application that performs one-way file system hashing I need to better define one-way hashing. Many of you reading this are probably saying, "I already know what a one-way hashing is, let's move on." However, this is such an important underpinning for computer forensics it is worthy of a good definition, possibly even a better one that you currently have.

One-way hashing algorithms' basic characteristics

1. The one-way hashing algorithm takes a stream of binary data as input; this could be a password, a file, an image of a hard drive, an image of a solid state drive, a network packet, 1's and 0's from a digital recording, or basically any continuous digital input.
2. The algorithm produces a message digest which is a compact representation of the binary data that was received as input.
3. It is infeasible to determine the binary input that generated the digest with only the digest. In other words, it is not possible to reverse the process using the digest to recover the stream of binary data that created it.
4. It is infeasible to create a new binary input that will generate a given message digest.
5. Changing a single bit of the binary input data will generate a unique message digest.
6. Finally, it is infeasible to find two unique arbitrary streams of binary data that produce the same digest.

Table 3.1 Popular One-Way Hashing Algorithms

Algorithm	Creator	Length (Bits)	Related standard
MD5	Ronald Rivest	128	RFC 1321
SHA-1	NSA and published by NIST	160	FIPS Pub 180
SHA-2	NSA and published by NIST	224 256 384 512	FIPS Pub 180-2 FIPS Pub 180-3 FIPS PUB 180-4
RIPEMD-160	Hans Dobbertin	160	Open Academic Community
SHA-3	Guido Bertoni, Joan Daemen, Michaël Peeters, and Gilles Van Assche	224, 256, 384, 512	FIPS-180-5

Popular cryptographic hash algorithms?

There are a number of algorithms that produce message digests. Table 3.1 provides background on some of the most popular algorithms.

What are the tradeoffs between one-way hashing algorithms?

The MD5 algorithm is still in use today, and for many applications the speed, convenience, and interoperability have made it the algorithm of choice. Due to attacks on the MD5 algorithm and the increased likelihood of collisions, many organizations are moving to SHA-2 (256 and 512 bits are the most popular sizes). Many organizations have opted to skip SHA-1 as it suffers from some of the same weaknesses as MD5.

Considerations for moving to SHA-3 are still in the future, and it will be a couple of years before broader adoption is in play. SHA-3 is completely different and was designed to be easier to implement in hardware to improve performance (speed and power consumption) for use in embedded or handheld devices. We will see how quickly the handheld devices' manufacturers adopt this newly established standard.

What are the best-use cases for one-way hashing algorithms in forensics?

Evidence preservation: When digital data are collected (for example, when imaging a mechanical or solid state drive), the entire contents—in other words every bit collected—are combined to create a unique one-way hashing value. Once completed the recalculation of the one-way hashing can be accomplished. If the new calculation matches the original, this can prove that the evidence has not been modified. This assumes of course that the original calculated hash value has been safeguarded against tampering since there is no held secret and the algorithms are available. Anyone could recalculate a hash, therefore the chain of custody of digital evidence, including the generated hash, must be maintained.

Search: One-way hashing values have been traditionally utilized to perform searches of known file objects. For example, if law enforcement has a collection of confirmed child-pornography files, the hashes could be calculated for each file. Then any suspect system could be scanned for the presence of this contraband by calculating the hash values of each file and comparing the resulting hashes to the known list of contraband hash values (those resulting from the child-pornography collection). If matches are found, then the files on the suspect system matching the hash values would be examined further.

Black Listing: Like the search example, it is possible to create a list of known bad hash files. These could represent contraband as with CP example, they could match known malicious code or cyber weapon files or the hashes of classified or proprietary documents. The discovery of hashes matching any of these Black Listed items would provide investigators with key evidence.

White Listing: By creating a list of known good or benign hashes (operating system or application executables, vendor supplied dynamic link libraries or known trustworthy application download files), investigators can use the lists to filter out files that they do not have to examine, because they were previously determined as a good file. Using this methodology you can dramatically reduce the number of files that require examination and then focus your attention on files that are not in the known good hash list.

Change detection: One popular defense against malicious changes to websites, routers, firewall configuration, and even operating system installations is to hash a "known good" installation or configuration. Then periodically you can re-scan the installation or configuration to ensure no files have changed. In addition, you must of course make sure no files have been added or deleted from the "known good" set.

Fundamental requirements

Now that we have a better understanding of one-way hashing and its uses, what are the fundamental requirements of our one-way file system hash application?

When defining requirements for any program or application I want to define them as succinctly as possible, and with little jargon, so anyone familiar with the domain could understand them—even if they are not software developers. Also, each requirement should have an identifier such that could be traced from definition, through design, development, and validation. I like to give the designers and developers room to innovate, thus I try to focus on WHAT not HOW during requirements definition (Table 3.2).

Table 3.2 Basic Requirements

Requirement number	Requirement name	Short description
000	Overview	The basic capability we are looking for is a forensic application that walks the file system at a defined starting point (for example, c:\ or /etc) and then generates a one-way hashing value for every file encountered
001	Portability	The application shall support Windows and Linux operating systems. As a general guideline, validation will be performed on Windows 7, Windows 8, and Ubuntu 12.04 LTS environments
002	Key functions	In addition to the one-way hashing generation, the application shall collect system metadata associated with each file that is hashed. For example, file attributes, file name, and file path at a minimum
003	Key results	The application shall provide the results in a standard output file format that offers flexibility
004	Algorithm selection	The application shall provide a wide diversity when specifying the one-way hashing algorithm(s) to be used
005	Error handling	The application must support error handling and logging of all operations performed. This will include a textual description and a timestamp

Design considerations

Now that I have defined the basic requirements for the application I need to factor in the design considerations. First, I would like to leverage or utilize as many of the built-in functions of the Python Standard Library as possible. Taking stock of the core capabilities, I like to map the requirements definition to Modules and Functions that I intend to use. This will then expose any new modules either from third party modules or new modules that need to be developed (Table 3.3).

One of the important steps as a designer or at least one of the fun parts is to name the program. I have decided to name this first program p-fish short for *Python-file system hashing.*

Next, based on this review of Standard Library functions I must define what modules will be used in our first application:

1. `argparse` for user input
2. `os` for file system manipulation
3. `hashlib` for one-way hashing
4. `csv` for result output (other optional outputs could be added later)
5. `logging` for event and error logging
6. Along with useful miscellaneous modules like `time`, `sys`, and `stat`

Table 3.3 Standard Library Mapping

Requirement	Design considerations	Library selection
User input (000, 003, 004)	Each of these requirements needs input from the user to accomplish the task. For example, 000 requires the user to specify the starting directory path. 003 requires that the user specify a suitable output format. 004 requires us to allow the user to specify the hash algorithm. Details of the exception handling or default settings need to be defined (if allowed)	For this first program I have decided to use the command line parameters to obtain input from the user. Based on this design decision I can leverage the argparse Python Standard Library module
Walk the file system (000, 001)	This capability requires the program to traverse the directory structure starting at a specific starting point. Also, this must work on both Windows and Linux platforms	The OS Module from the Standard Library provides key methods that provide the ability to walk the file system, OS also provides abstraction which will provide cross platform compatibility. Finally, this module contains cross platform capabilities that provide access to metadata associated with files
Meta data collection (003)	This requires us to collect the directory path, filename, owner, modified/access/created times, permissions, and attributes such as read only, hidden, system or archive	
File hashing (000)	I must provide flexibility in the Hashing algorithms that the users could select. I have decided to support the most popular algorithms such as MD5 and several variations of SHA	The Standard Library module hashlib provides the ability to generate one-way hashing values. The library supports common hash algorithms such as "md5," "sha1," "sha224," "sha256," "sha384," "sha512." This should provide a sufficient set of selection for the user
Result output (003)	To meet this requirement I must be able to structure the program output to support a format that provides flexibility	The Standard Library offers multiple options that I could leverage. For example, the csv module provides the ability to create comma separated value output, whereas the json module (Java Object Notation) provides encoder and decoders for JSON objects and finally the XML module could be leveraged to create XML output

Continued

Table 3.3 Standard Library Mapping—cont'd

Requirement	Design considerations	Library selection
Logging and error handling	I must expect that errors will occur during our walk of the file system, for example I might not have access to certain files, or certain files may be orphaned, or certain files maybe locked by the operating system or other applications. I need to handle these error conditions and log any notable events. For example, I should log information about the investigator, location, date and time, and information that pertains to the system that are walked	The Python Standard Library includes a `logging` facility which I can leverage to report any events or errors that occur during processing

Program structure

Next, I need to define the structure of our program, in other words how I intend to put the pieces together. This is critical, especially if our goal is to reuse components of this program in future applications. One way to compose the components is with a couple simple diagrams as shown in Figures 3.2 and 3.3.

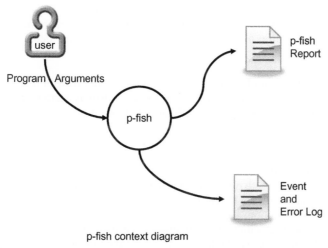

p-fish context diagram

FIGURE 3.2

Context diagram: Python-file system hashing (p-fish).

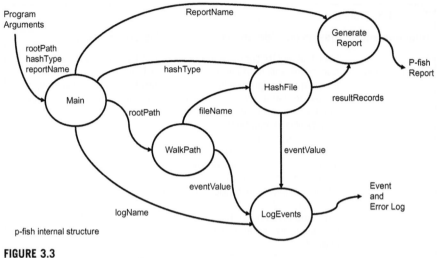

FIGURE 3.3

p-fish internal structure.

The context diagram is very straightforward and simply depicts the major inputs and outputs of the proposed program. A user specifies the program arguments, p-fish takes those inputs and processes (hashes, extracts metadata, etc.) the file system produces a report and any notable events or errors to the "p-fish report" and the "p-fish event and error log" files respectively.

Turning to the internal structure I have broken the program down into five major components. The `Main` program, `ParseCommandLine` function, `WalkPath` function, `HashFile` functions, `CSVWriter` class and logger (note logger is actually the Python logger module), that is utilized by the major functions of pfish. I briefly describe the operation of each below and during the code walk through section a more detailed line by line explanation of how each function operates is provided.

Main function
The purpose of the Main function is to control the overall flow of this program. For example, within Main I set up the Python logger, I display startup and completion messages, and keep track of the time. In addition, Main invokes the command line parser and then launches the `WalkPath` function. Once `WalkPath` completes Main will log the completion and display termination messages to the user and the log.

ParseCommandLine
In order to provide smooth operation of p-fish, I leverage parseCommandLine to not only parse but also validate the user input. Once completed, information that is germane to program functions such as `WalkPath`, `HashFile`, and `CSVWrite` is available from parser-generated values. For example, since the `hashType` is specified by the user, this value must be available to `HashFile`. Likewise the `CSVWriter` needs the path where the resulting pfish report will be written, and `WalkPath` requires the starting or `rootPath` to start the walk.

WalkPath function

The `WalkPath` function must start at the root of the directory tree or path and traverse every directory and file. For each valid file encountered it will call the `HashFile` function to perform the one-way hashing operations. Once all the files have been processed `WalkPath` will return control back to Main with the number of files successfully processed.

HashFile function

The `HashFile` function will open, read, hash, and obtain metadata regarding the file in question. For each file, a row of data will be sent to the `CSVWriter` to be included in the p-fish report. Once the file has been processed, `HashFile` will return control back to `WalkPath` in order to fetch the next file.

CSVWriter (class)

In order to provide an introduction to class and object usage I decided to create `CSVWriter` as a class instead of a simple function. You will see more of this in upcoming cookbook chapters but `CSVWriter` sets up nicely for a class/object demonstration. The csv module within the Python Standard Library requires that the "writer" be initialized. For example, I want the resulting csv file to have a header row made up of a static set of columns. Then subsequent calls to writer will contain data that fills in each row. Finally, once the program has processed all the files the resulting csv report must be closed. Note that as I walk through the program code you may wonder why I did not leverage classes and objects more for this program. I certainly could have, but felt for the first application I would create a more function-oriented example.

Logger

The built-in Standard Library logger provides us with the ability to write messages to a log file associated with p-fish. The program can write information messages, warning messages, and error messages. Since this is intended to be a forensic application, logging operations of the program is vital. You can expand the program to log additional events in the code, they can be added to any of the _pfish functions.

Writing the code

I decided to create two files, mainly to show you how to create your own Python module and also to give you some background on how to separate capabilities. For this first simple application, I created (1) pfish.py and (2) _pfish.py. As you may recall, all modules that are created begin with an underscore and since _pfish.py contains all the support functions for pfish I simply named it _pfish.py. If you would like to split out the modules to better separate the functions you could create separate modules for the `HashFile` function, the `WalkPath` function, etc. This is a decision that is typically based on how tightly or loosely coupled the functions are, or better stated, whether you wish to reuse individual functions later that need to standalone. If that is the case, then you should separate them out.

In Figure 3.4 you can see my IDE setup for the project pfish. You notice the project section to the far upper right that specifies the files associated with the project. I also have both files open—you can see the two tabs far left about half way down

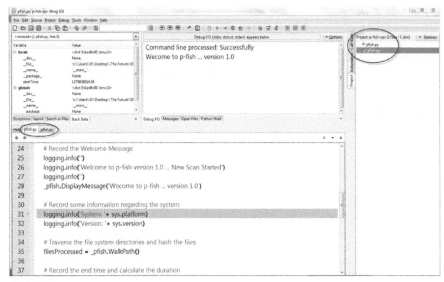

FIGURE 3.4

p-fish WingIDE setup.

where I can view the source code in each of the files. As you would expect in the upper left quadrant, you can see the program is running and the variables are available for inspection. Finally, in the upper center portion of the screen you can see the current display messages from the program reporting that the command line was processed successfully and the welcome message for pfish.

CODE WALK-THROUGH

I will be inserting dialog as I discuss each code section. The code walk-through will give you an in-depth look at all the code associated with the program. I will be first walking through each of the key functions and then will provide you with a complete listing of both files.

Examining main—code walk-through

The embedded commentary is represented in italics, while the code itself is represented in a fixed-sized font.

```
# p-fish : Python File System Hash Program
# Author: C. Hosmer
# July 2013
# Version 1.0
#
```

The main program code is quite straightforward. At the top as you would expect, you see the import statements that make the Python Standard Library modules available for our use. What you have not seen before is the import statement referencing our own module in this case _pfish. Since I will be calling functions from Main that exist in our module, the module must import our own module _pfish.

```
import logging    # Python Library logging functions
import time       # Python Library time manipulation functions
import sys        # Python Library system specific parameters
import _pfish     # _pfish Support Function Module

if __name__ == '__main__':
    PFISH_VERSION = '1.0'
    # Turn on Logging
```

Next, you can see my initialization of the Python logging system. In this example I have hard-wired the log to be stored in the file aptly named pFishLog.log. I set the logging level to DEGUG and specified that I wanted the Time and Date recorded for each log event. By setting the level to DEBUG (which is the lowest level) this will ensure all messages sent to the logger will be visible.

```
    logging.basicConfig(filename='pFishLog.log',level=logging.
    DEBUG,format='%(asctime)s %(message)s')
```

Next, I pass control to process the command line arguments by calling the _pfish. ParseCommandLine() function. I must prefix the function with _pfish, since the function exists in the _pfish module. If the parse is successful, the function will return here, if not, it will post a message to the user and exit the program. I will take a deeper look at the operation of ParseCommandLine() in the next section.

```
    # Process the Command Line Arguments
    _pfish.ParseCommandLine()
```

I need to record the current starting time of the application in order to calculate elapsed time for processing. I use the Standard Library function time.time() to acquire the time elapsed in seconds since the epoch. Note, forensically this is the time of the system we are running on, therefore if the time is a critical element in your investigation you should sync your system clock accordingly.

```
    # Record the Starting Time
    startTime = time.time()
```

Next the program posts a message to the log reporting the start of the scan and display this on the user screen only if the verbose option was selected on the command line (more about this when I examine the ParseCommandLine function). Notice that I used a CONSTANT to hold the version number instead of just embedding a magic number. Now we can just modify the CONSTANT in the future. Then anywhere PFISH_VERSION is used it will display the proper version number. I also logged the system platform and version in case there is a question in the future about the system that was used to process these data. This would be a great place to add information about the organization, investigator name, case number, and other information that is relevant to the case.

```
# Post the Start Scan Message to the Log
logging.info('Welcome to p-fish version 1.0 ... New Scan Started')
_pfish.DisplayMessage('Welcome to p-fish ... version 1.0')
```

Note, since I created a constant PFISH_VERSION, we could use that to make the source code easier to maintain. That would look something like:

_pfish.DisplayMessage('Welcome to p-fish ... '+ PFISH_VERSION)

```
# Record some information regarding the system
logging.info('System: '+ sys.platform)
logging.info('Version: '+ sys.version)
```

Now the main program launches the WalkPath *function within the* _pfish *module that will traverse the directory structure starting at the predefined root path. This function returns the number of files that were successfully processed by* WalkPath *and* HashFile. *As you can see I use this value along with the ending time to finalize the log entries. By subtracting the* startTime *from the* endTime *I can determine the number of seconds it took to perform the file system hashing operations. You could convert the seconds into days, hours, minutes, and seconds of course.*

```
# Traverse the file system directories and hash the files
filesProcessed = _pfish.WalkPath()

# Record the end time and calculate the duration
endTime = time.time()
duration = endTime - startTime

logging.info('Files Processed: '+ str(filesProcessed) )
logging.info('Elapsed Time: '+ str(duration) +' seconds')

logging.info('Program Terminated Normally')

_pfish.DisplayMessage("Program End)"
```

ParseCommandLine()

In the design section I made a couple of decisions that drove the development:

1. I decided that this first application would be a command line program.
2. I decided to provide several options to the user to manipulate the behavior of the program. This has driven the design and implementation of the command line options.

Based on this I provided the following command line options to the program.

Option	Description	Notes
-v	Verbose, if this option is specified then any calls to the `DisplayMessage()` function will be displayed to the standard output device, otherwise the program will run silently	
--MD5 --SHA256 --SHA512	Hash type selection, the user must specify the one-way hashing algorithm that would be utilized	The selection is mutually exclusive and at least one must be selected or the program will abort
-d	`rootPath`, this allows the user to specify the starting or root path for the walk	The directory must *exist* and must be *readable* or the program will abort
-r	`reportPath`, this allows the user to specify the directory where the resulting .csv file will be written	The directory must *exist* and must be *writable* or the program will abort

Even though at first some of these requirements might seem difficult, the `argparse` Standard Library provides great flexibility in handling them. This allows us to catch any possible user errors prior to program execution and also provides us with a way to report problems to the user to handle the exceptions.

```
def ParseCommandLine():
```

The majority of the process of using `argparse` *is knowing how to setup the parser. If you set the parser up correctly it will do all the hard work for you. I start by creating a new parser named "parser" and simply give it a description. Next, I add a new argument in this case –v or verbose. The option is –v and the resulting variable that is used is* `verbose`. *The help message associated with the argument is used by the help system to inform the user on how to use pfish. The –h option is built-in and requires no definition.*

```
parser = argparse.ArgumentParser('Python file system hashing ..
p-fish')

parser.add_argument('-v', '--verbose' help='allows progress messages to
be displayed', action='store_true')
```

The next section defines a mutually exclusive group of arguments for selecting the specific hash type the user would like to generate. If you wanted to add in another option, for example sha384, you would simply add another argument to the group and follow the same format. Since I specified under the add_mutually_exclusive_group the option **required=True,** `argparse` *will make sure that the user has only specified one argument and at least one.*

```
# setup a group where the selection is mutually exclusive ## and required.

group = parser.add_mutually_exclusive_group(required=True)

group.add_argument('--md5', help = 'specifies MD5 algorithm',
action='store_true')
```

```
group.add_argument('--sha256',    help = 'specifies SHA256
algorithm', action='store_true')
```

```
group.add_argument('--sha512',    help = 'specifies SHA512
algorithm', action='store_true')
```

*Next I need to specify the starting point of our walk, and where the report should be created. This works the same as the previous setup, except I have added the **type** option. This requires* argparse *to validate the type I have specified. In the case of the –d option, I want to make sure that the* rootPath *exists and is readable. For the* reportPath, *it must exist and be writable. Since* argparse *does not have built-in functions to validate a directory, I created the functions* ValidateDirectory() *and* ValidateDirectoryWritable(). *They are almost identical and they use Standard Library operating system functions to validate the directories as defined.*

```
parser.add_argument('-d', '--rootPath', type=
ValidateDirectory, required=True, help="specify the root
path for hashing)"
```

```
parser.add_argument('-r', '--reportPath', type=
ValidateDirectoryWritable, required=True, help="specify the
path for reports and logs will be written)"
```

```
# create a global object to hold the validated arguments,
# # these will be available then to all the Functions
within # the _pfish.py module
```

```
global gl_args
global gl_hashType
```

Now the parser can be invoked. I want to store the resulting arguments (once validated) in a global variable so they can be accessible by the functions within the _pfish module. This would be a great opportunity to create a class to handle this which would avoid the use of the global variables. This is done in Chapter 4.

```
gl_args = parser.parse_args()
```

If the parser was successful (in other words argparse *validated the command line parameters), I want to determine which hashing algorithm the user selected. I do that by examining each value associated with the hash types. If the user selected sha256 for example, the* gl_args.sha256 *would be True and md5 and sha512 would be false. Therefore, by using a simple if/elif language routine I can determine which was selected.*

```
if gl_args.md5:
    gl_hashType = 'MD5'
elif gl_args.sha256:
    gl_hashType = 'SHA256'
elif gl_args.sha512:
    gl_hashType = 'SHA512'
else:
    gl_hashType = "Unknown"
```

```
        logging.error('Unknown Hash Type Specified')

    DisplayMessage("Command line processed: Successfully)"
    return
```

ValiditingDirectoryWritable

As mentioned above, I needed to create functions to validate the directories provided by the users for both the report and starting or root path of the Walk. I accomplish this by leveraging the Python Standard Library module os. I leverage both the os.path. isdir and os.access methods associated with this module.

```
    def ValidateDirectoryWritable(theDir):
```

I first check to see if in fact the directory string that the user provided exists. If the test fails then I raise an error within argparse *and provide the message "Directory does not exist." This message would be provided to the user if the test fails.*

```
    # Validate the path is a directory
    if not os.path.isdir(theDir):
            raise argparse.ArgumentTypeError('Directory does not
            exist')
```

Next I validate that write privilege is authorized to the directory and once again if the test fails I raise an exception and provide a message.

```
    # Validate the path is writable
    if os.access(theDir, os.W_OK):
            return theDir
    else:
            raise argparse.ArgumentTypeError('Directory is not writable')
```

Now that I have completed the implementation of the ParseCommandLine function, let us examine a few examples of how the function rejects improper command line arguments. In Figure 3.5, I created four improperly formed command lines:

(1) I mistyped the root directory as TEST_DIR instead of simply TESTDIR
(2) I mistyped the –sha512 parameter as –sha521
(3) I specified two hash types –sha512 and –md5
(4) Finally, I did not specify any hash type

As you can see in each case, ParseCommandLine rejected the command.

In order to get the user back on track they simply have to utilize the –h or help option as shown in Figure 3.6 to obtain the proper command line argument instructions.

WalkPath

Now let us walk through the WalkPath function that will traverse the directory structure, and for each file will call the HashFile function. I think you will be pleasantly surprised how simple this is.

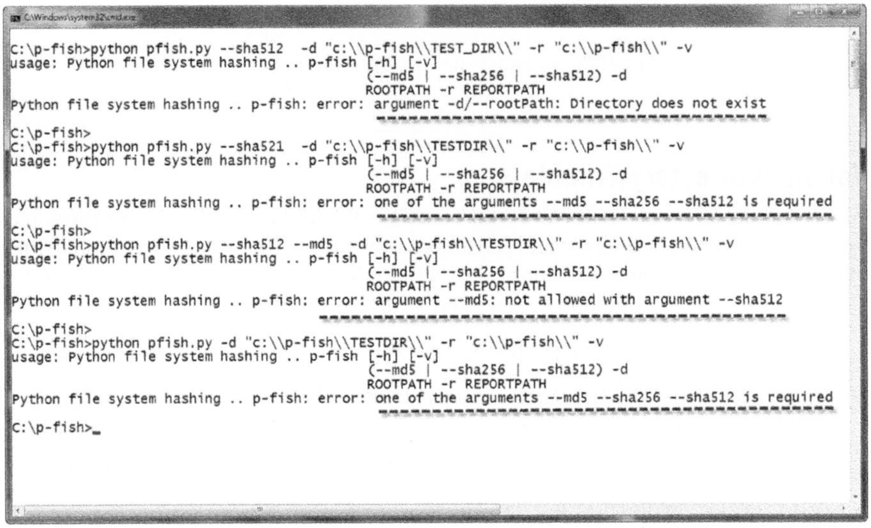

FIGURE 3.5

Demonstration of ParseCommandLine.

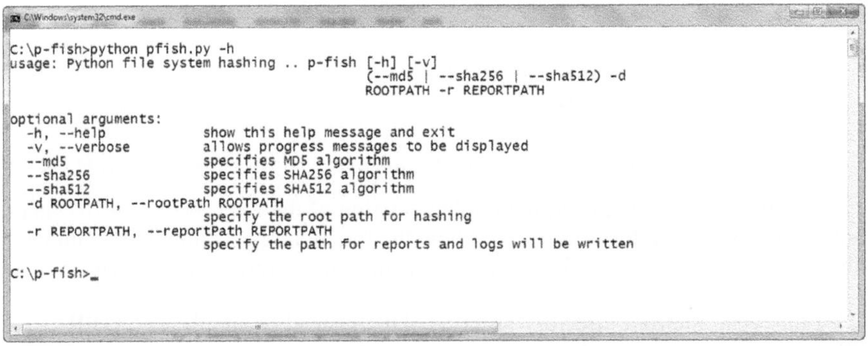

FIGURE 3.6

pfish –h command.

```
def WalkPath():
```

I first initialize the variable processCount *in order to count the number of successfully processed files and I post a message to the log file to document the root path value.*

```
processCount = 0
errorCount = 0

log.info('Root Path: ' + gl_args.rootPath)
```

Next I initialize the CSVWriter *with the* reportPath *provided on the command line by the user. I also provide the* hashType *selected by the user so it can be included in the Header line of the CSV file. I will cover the* CSVWriter *class later in this chapter.*

```
oCVS = _CSVWriter(gl_args.reportPath+'fileSystemReport.csv',
gl_hashType)

# Create a loop that process all the files starting
# at the rootPath, all sub-directories will also be
# processed
```

Next I create a loop using the os.walk *method and the* rootpath *specified by the user. This will create a list of file names that is processed in the next loop. This is done for each directory found within the path.*

```
for root, dirs, files in os.walk(gl_args.rootPath):

        # for each file obtain the filename and call the
        # HashFile Function
```

The next loop processes each file in the list of files and calls the function HashFile *with the file name joined with the path, along with the simple file name for use by* HashFile. *The call also passes* HashFile *with access to the CVS writer so that the results of the hashing operations can be written to the CVS file.*

```
for file in files:
    fname = os.path.join(root, file)
    result = HashFile(fname, file, oCVS)

    # if successful then increment ProcessCount
```

The process and error counts are incremented accordingly

```
    if result is True:
        processCount += 1
    # if not successful, the increment the ErrorCount
    else:
        errorCount += 1
```

Once all the directories and files have been processed the CVSWriter *is closed and the function returns to the main program with the number of successfully processed files.*

```
oCVS.writerClose()
return(processCount)
```

HashFile

Below is the code for the HashFile function, it is clearly the longest for this program, but also quite simple and straightforward. Let us walk through the process.

```
def HashFile(theFile, simpleName, o_result):
```

For each file several items require validation before we attempt to hash the file.
(1) Does the path exist
(2) Is the path a link instead of an actual file
(3) Is the file real (making sure it is not orphaned)
For each of these tests there is a corresponding log error that is posted to the log
file if failure occurs. If the file is bypassed the program will simply return to
WalkFile *and process the next file.*

```
# Verify that the path is valid
if os.path.exists(theFile):
    #Verify that the path is not a symbolic link
    if not os.path.islink(theFile):
        #Verify that the file is real
        if os.path.isfile(theFile):
```

The next part is a little tricky. Even through our best efforts to determine the existence
of the file, there may be cases where the file cannot be opened or read. This could be
caused by permission issues, the file is locked or possibly corrupted. Therefore, I uti-
lize the try methods while attempting to open and then read from the files. Note that
I'm careful to open the file as read-only the "rb" *option. Once again if an error*
occurs a report is generated and logged and the program moves on to the next file.

```
try:
        #Attempt to open the file
        f = open(theFile, 'rb')
    except IOError:
        #if open fails report the error
        log.warning('Open Failed: ' + theFile)
        return
    else:
        try:
            # Attempt to read the file
            rd = f.read()
        except IOError:
            # if read fails, then close the file and
            # report error
            f.close()
            log.warning('Read Failed: ' + theFile)
            return
        else:
            #success the file is open and we can
            #read from it
            #lets query the file stats
```

Once the file has been successfully opened and verified that reading from the file
is allowed, I extract the attributes associated with the file. These include owner,
group, size, MAC times, and mode. I will include these in the record that is posted
to the CSV file.

```
theFileStats = os.stat(theFile)
    (mode, ino, dev, nlink, uid, gid, size,
    atime, mtime, ctime) = os.stat(theFile)

# Display progress to the user

DisplayMessage("Processing File: " + theFile)

# convert the file size to a string
fileSize = str(size)

# convert the MAC Times to strings

modifiedTime = time.ctime(mtime)
accessTime = time.ctime(atime)
createdTime = time.ctime(ctime)

# convert the owner, group and file mode

ownerID = str(uid)
groupID = str(gid)
fileMode = bin(mode)
```

Now that the file attributes have been collected the actual hashing of the file occurs. I need to hash the file as specified by the user (i.e., which one-way hashing algorithm should be utilized). I'm using the Python Standard Library module hashlib *as we experimented with in Chapter 2.*

```
#process the file hashes

if gl_args.md5:
    #Calcuation the MD5
    hash = hashlib.md5()
    hash.update(rd)
    hexMD5 = hash.hexdigest()
    hashValue = hexMD5.upper()
elif gl_args.sha256:
    #Calculate the SHA256
    hash=hashlib.sha256()
    hash.update(rd)
    hexSHA256 = hash.hexdigest()
    hashValue = hexSHA256.upper()
elif gl_args.sha512:
    #Calculate the SHA512
    hash=hashlib.sha512()
    hash.update(rd)
    hexSHA512 = hash.hexdigest()
    hashValue = hexSHA512.upper()
else:
    log.error('Hash not Selected')
#File processing completed
#Close the Active File
```

Now that processing of the file is complete the file must be closed. Next I use the CSV class to write out the record to the report file and return successfully to the caller in this case WalkPath.

```
            f.close()

                        # write one row to the output file

                        o_result.writeCSVRow(simpleName,
                        theFile, fileSize, modifiedTime,
                        accessTime, createdTime, hashValue,
                        ownerID, groupID, mode)
                        return True
```

This section posts the warning messages to the log file relating to problems encountered processing the file.

```
        else:
            log.warning('[' + repr(simpleName) + ', Skipped NOT a File' + ']')
            return False
        else:
            log.warning('[' + repr(simpleName) + ', Skipped Link
            NOT a File' + ']')
            return False
    else:
            log.warning('[' + repr(simpleName) + ', Path does NOT exist' + ']')
        return False
```

CSVWriter

The final code walk-through section I will cover in this chapter is the CSVWriter. As I mentioned earlier, I created this code as a class instead of a function to make this more useful and to introduce you to the concept of classes in Python. The class only has three methods, the constructor or init, writeCSVRow, and writerClose. Let us examine each one.

```
    class _CSVWriter:
```

The constructor or init method accomplishes three basic initializations:
(1) Opens the output csvFile
(2) Initializes the csv.writer
(3) Writes the header row with the names of each column
If any failure occurs during the initialization an exception is thrown and a log entry is generated.

```
    def __init__(self, fileName, hashType):
        try:
                # create a writer object and write the header row
                self.csvFile = open(fileName, 'wb')
```

```
         self.writer = csv.writer(self.csvFile,
            delimiter=',', quoting=csv.QUOTE_ALL)
         self.writer.writerow( ('File', 'Path', 'Size',
            'Modified Time', 'Access Time', 'Created Time',
         hashType, 'Owner', 'Group', 'Mode') )
      except:
            log.error('CSV File Failure')
```

The second method writeCSVRow *receives a record from* HashFile *upon successful completion of each file hash. The method then uses the csv writer to actually place the record in the report file.*

```
def writeCSVRow(self, fileName, filePath, fileSize, mTime,
      aTime, cTime, hashVal, own, grp, mod):

            self.writer.writerow( (fileName, filePath,
                fileSize, mTime, aTime, cTime, hashVal, own,
                grp, mod))
```

Finally, the writeClose method, as you expect, simply closes the csvFile.

```
def writerClose(self):
            self.csvFile.close()
```

Full code listing pfish.py

```
#
# p-fish : Python File System Hash Program
# Author: C. Hosmer
# July 2013
# Version 1.0
#
import logging        # Python Standard Library Logger
import time           # Python Standard Library time functions
import sys            # Python Library system specific parameters
import _pfish         # _pfish Support Function Module

if __name__ == '__main__':

    PFISH_VERSION = '1.0'

    # Turn on Logging
    logging.basicConfig(filename='pFishLog.log',level=logging.DEBUG,
    format='%(asctime)s %(message)s')

    # Process the Command Line Arguments
    _pfish.ParseCommandLine()

    # Record the Starting Time
```

```
startTime = time.time()

# Record the Welcome Message
logging.info(")
logging.info('Welcome to p-fish version '+ PFISH_VERSION +'... New Scan
Started')
logging.info(")
_pfish.DisplayMessage('Welcome to p-fish ... version '+
PFISH_VERSION)

# Record some information regarding the system
logging.info('System: '+ sys.platform)
logging.info('Version: '+ sys.version)

# Traverse the file system directories and hash the files
filesProcessed = _pfish.WalkPath()

# Record the end time and calculate the duration
endTime = time.time()
duration = endTime - startTime
logging.info('Files Processed: '+ str(filesProcessed) )
logging.info('Elapsed Time: '+ str(duration) +' seconds')
logging.info(")
logging.info('Program Terminated Normally')
logging.info(")

_pfish.DisplayMessage("Program End")
```

Full code listing _pfish.py

```
#
# pfish support functions, where all the real work gets done
#
# Display Message()        ParseCommandLine()        WalkPath()
# HashFile()               class _CVSWriter
# ValidateDirectory()      ValidateDirectoryWritable()
#

import os            #Python Standard Library - Miscellaneous
                     operating system interfaces
import stat          #Python Standard Library - functions for
                     interpreting os results
import time          #Python Standard Library - Time access and
                     conversions functions
import hashlib       #Python Standard Library - Secure hashes and
                     message digests
import argparse      #Python Standard Library - Parser for command-
                     line options, arguments
import csv           #Python Standard Library - reader and writer for
                     csv files
```

```
import logging          #Python Standard Library - logging facility

log = logging.getLogger('main._pfish')

#
# Name: ParseCommand() Function
#
# Desc: Process and Validate the command line arguments
#           use Python Standard Library module argparse
#
# Input: none
#
# Actions:
#               Uses the standard library argparse to process the
#               command line
#               establishes a global variable gl_args where any of the
#               functions can
#               obtain argument information
#
def ParseCommandLine():

    parser = argparse.ArgumentParser('Python file system hashing ..
    p-fish')

    parser.add_argument('-v', '--verbose', help='allows progress messages
    to be displayed', action='store_true')

    # setup a group where the selection is mutually exclusive and
    required.
    group = parser.add_mutually_exclusive_group(required=True)
    group.add_argument('--md5',    help = 'specifies MD5 algorithm',
    action='store_true')
    group.add_argument('--sha256',   help = 'specifies SHA256
    algorithm', action='store_true')
    group.add_argument('--sha512',   help = 'specifies SHA512
    algorithm', action='store_true')

    parser.add_argument('-d', '--rootPath', type=
    ValidateDirectory, required=True, help="specify the root
    path for hashing")
    parser.add_argument('-r', '--reportPath', type=
    ValidateDirectoryWritable, required=True, help="specify the
    path for reports and logs will be written")

    # create a global object to hold the validated arguments, these will be
    available then
    # to all the Functions within the _pfish.py module

    global gl_args
    global gl_hashType

    gl_args = parser.parse_args()
```

```
            if gl_args.md5:
                gl_hashType = 'MD5'
            elif gl_args.sha256:
                gl_hashType = 'SHA256'
            elif gl_args.sha512:
                gl_hashType = 'SHA512'
            else:
                gl_hashType = "Unknown"
                logging.error('Unknown Hash Type Specified')

            DisplayMessage("Command line processed: Successfully")

            return

# End ParseCommandLine==================================

#
# Name: WalkPath() Function
#
# Desc: Walk the path specified on the command line
#             use Python Standard Library module os and sys
#
# Input: none, uses command line arguments
#
# Actions:
#             Uses the standard library modules os and sys
#             to traverse the directory structure starting a root
#             path specified by the user. For each file discovered,
#             WalkPath
#             will call the Function HashFile() to perform the file
#             hashing
#

def WalkPath():

    processCount = 0
    errorCount = 0

    oCVS = _CSVWriter(gl_args.reportPath+'fileSystemReport.csv',
    gl_hashType)

    # Create a loop that process all the files starting
    # at the rootPath, all sub-directories will also be
    # processed

    log.info('Root Path: '+ gl_args.rootPath)

    for root, dirs, files in os.walk(gl_args.rootPath):

        # for each file obtain the filename and call the HashFile Function
        for file in files:
            fname = os.path.join(root, file)
```

```
        result = HashFile(fname, file, oCVS)

        # if hashing was successful then increment the ProcessCount
        if result is True:
            processCount += 1
        # if not successful, the increment the ErrorCount
        else:
            ErrorCount += 1

    oCVS.writerClose()

    return(processCount)

#End WalkPath=============================================

#
# Name: HashFile Function
#
# Desc: Processes a single file which includes performing a hash of the
        file
#                and the extraction of metadata regarding the file processed
#                use Python Standard Library modules hashlib, os, and sys
#
# Input: theFile = the full path of the file
#                simpleName = just the filename itself
#
# Actions:
#                Attempts to hash the file and extract metadata
#                Call GenerateReport for successful hashed files
#
def HashFile(theFile, simpleName, o_result):

    # Verify that the path is valid
    if os.path.exists(theFile):

        #Verify that the path is not a symbolic link
        if not os.path.islink(theFile):

            #Verify that the file is real
            if os.path.isfile(theFile):

                try:
                    #Attempt to open the file
                    f = open(theFile, 'rb')
                except IOError:
                    #if open fails report the error
                    log.warning('Open Failed: ' + theFile)
                    return
                else:
                    try:
                        # Attempt to read the file
```

```
            rd = f.read()
    except IOError:
        # if read fails, then close the file and
        report error
        f.close()
        log.warning('Read Failed: ' + theFile)
        return
else:
        #success the file is open and we can read from it
        #lets query the file stats

        theFileStats = os.stat(theFile)
        (mode, ino, dev, nlink, uid, gid, size, atime,
        mtime, ctime) = os.stat(theFile)

        #Print the simple file name
        DisplayMessage("Processing File: " + theFile)

        # print the size of the file in Bytes
        fileSize = str(size)

        #print MAC Times
        modifiedTime = time.ctime(mtime)
        accessTime = time.ctime(atime)
        createdTime = time.ctime(ctime)

        ownerID = str(uid)
        groupID = str(gid)
        fileMode = bin(mode)

        #process the file hashes

        if gl_args.md5:
            #Calcuation and Print the MD5
            hash = hashlib.md5()
            hash.update(rd)
            hexMD5 = hash.hexdigest()
            hashValue = hexMD5.upper()
        elif gl_args.sha256:
            hash=hashlib.sha256()
            hash.update(rd)
            hexSHA256 = hash.hexdigest()
            hashValue = hexSHA256.upper()
        elif gl_args.sha512:
            #Calculate and Print the SHA512
            hash=hashlib.sha512()
            hash.update(rd)
            hexSHA512 = hash.hexdigest()
            hashValue = hexSHA512.upper()
        else:
            log.error('Hash not Selected')
```

```
                    #File processing completed
                    #Close the Active File
                    print "=============================="
                    f.close()

                    # write one row to the output file

                    o_result.writeCSVRow(simpleName, theFile,
                    fileSize, modifiedTime, accessTime, createdTime,
                    hashValue, ownerID, groupID, mode)
                    return True
            else:
                log.warning('[' + repr(simpleName) + ', Skipped NOT a
                File' + ']')
                return False
        else:
                log.warning('[' + repr(simpleName) + ', Skipped Link NOT a
                File' + ']')
            return False
else:
                log.warning('[' + repr(simpleName) + ', Path does NOT
                exist' + ']')
return False

# End HashFile Function ===================================

#
# Name: ValidateDirectory Function
#
# Desc: Function that will validate a directory path as
#         existing and readable. Used for argument validation only
#
# Input: a directory path string
#
# Actions:
#             if valid will return the Directory String
#
#             if invalid it will raise an ArgumentTypeError within
            argparse
#             which will in turn be reported by argparse to the user
#
def ValidateDirectory(theDir):

    # Validate the path is a directory
    if not os.path.isdir(theDir):
        raise argparse.ArgumentTypeError('Directory does not exist')

    # Validate the path is readable
    if os.access(theDir, os.R_OK):
        return theDir
    else:
```

```
            raise argparse.ArgumentTypeError('Directory is not readable')

#End ValidateDirectory =====================================
#
# Name: ValidateDirectoryWritable Function
#
# Desc: Function that will validate a directory path as
#           existing and writable. Used for argument validation only
#
# Input: a directory path string
#
# Actions:
#               if valid will return the Directory String
#
#               if invalid it will raise an ArgumentTypeError within
#               argparse
#               which will in turn be reported by argparse to the user
#

def ValidateDirectoryWritable(theDir):

    # Validate the path is a directory
    if not os.path.isdir(theDir):
        raise argparse.ArgumentTypeError('Directory does not exist')

    # Validate the path is writable
    if os.access(theDir, os.W_OK):
        return theDir
    else:
        raise argparse.ArgumentTypeError('Directory is not writable')

#End ValidateDirectoryWritable ============================

#=========================================================
#
# Name: DisplayMessage() Function
#
# Desc: Displays the message if the verbose command line option is present
#
# Input: message type string
#
# Actions:
#               Uses the standard library print function to display the
#               message
#
def DisplayMessage(msg):

    if gl_args.verbose:
        print(msg)
```

```
        return

#End DisplayMessage=====================================
#
# Class: _CSVWriter
#
# Desc: Handles all methods related to comma separated value operations
#
# Methods constructor:      Initializes the CSV File
#                writeCVSRow:    Writes a single row to the csv file
#                writerClose:    Closes the CSV File

class _CSVWriter:

    def __init__(self, fileName, hashType):
        try:
            # create a writer object and then write the header row
            self.csvFile = open(fileName, 'wb')
            self.writer = csv.writer(self.csvFile, delimiter=',',
            quoting=csv.QUOTE_ALL)
            self.writer.writerow( ('File', 'Path', 'Size', 'Modified Time',
            'Access Time', 'Created Time', hashType, 'Owner', 'Group', 'Mode') )
        except:
            log.error('CSV File Failure')

    def writeCSVRow(self, fileName, filePath, fileSize, mTime, aTime,
    cTime, hashVal, own, grp, mod):

        self.writer.writerow( (fileName, filePath, fileSize, mTime,
        aTime, cTime, hashVal, own, grp, mod))

    def writerClose(self):
        self.csvFile.close()
```

RESULTS PRESENTATION

Now that the walk-through has been completed and I have gone through a deep dive into the code, let us take a look at the results. In Figure 3.7, I executed the program with the following options:

C:\p-fish > Python pfish.py --md5 -d "c:\\p-fish\\TESTDIR\\" -r "c:\\p-fish\\" –v

The –v or verbose option was selected and the program displayed information regarding every file processed was selected as expected.

In Figure 3.8, I examine the c:\p-fish directory and discover that two files were created there, which are the two resulting files for the pfish.py.

1. fileSystemReport.csv
2. pFishLog.log

```
   -d ROOTPATH, --rootPath ROOTPATH
                    specify the root path for hashing
   -r REPORTPATH, --reportPath REPORTPATH
                    specify the path for reports and logs will be written

C:\p-fish>python pfish.py --md5 -d "c:\\p-fish\\TESTDIR\\" -r "c:\\p-fish\\" -v
Command line processed: Successfully
Wecome to p-fish ... version 1.0
Processing File: c:\\p-fish\\TESTDIR\hpwmd121.dat
=================================================
Processing File: c:\\p-fish\\TESTDIR\hpwpr103.dat
=================================================
Processing File: c:\\p-fish\\TESTDIR\hpwpr104.dat
=================================================
Processing File: c:\\p-fish\\TESTDIR\hpwpr110.dat
=================================================
Processing File: c:\\p-fish\\TESTDIR\hpwpr111.dat
=================================================
Processing File: c:\\p-fish\\TESTDIR\Before and After\124.JPG
=================================================
Processing File: c:\\p-fish\\TESTDIR\Before and After\210.JPG
=================================================
Processing File: c:\\p-fish\\TESTDIR\Before and After\291.JPG
=================================================
Processing File: c:\\p-fish\\TESTDIR\Before and After\292.JPG
=================================================
Processing File: c:\\p-fish\\TESTDIR\Before and After\293.JPG
=================================================
```

FIGURE 3.7

Test run of pfish.py.

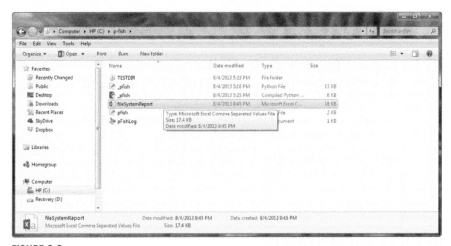

FIGURE 3.8

Result directory after pfish execution.

By choosing to leverage the Python `csv` module to create the report file Windows already recognizes it as a file that Microsoft Excel can view. Opening the file we see the results in Figure 3.9, a nicely formatted column report that can now manipulate with Excel (sort columns, search for specific values, arrange in date order, and examine each of the results). You notice that the hash value is in a column named MD5 that is labeled as such because I passed the appropriate heading value during the initialization of the `csv`.

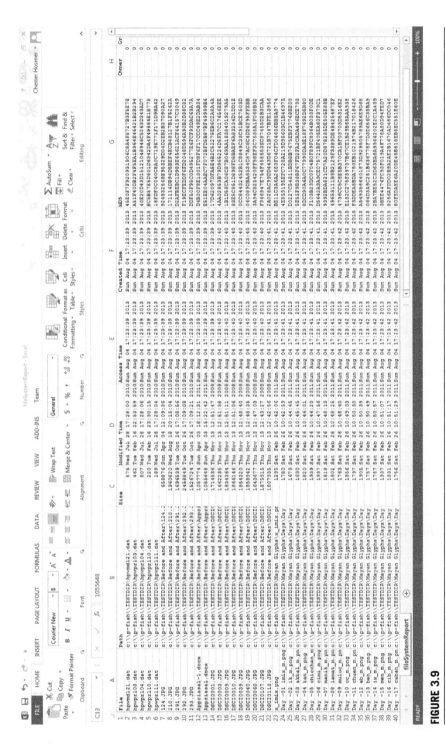

FIGURE 3.9

Examining the Result File with Microsoft Excel.

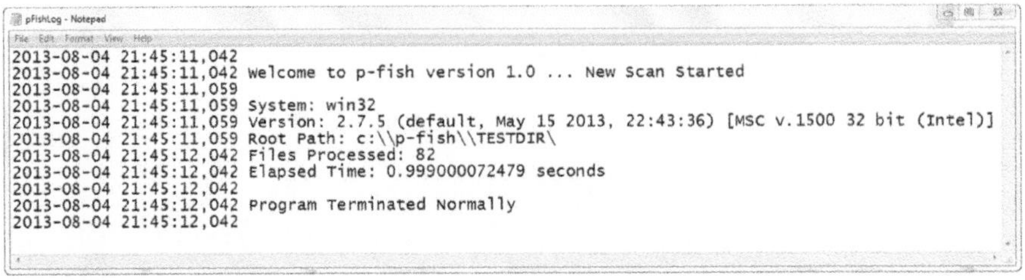

```
2013-08-04 21:45:11,042
2013-08-04 21:45:11,042 Welcome to p-fish version 1.0 ... New Scan Started
2013-08-04 21:45:11,059
2013-08-04 21:45:11,059 System: win32
2013-08-04 21:45:11,059 Version: 2.7.5 (default, May 15 2013, 22:43:36) [MSC v.1500 32 bit (Intel)]
2013-08-04 21:45:11,059 Root Path: c:\\p-fish\\TESTDIR\
2013-08-04 21:45:12,042 Files Processed: 82
2013-08-04 21:45:12,042 Elapsed Time: 0.999000072479 seconds
2013-08-04 21:45:12,042
2013-08-04 21:45:12,042 Program Terminated Normally
2013-08-04 21:45:12,042
```

FIGURE 3.10

Contents of the pFishLog file.

The generated pFishLog.log file results are depicted in Figure 3.10. As expected we find the welcome message, the details regarding the Windows environment, the root path that was specified by the user, the number of files processed, and the elapsed time of just under 1 s. In this example no errors were encountered and the program terminated normally.

Moving to a Linux platform for execution only requires us to copy two Python Files.

1. pfish.py
2. _pfish.py

Execution under Linux (Ubuntu version 12.04 LTS in this example) works ***without*** changing any Python code and produces the following results shown in Figures 3.11–3.13.

You notice that the pFishLog file under Linux has a number of warnings; this is due to lack of read access to many of the files within the /etc directory at the user privilege level I was running and due to some of the files being locked because they were in use.

CHAPTER REVIEW

In this chapter I created our first useable Python forensics application. The pfish.py program executes on both Windows and Linux platforms and through some ingenuity I only used Python Standard Library modules to accomplish this along with our own code. I also scratched the surface with `argparse` allowing us to not only parse the command line but also validate command line parameters before they were used by the application.

I also enabled the Python logger and reported events and errors to the logging system to provide a forensic record of our actions. I provided the user with the capability of selecting among the most popular one-way hashing algorithms and the program extracted key attributes of each file that was processed. I also leveraged the `cvs` module to create a nicely formatted output file that can be opened and processed by standard applications on both Windows and Linux systems. Finally, I implemented our first class in Python with many more to come.

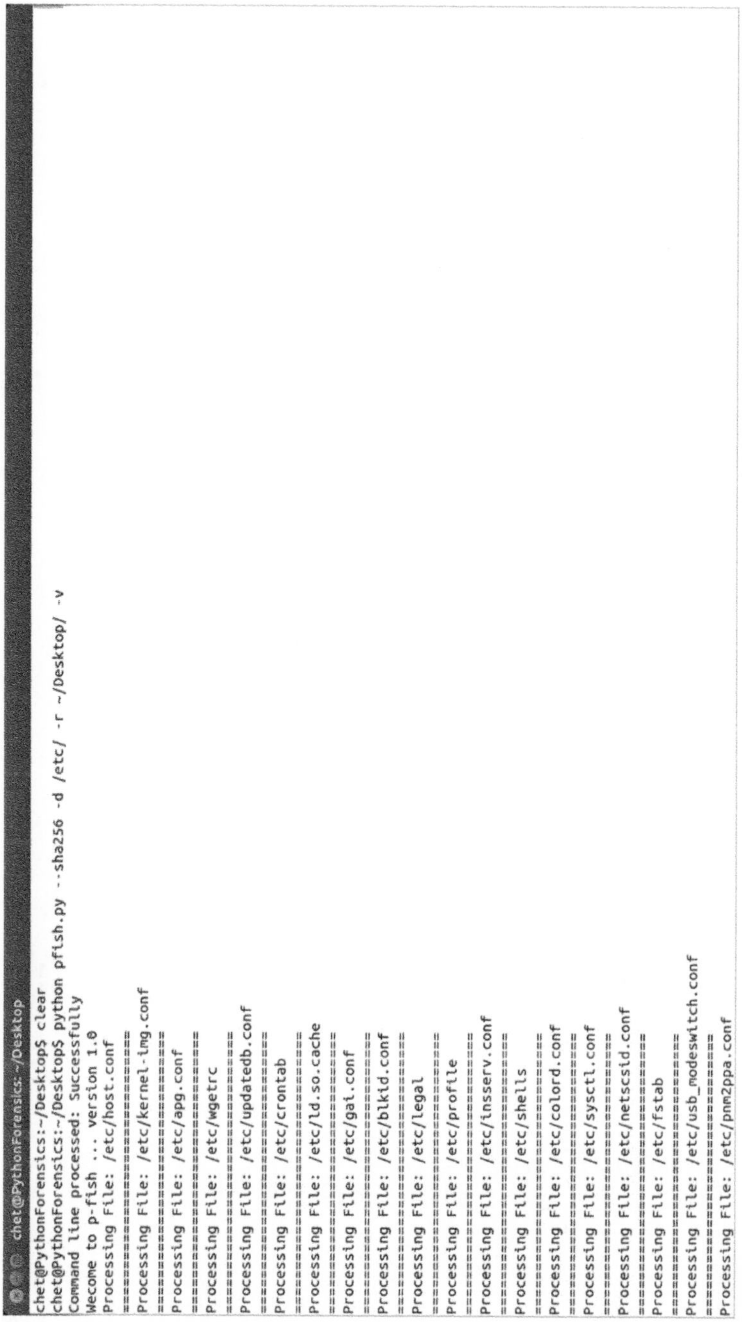

```
  chet@PythonForensics: ~/Desktop
chet@PythonForensics:~/Desktop$ clear
chet@PythonForensics:~/Desktop$ python pfish.py --sha256 -d /etc/ -r ~/Desktop/ -v
Command line processed: Successfully
Wecome to p-fish ... version 1.0
Processing File: /etc/host.conf
========================
Processing File: /etc/kernel-img.conf
========================
Processing File: /etc/apg.conf
========================
Processing File: /etc/wgetrc
========================
Processing File: /etc/updatedb.conf
========================
Processing File: /etc/crontab
========================
Processing File: /etc/ld.so.cache
========================
Processing File: /etc/gai.conf
========================
Processing File: /etc/blkid.conf
========================
Processing File: /etc/legal
========================
Processing File: /etc/profile
========================
Processing File: /etc/insserv.conf
========================
Processing File: /etc/shells
========================
Processing File: /etc/colord.conf
========================
Processing File: /etc/sysctl.conf
========================
Processing File: /etc/netscsid.conf
========================
Processing File: /etc/fstab
========================
Processing File: /etc/usb_modeswitch.conf
========================
Processing File: /etc/pnm2ppa.conf
```

FIGURE 3.11

Linux Command Line Execution.

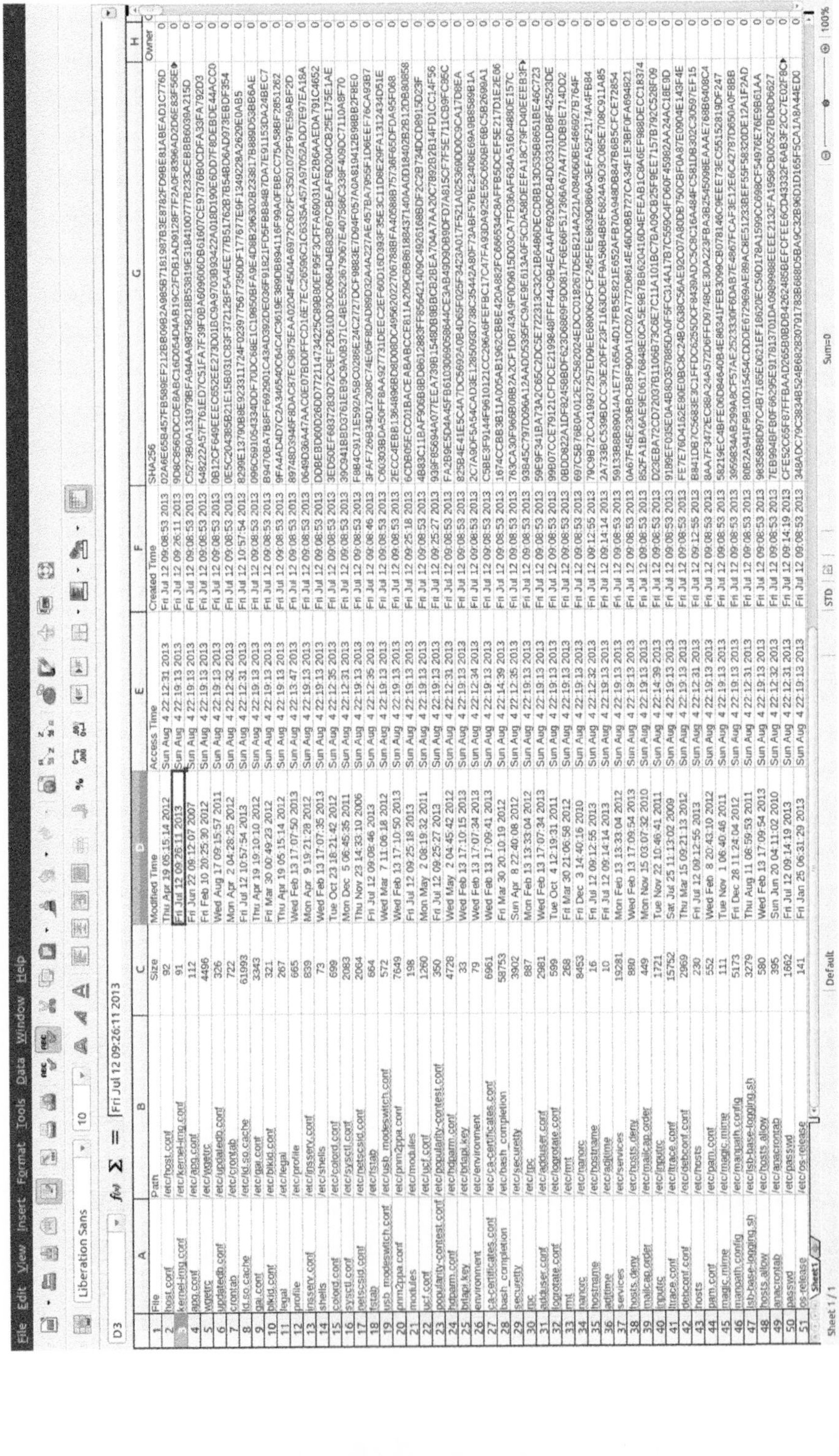

FIGURE 3.12

Linux Execution Results pfish Result File.

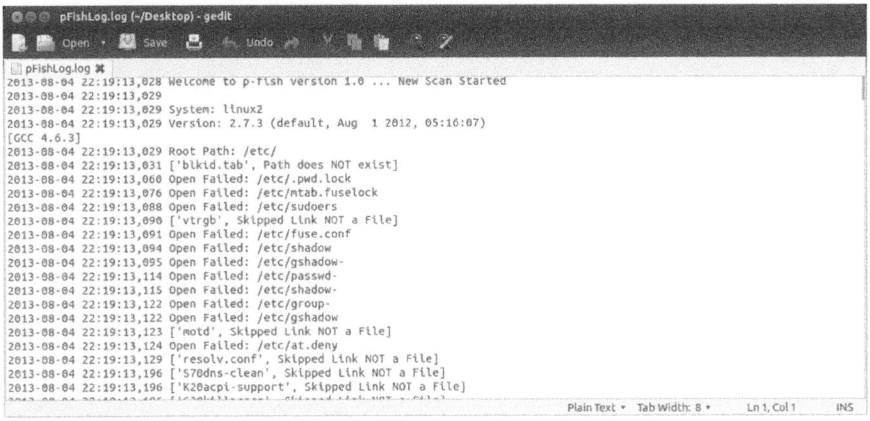

FIGURE 3.13

Linux Execution Results pFishLog File.

SUMMARY QUESTIONS

1. If you wanted to add additional one-way hashing algorithms, which functions would you need to modify? Also, by using just the Python Standard Library what other one-way hashing algorithms are readily available.
2. If you wanted to eliminate the need of the two global variables how could you easily accomplish this by using classes? What function would you convert to a class and what methods would you need to create?
3. What other events or elements do you think should be logged? How would you go about doing that?
4. What additional columns would you like to see in the report and how would you obtain the additional information?
5. What additional information (such as Investigator name or case number) should be included in the log. How would you obtain that information?

LOOKING AHEAD

In Chapter 4, I will be continuing with the cookbook section by tackling searching and indexing of forensic data.

Additional Resources

Hosmer C. Using SmartCards and digital signatures to preserve electronic evidence. In: SPIE proceedings, vol. 3576. Forensic Technologies for Crime Scene and the Laboratory I. The paper was initially presented at the investigation and forensic science technologies symposium; 1998. Boston, MA, http://proceedings.spiedigitallibrary.org/proceeding.aspx?articleid=974141 [01.11.1998].

Kim G. The design and implementation of tripwire: a file system integrity checker. Purdue ePubs computer science technical reports, 1993. http://docs.lib.purdue.edu/cstech/1084/.

Forensic Searching and Indexing Using Python

4

CHAPTER CONTENTS

INTRODUCTION

Searching is certainly one of the pillars of forensic investigation and today a search is only as good as the investigator running it. Knowing what to search for, where to search for it (in a file, in deleted files, slack space, e-mail files, a database, or application data), and then interpreting the search results requires both experience and knowledge of criminal behavior. Over the past several years we have seen the emergence of indexing of evidence and we have also seen frustration with the performance of indexing methods. The Python programming language has several built-in language mechanisms along with Standard Library modules that will assist in both searching and indexing.

There are many reasons for searching and indexing, and I want to make sure we examine more than just simple keywords, names, hashes, etc. So what is the underlying reason or rationale why we search? Referencing fictional works or characters is always a risk when writing a book like this, but in this case I believe it works. Most of us have read some if not all of the works of Sir Arthur Conan Doyle's Sherlock Holmes novels and short stories. In these fictional accounts, Holmes uses both deductive and inductive reasoning to create theories about the crime and profiles of the suspects, victims, and even bystanders.

Deductive reasoning takes no risk, in other words if you have verifiable facts along with a valid argument the conclusion must be true. For example:

1. All men are mortal
2. Socrates was a man
   Therefore, Socrates was mortal.
   Inductive reasoning on the other hand takes risks and uses probabilities. For example:

1. John always leaves for the office at 6:00 AM
2. He punches in between 7:30 and 7:45 AM each day
3. John left home today promptly at 6:00 AM verified by a surveillance camera and punched in at work at 7:42 AM.
   Therefore, John could not have committed a murder at 7:05 AM that occurred over 3 miles from the office.

The basis of these hypotheses whether based on deductive or inductive reasoning is *facts*. Therefore, I believe the reason to search and index is to discover facts that we then use to create theories and hypothesis. I know this may seem brutally obvious, but then again we sometimes narrow in on a theory before we have any trustworthy facts. This is especially true in the digital world where we can be quick to judge as the saying goes "because I saw it on the Internet" when in fact the Internet or digital data have been manipulated to skew the facts.

Seasoned investigators understand this and are typically very thorough in their investigation of digital crime scenes. I have had the privilege of working with many such investigators and they are tenacious in validation of digital evidence. I cannot tell you how many times I have been asked "are you sure about that?" or "can you prove that" or even "how else could this have happened?" Finally, we need to be conscious in our searching to discover both inculpatory and exculpatory evidence and make sure both types of facts are recorded before we create theories or hypothesis.

Inculpatory evidence supports a defined hypothesis
   Exculpatory evidence is contradictory to a defined hypothesis

The question then becomes what facts do we wish to discover? Fundamentally, the answer is who, what, where, when, and how or to be slightly more specific, here are small set of examples.

You might be wondering about the "Why" of the search. We tend not to think about why as in many cases this is generated by the investigator, through experience, intuition, and deep understanding regarding the circumstances that surround the case.

- What documents exist and what is their content or relevance? When were they created, modified, last accessed, when and how many times were they printed? Were the documents stored or written to a flash device or stored in the cloud? Where did they originate?
- What multimedia files exist and where did they originate? For example, were they downloaded from the Internet or recorded or snapped by the suspect or victim. If so, what camera or recording device was used?
- Who is the suspect(s) we are investigating and what do we know about them? Do we have a photograph, phone numbers, e-mail addresses, home address, where do they work, when and where have they traveled, do they own a vehicle(s), if so what make, model, year, and plate number? Do they have an alias (physical world or cyber world)?
- Who are their known associates, what do we know about them?

I think you get the idea, the questions that we might ask during a search are vast with some being very specific and others more general. In this chapter, we certainly cannot solve all of these issues, but we can scratch the surface and create Python programs that will assist us now and be able to be evolved in the future.

KEYWORD CONTEXT SEARCH

Keyword searching with context is the ability to perform a search of a data object like a disk image or a memory snapshot, and discover keywords or phrases that relate to a specific context or category. For example, I might want to perform a search of a disk image for each occurrence of the following list of street names for the drug cocaine:

blow, C, candy, coke, do a line, freeze, girl, happy dust, mama coca, mojo, monster, nose, pimp, shot, smoking gun, snow, sugar, sweet stuff, white powder, base, beat, blast, casper, chalk, devil drug, gravel, hardball, hell, kryptonite, love, moonrocks, rock, scrabble, stones, and tornado.

How can this be accomplished easily in Python?

In order to tackle keyword searching with Python we must first address several simple issues. First, how should we store the search words or phrases? Python has several built-in data types that are ideally suited to handle such lists each with their own unique capabilities and rules. The basic types are *sets*, *lists*, and *dictionaries*. My preference would be to create a *set* to hold the search words and phrases. Sets in Python provide a nice way of dealing with this type of data mainly due to the fact that they automatically eliminate duplicates, they are trivial to implement, and they can easily be tested for members.

The code below demonstrates the basics. I start by initializing an empty set named *searchWords*. Next, the code opens and then reads the file *narc.txt* that contains narcotic-related words and phrases. I of course include exception handling for the file operations to ensure we successfully opened and then can read each line from the file. Next, I print out the list of search words and phrases that were loaded line by line (notice one word or phrase per line) and then search the list for the word "kryptonite" and either print "Found word" if the word exists in the search words list or "not found" if the word does not exist. One fine point, I specify *line.strip()* when adding the words to the set searchWords. This strips the newline characters that exist at the end of each line.

```
import sys
searchWords = set()
try:
    fileWords = open('narc.txt')
    for line in fileWords:
        searchWords.add(line.strip())
except:
    print("file handling error)"
    sys.exit()
print(searchWords)
if ('kryptonite' in searchWords):
    print("Found word)"
else:
  print("not found)"
```

Executing the code produces the following output:
Starting with the contents of the set:

{'shot', 'devil drug', 'do a line', 'scrabble', 'casper', 'hell', 'kryptonite', 'mojo', 'blow', 'stones tornado', 'white powder', 'smoking gun', 'happy dust', 'gravel', 'hardball', 'moonrocks', 'monster', 'beat', 'snow sugar', 'coke', 'rock', 'base', 'blast', 'pimp', 'sweet stuff', 'candy', 'chalk', 'nose', 'mama coca', 'freeze girl'}

Then printing out the results of the search for kryptonite produces
Found word
This simple code then solves two fundamental challenges:

(1) Reading a list into a set from a file
(2) Searching a set to determine if an entry exits in a set.

Next, we have to solve the problem of extracting words and phrases from the target of a search. Almost always this requires that a binary file or stream be parsed. These binary data could be a memory snapshot, a disk image or a snapshot of network data. The key is the data would be either unformatted or formatted based on one of hundreds of standards, some open and some proprietary with text and binary data intertwined. Therefore, if we would like to develop a simple search tool that could extract and compare text strings without regard to the format or content, how might we accomplish this?

The first challenge would be to define what Python data object we would use to hold these binary data. For this I have chosen the Python object *bytearray* as this fits our criteria exactly. As the name implies *bytearrays* are simply a series of bytes (a byte being and unsigned 8-bit value) starting at the zero array element and extending to the end of the array. I am going to take advantage of a couple of Python specialties, for example, loading a file into a *bytearray*, the core code to do so is only two lines.

The first line opens a file for reading in binary mode. Whereas the second line reads the contents of the file into a *bytearray* named baTarget. You notice that I prefix the object Target with "ba" this simply makes the code more readable and anyone will immediately recognize that the object is of type *bytearray*. Also, note this code is just an illustration. In the real program, we have to check the return values from the function calls and make sure there are no errors, I will illustrate that technique when we get to the actual program.

```
targetFile = open('file.bin', 'rb')
baTarget = bytearray(targetFile.read())
```

One of the immediate questions you might have is, "how do I know how many bytes were loaded into the *bytearray*?" This is handled just like any other Python object by using the *len* function.

sizeOfTarget = len(baTarget)

In Figure 4.1, we can see the object *baTarget* that was created and also the *sizeOfTarget* that was determined of *baTarget* using the *len* function.

Variable	Value
locals	< dict 0x202e930; len=7 >
baTarget	< huge bytearray 0x1f255f0 >
baTargetCopy	< huge bytearray 0x1f255f0 >
fileWords	< closed file 'c:\\pytest\\narc.txt', mode 'r' at 0x01FAED30 >
line	'tornado\n'
⊞ searchWords	< set 0x1fc6120; len=27 >
sizeOfTarget	77650
targetFile	< closed file 'c:\\pytest\\capture.raw', mode 'rb' at 0x01FAED88 >

FIGURE 4.1

Snapshot of stackdata displaying the baTarget object and the size in bytes of the baTarget bytearray.

Fundamental requirements

Now that I have defined the new language and data elements we intend to use for our simple text search, I want to define the basic requirements of the program as shown in Table 4.1.

Design considerations

Now that I have defined the basic requirements for the application, I need to factor in the design considerations. For the search program, I will be using Python Standard Library modules and the specialized code we developed for parsing the target file. Table 4.2 covers the basic mapping of requirements to modules and functions that will be utilized.

Next, I want to define the overall design of the search capability. As with the p-fish program we developed in Chapter 3, I will be using the command line and command line arguments to specify the inputs to the program. For the search results, I will be directing the output to standard output using some specialized methods developed to render the data for easy interpretation. Finally, I will be using the built-in logging functions to complete the forensic nature of the search (Figure 4.2).

Turning to the internal structure, I have broken the program down into four main components. The `Main program`, `ParseCommandLine` function, the actual `Search-Words` function, `PrintBuffer` functions for outputting the results, and `logger` (note logger is actually the Python logger module), that is utilized by the major functions of p-search. I briefly describe the operation of each below and during the code

Table 4.1 Basic Requirements

Requirement number	Requirement name	Short description
SRCH-001	Command Line Arguments	Allow the user to specify a file containing keywords (ASCII in this example) Allow the user to specify a file containing a binary file to search Allow the user to specify verbose output regarding the progress of search
SRCH-002	Log	The program must produce a forensic audit log
SRCH-003	Performance	The program should perform the search efficiently
SRCH-004	Output	The program should identify any of the keywords found in the binary file and provide a Hex/ASCII printout, the offset where the keyword was found along with the surrounding values in order to provide context
SRCH-005	Error Handling	The application must support error handling and logging of all operations performed. This will include a textual description and a timestamp

Table 4.2 Standard Library Mapping

Requirement	Design considerations	Library selection
User Input (001)	User input for keyword and target file	I will be using argparse from the Standard Library module to obtain input from the user
Performance (003)	Selecting the right language and library objects to process the data is important when designing a search method	I will be using Python *sets* and *bytearrays* to handle the data related to searching which will increase performance and make the search process extensible
Output (004)	The search results must be provided in a meaningful manner. In other words, mapping the identified keywords to the offset in the file along with pre- and postdata that surround the identified keywords	I will be using the Standard Library print function to accomplish this, but instead of writing the result to a file directly, I am going to write the data to standard out, the user can then pipe the output if they wish to a file or into other programs or functions
Logging and error handling (002 and 005)	Errors may occur during the processing of the keyword and target file. Therefore, handling these potential errors must be rigorous	The Python Standard Library includes a logging facility which I can leverage to report any events or errors that occur during processing

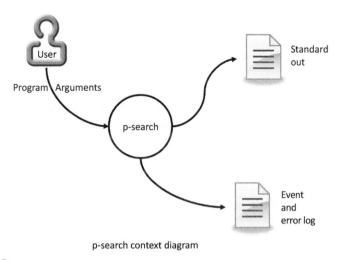

p-search context diagram

FIGURE 4.2

p-search context diagram.

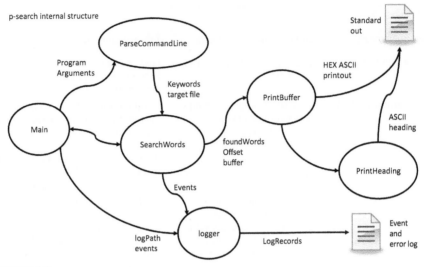

FIGURE 4.3

p-search internal structure.

walk-through section a more detailed line by line explanation of how each function operates is provided (Figure 4.3).

Main function

The purpose of the Main function is to control the overall flow of this program. For example, within Main, I setup the Python logger, I display startup and completion messages, and keep track of the time. In addition, Main invokes the command line parser and then launches the SearchWords function. Once SearchWords completes, Main will log the completion and display termination messages to the user and the log.

ParseCommandLine

In order to provide smooth operation of p-search, I leverage the ParseCommandLine to not only parse but also validate the user input. Once completed, information that is needed by the core search method will be available via the parser.

SearchWords function

SearchWords is the core of the p-search program. The objective is to make this function as quick and accurate as possible. In this example, we are only searching for ASCII text strings or words. This provides a huge advantage and we can set the search up in a way that is quick and effective. The algorithm performs the search in two passes over the *baTarget bytearray*. The first pass converts any byte that is not an alpha character to a zero. The second pass collects sequences of alpha characters. If the consecutive alpha character sequence is greater than or equal to

MIN_WORD and less than or equal to *MAX_WORD* before encountering a zero, the characters are collected and then compared to the *set* of keywords. Note MIN_-WORD and MAX_WORD will be defined as constants. In the future, they could be command line arguments to the search.

PrintBuffer functions

The PrintBuffer function is called by `SearchWords` whenever a keyword match is discovered. Then the offset within the file and Hex/ASCII display are sent to standard out.

logger

The built-in Standard Library *logger* provides us with the ability to write messages to a log file associated with *p-search*. The program can write information messages, warning messages, and error messages. Since this is intended to be a forensic application, logging operations of the program are vital. You can expand the program to log additional events in the code; they can be added to any of the *_p-search* functions.

Writing the code

Once again, I broke the code into source files *p-search.py* and *_p-search.py*, where _p-search.py provides the support and heavy lifting functions of p-search. In Figure 4.4 you can see the WingIDE environment along with the p-search program running. The upper left corner displays the local and global variables. In the upper

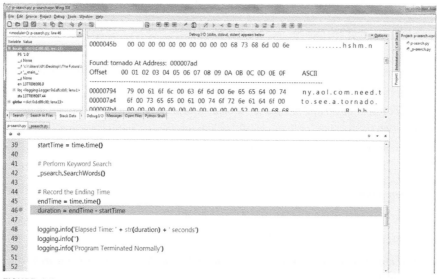

FIGURE 4.4

WingIDE p-search execution.

center panel you get a glimpse of the program output showing the match of the word "tornado" along with the detailed Hex/ASCII representation of the output. On the far right, the files associated with the program are listed. Finally, in the bottom portion of the screen you can see the source code for the program. In the following section, we will walk-through the important code elements to disclose the detailed method and approach I have taken.

CODE WALK-THROUGH

I will be inserting dialog as I discuss each code section. The code walk-through will give you an in-depth look at all the codes associated with the program. I will be first walking through each of the key functions and then will provide you with a complete listing of both *p-search.py* and *_p-search.py*.

Examining Main—code walk-through

```python
import logging
import time
import _psearch
```

For the main program we need to import logging to record forensic events and time to calculate the duration of program execution both from the Python Standard Library. We also import our _psearch module that contains the supporting and core functions of p-search

```python
if __name__ == '__main__':
    P-SEARCH_VERSION = '1.0'
    # Turn on Logging

    logging.basicConfig(filename='pSearchLog.log',level=logging.DEBUG,
    format='%(asctime)s %(message)s')
```

Next I invoke command line parser to obtain the program arguments passed in by the user.

```python
    # Process the Command Line Arguments

    _psearch.ParseCommandLine()
```

I then setup logging to occur and send the startup events to the logger.

```python
    log = logging.getLogger('main._psearch')

    log.info("p-search started)"
```

I record the start time of execution in order calculate duration when the search is complete.

```python
    # Record the Starting Time

    startTime = time.time()
```

Next, I invoke the SearchWords function. Note that this functions is contained in the _psearch module thus I need to prefix the call with the module name _psearch.

```
# Perform Keyword Search

    _psearch.SearchWords()
```

I record the end time and calculate the duration and make the final entries in the log.

```
    # Record the Ending Time

    endTime = time.time()
    duration = endTime - startTime

    logging.info('Elapsed Time: '+ str(duration) +' seconds')
    logging.info('')
    logging.info('Program Terminated Normally')
```

Examining _p-search functions—code walk-through

The remaining functions are contained in the _p-search.py file. The file starts by importing the needed modules. These include *argparse* for processing command line arguments. The *os* module is for handling file I/O operations. Finally, logging is used for forensic logging capabilities.

```
import argparse
import os
import logging
```

Examining ParseCommandLine

For the p-search program, we only require two parameters from the user—the full path name of the file containing the keywords to search along with the full path name of the file we wish to search. The verbose option is optional and when it is not provided the program messages will be suppressed (Table 4.3).

As you can see the ParseCommandLine prepares for three arguments verbose, keywords and srchTarget. Keywords and search target are required parameters and they are both validated by the function ValidateFileName().

```
def ParseCommandLine():
    parser = argparse.ArgumentParser('Python Search')

    parser.add_argument('-v', '--verbose', help="enables printing of
    program messages", action='store_true')

    parser.add_argument('-k', '--keyWords', type= ValidateFileRead,
    required=True, help="specify the file containing search words)"

    parser.add_argument('-t', '--srchTarget', type= ValidateFileRead,
    required=True, help="specify the target file to search)"
```

Table 4.3 p-search command line argument definition

Option	Description	Notes
-v	Verbose, if this option is specified then any calls to the `DisplayMessage()` function will be displayed to the standard output device, otherwise the program will run silently	
-k	`Keyword`, this allows the user to specify the path of the file containing the keywords	The file must *exist* and must be *readable* or else the program will abort
-t	`Target`, this allows the user to specify the path of the file to be searched	The file must *exist* and must be *readable* or else the program will abort

Next we establish a global variable to hold results of parse_args operations. Any invalid entries will automatically abort processing.

```
global gl_args
gl_args = parser.parse_args()
DisplayMessage("Command line processed: Successfully)"
return
```

One of the nice features of `argparse` is the ability to include a help message with each entry. Then whenever the user specifies -h on the command line `argparse` automatically assembles the appropriate response. This allows the developer to provide as much information as possible to assist the user in providing the correct response, so be verbose. Figure 4.5 depicts the operation of the -h option for p-search.

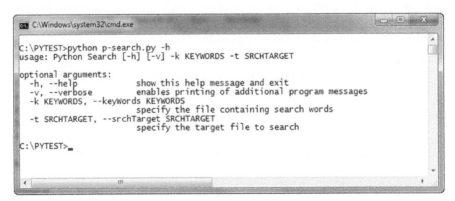

FIGURE 4.5

p-search execution using only the -h or help option.

Examining ValidateFileRead(theFile)

This function supports the `ParseCommandLine` and `parser.parse_args()` by validating any filenames provided by the user. The function first ensures that the file exists and then verifies that the file is readable. Failing either of these checks will result in the program aborting and will raise the appropriate exception.

```
def ValidateFileRead(theFile):

  # Validate the path is a valid

    if not os.path.exists(theFile):
        raise argparse.ArgumentTypeError('File does not exist')

    # Validate the path is readable

    if os.access(theFile, os.R_OK):
        return theFile
    else:
        raise argparse.ArgumentTypeError('File is not readable')
```

Examining the SearchWords function

The core of p-search is the `SearchWords` function which compares the keywords provided by the user with the contents of the target file specified. We will take a deep dive line by line of `SearchWords`.

```
def SearchWords():
```

> *# Create an empty set of search words*

As I mentioned in the design considerations, I decided to use a Python set object to hold the keywords to search. To do this I simply assign `searchWords` *as a set object.*

```
        searchWords = set()
```

Next, I need to load the keywords from the file specified by the user in the command line arguments. I do this using the 'try, except, finally' method to ensure we trap or capture any failures.

```
    # Attempt to open and read search words
    try:
```
> *fileWords = open(gl_args.keyWords)*

Once we successfully open the keywords file I process each line striping the words from the line and adding it to the `searchWords` *set.*

```
        for line in fileWords:
```
> *searchWords.add(line.strip())*
```
    except:
```

Any exceptions encountered are logged and the program is aborted

```
        log.error('Keyword File Failure:'+gl_args.keyWords)
        sys.exit()
    finally:
```

Once all the lines have been processed successfully, the file is closed.

```
        fileWords.close()
```

```
    # Create Log Entry Words to Search For
```

Next, I write entries into the forensic log to record the words that are to be included in the search.

```
    log.info('Search Words')
    log.info('Input File:'+gl_args.keyWords)
    log.info(searchWords)
```

```
    # Attempt to open and read the target file
    # and directly load the file into a bytearray
```

Now that I have the keywords to search for, I will read the target file provided and store the data into a Python byte array object.

```
    try:
        targetFile = open(gl_args.srchTarget, 'rb')
        baTarget = bytearray(targetFile.read())
    except:
```

Any exceptions will be caught, logged and the program will exit.

```
        log.error('Target File Failure:'+gl_args.srchTarget)
        sys.exit()
    finally:
        targetFile.close()
```

I record the size of the target file on success.

```
    sizeOfTarget = len(baTarget)
```

```
    # Post to log
```

I also post this information to the forensic log file.

```
    log.info('Target of Search:'+gl_args.srchTarget)
    log.info('File Size:'+str(sizeOfTarget))
```

I'm going to modify baTarget *by substituting zero for all not alpha characters. In order to ensure that I can display the original contents of the target file, I make a copy.*

```
    baTargetCopy = baTarget
    # Search Loop
    # step one, replace all non characters with zero's
```

The first search step is to traverse the target and replace all non alpha characters with zero to make the search of words much easier and faster. The loop below starts at the beginning of the file and performs the replacement.

```
for i in range(0, sizeOfTarget):
    character = chr(baTarget[i])
    if not character.isalpha():
        baTarget[i] = 0

# step # 2 extract possible words from the bytearray
# and then inspect the search word list
```

Now that the bytearray baTarget only contains valid alpha characters and zeros I can count any consecutive alpha character sequences and if the sequence meets the size characteristics defined I can check the collected sequences of characters against the smaller keyword list

```
# create an empty list of not found items
```

To be thorough, I'm creating a list of notFound *character sequences that meet our criteria of sequences of characters, but do not match the keywords specified by the user.*

```
notFound = []
```

Now I begin the actual search. I simply check each byte and if it qualifies as a character I increase the count by one. If I encounter a zero, I stop the count and see if I have encountered enough consecutive characters to qualify as a possible word. If I don't then I set the count back to zero and continue the search. If on the other hand the count meets the criteria for the minimum and maximum number of characters I have a possible word.

```
cnt = 0
for i in range(0, sizeOfTarget):
    character = chr(baTarget[i])
    if character.isalpha():
        cnt += 1
    else:
        if (cnt >= MIN_WORD and cnt <= MAX_WORD):
            newWord = ""
```

If I have a sequence that meets the criteria I need to collect the characters that I have now skipped. One of the tricks is to not bother collecting or building possible strings until you meet the criteria. Once the criteria is met I backtrack and pull the consecutive letters together and store them in the variable newWord*. I use the* newWord *variable to search the set of keywords.*

```
for z in range(i-cnt, i):
    newWord = newWord + chr(baTarget[z])
```

To search the set of keywords stored in the set seachWords*, I simply write the one line test. This is the power of properly choosing the correct object type for storing the keywords.*

```
if (newWord in searchWords):
```

If I get a hit in the searchWord list, I call the PrintBuffer function with the details of the hit which includes the word I found, the offset in the buffer, the saved unmodified buffer, where to start printing the result and where to stop.

```
    PrintBuffer(newWord,  i-cnt,  baTargetCopy,  i-  PREDECESSOR_
    SIZE, WINDOW_SIZE)
        print
    else:
        notFound.append(newWord)
        cnt = 0
else:
    cnt = 0
```

After I have processed the complete bytearray, I also print out the notFound list I created, this will give the investigator additional possible words to consider that were not in the keyword list.

```
PrintNotFound(notFound)
# End of SearchWords Function
```

Examining the PrintBuffer function

Most of us that investigate cybercrime for a living use Hex editors or viewers quite often. The `PrintBuffer` function is a very simple Hex and ASCII viewer written in Python. It is simple to ensure that it will run on almost any platform (Windows, Linux, Mac, and even mobile devices). The trick is to not get fancy, but instead just provide the facts. Let us take a look how this can be accomplished with just a few lines of Python code.

```
def PrintBuffer(word, directOffset, buff, offset, hexSize):
```

The inputs to the function are as follows:
  word: The alpha string that was identified
  directOffset: The offset in the target file to the beginning of the alpha string
  buff: The actual buffer
  offset: The offset where the Hex/ ASCII Window should start
  hexSize: What is the size in bytes that should be displayed
  I start by printing the basic facts, the word and offset where the string was found.

```
print "Found: "+ word + " At Address: ",
print "%08x " % (directOffset)
```

Next, I print the heading which prints the following heading.

```
Offset 00 01 02 03 04 05 06 07 08 09 0A 0B 0C 0D 0E 0 F ASCII
    PrintHeading()
```

Next, I just need to print the Hex and ASCII values found in the buffer starting that the specified offset. The outer loop continues in 16 value chunks since each line

*will hold the next 16 values. Since we are printing this out in Hex this makes the
most sense.*

```
for i in range(offset, offset+hexSize, 16):
    for j in range(0,17):
```

*The inside loop then needs to print each of the next 16 bytes in hex. I start by print-
ing the offset value in hex leaving the appropriate amount of same. Note also, that
I use the syntax %08x which allows for an 8 digit Hex address zero filled. This
should be plenty for this demonstration application.*

```
        if (j == 0):
            print "%08x " % i,
        else:
            byteValue = buff[i+j]
            print "%02x " % byteValue,
    print "        ",
```

*Next we repeat this loop but this time we print the ASCII character representation
instead of the Hex values.*

```
for j in range (0,16):
    byteValue = buff[i+j]
```

*To avoid any special characters we only print the ASCII printable set and then
replace the other values with a period.*

```
        if (byteValue >= 0x20 and byteValue <= 0x7f):
            print "%c" % byteValue,
        else:
            print '.',
    print
# End Print Buffer
```

RESULTS PRESENTATION

Now that the walk-through has been completed and I have gone through a deep dive
into the code, let us take a look at the results. Figure 4.6 is a snapshot of the directory
that contains all the requisite files. This includes the two Python program files
p-search.py and *_p-search.py*. It includes the *narc.txt* file that contains the search
words. *Capture.raw* is a file containing binary data that we wish to search. *pSear-
chLog.log* is the forensic log file output from p-search and finally *results.txt* is a file
containing the standard output results that were piped to a file for easy viewing.

Figure 4.7 lists the file containing the drug-related keywords that we intend to
search for.

Figure 4.8 is the direct output of the program starting with the command line
entry which specified that the results be piped to the file *results.txt*. Also included
is the *results.txt* file. You can see that we identified three hits in the target file, they
include sugar, tornado, and moonrocks. You also see the Hex/ASCII printout generated by the program along with the unidentified words at the bottom.

FIGURE 4.6

Execution test directory for p-search.

FIGURE 4.7

Keyword file dump.

Finally in Figure 4.9, you see the contents of the log file generated by *p-search* that includes the start message, the search word file, and contents. Also included is the name and size of the target file *capture.raw*. Finally, you see the elapsed time for execution in seconds and the program termination message.

To round out this example and demonstrate the portability, I have included two additional screenshots running the unmodified p-search program on both a Linux machine (Figure 4.10) and iMac (Figure 4.11).

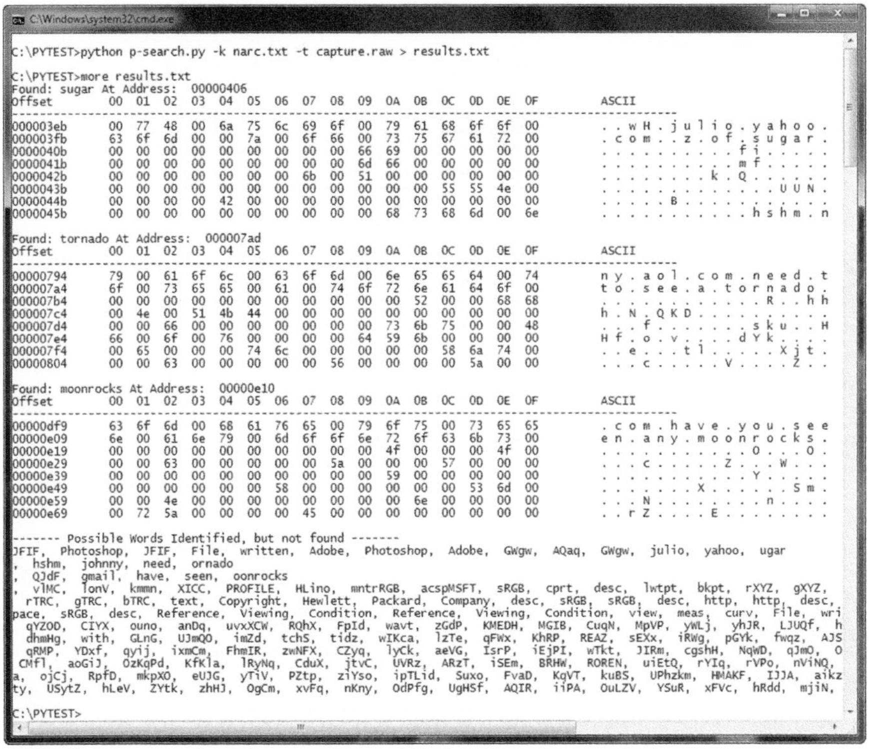

FIGURE 4.8

p-search sample execution.

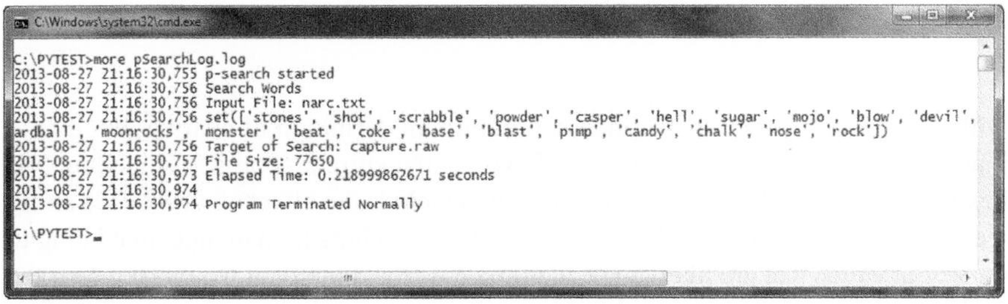

FIGURE 4.9

Log file contents post execution.

INDEXING

Indexing provides the investigator with a different look at the data and potential evidence contained within a file, disk image, memory snapshot, or network trace. Instead of determining what keywords to look for, we want p-search to provide us

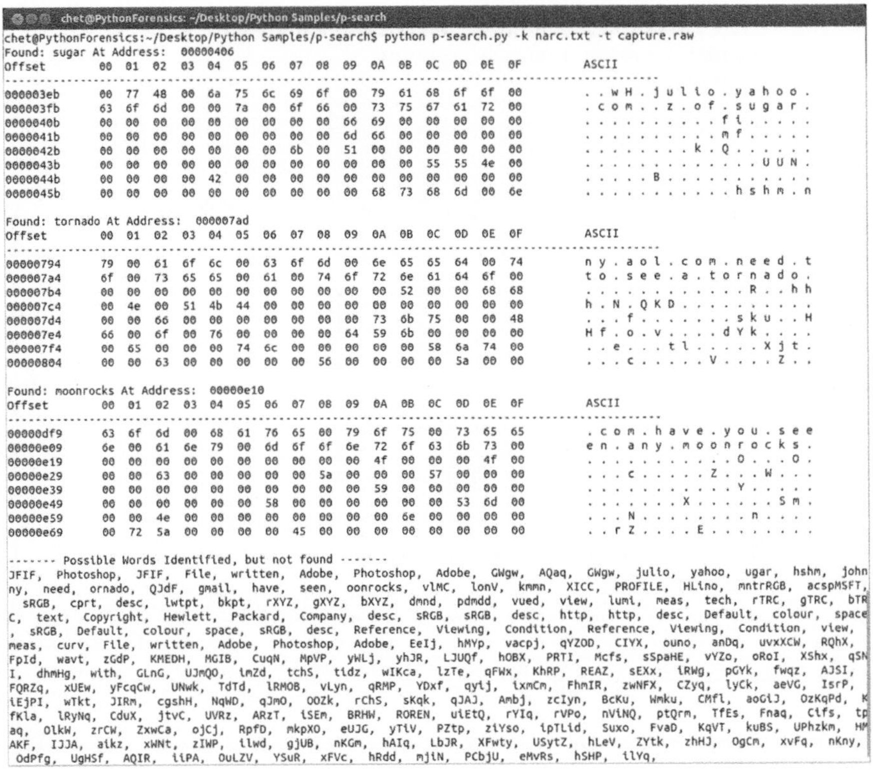

FIGURE 4.10

Execution of p-search running on Ubuntu Linux 12.04 LTS.

with a list of all the words that meet the minimum definition of a string, but do not match any of the defined key words. However, the current approach is lacking two key pieces of data. The first is simple, I need to include the offset of where each string was found in the target file. The second problem is a bigger challenge, that being to only print words that are likely to be legitimate words. Finally, it would be nice if the words were provided in a sorted list.

To handle the more difficult problem of identifying strings that have a high probability of being words, I have devised an approach that works exceptionally well and is fast. I depict the basic concept in Figure 4.12. I first process known words with an algorithm that produces a numeric weight based on the internal characteristics of each word.

Once a numeric weight is calculated for the word, the weights are sorted and any duplicates are removed. The key here is to process a large list of words. For this example, I used a dictionary containing over 600,000 words. This produces a matrix

```
janet-hosmers-imac:p-search janet$ python p-search.py -k narc.txt -t capture.raw -m matrix.txt
Found: sugar At Address:   00000406
Offset      00  01  02  03  04  05  06  07  08  09  0A  0B  0C  0D  0E  0F       ASCII
---------------------------------------------------------------------------
000003eb    00  77  48  00  6a  75  6c  69  6f  00  79  61  68  6f  6f  00     . . w H . j u l i o . y a h o o .
000003fb    63  6f  6d  00  00  7a  00  6f  66  00  73  75  67  61  72  00     . c o m . . z . o f . s u g a r .
0000040b    00  00  00  00  00  00  00  00  00  66  69  00  00  00  00  00     . . . . . . . . . f i . . . . .
0000041b    00  00  00  00  00  00  00  00  00  6d  66  00  00  00  00  00     . . . . . . . . . m f . . . . .
0000042b    00  00  00  00  00  00  00  6b  00  51  00  00  00  00  00  00     . . . . . . . k . Q . . . . . .
0000043b    00  00  00  00  00  00  00  00  00  00  00  55  55  4e  00     . . . . . . . . . . . U U N .
0000044b    00  00  00  00  42  00  00  00  00  00  00  00  00  00  00  00     . . . . B . . . . . . . . . . .
0000045b    00  00  00  00  00  00  00  00  00  00  68  73  68  6d  00  6e     . . . . . . . . . . h s h m . n

Found: tornado At Address:   000007ad
Offset      00  01  02  03  04  05  06  07  08  09  0A  0B  0C  0D  0E  0F       ASCII
---------------------------------------------------------------------------
00000794    79  00  61  6f  6c  00  63  6f  6d  00  6e  65  65  64  00  74     n y . a o l . c o m . n e e d . t
000007a4    6f  00  73  65  65  00  61  00  74  6f  72  6e  61  64  6f  00     t o . s e e . a . t o r n a d o .
000007b4    00  00  00  00  00  00  00  00  00  00  52  00  00  68  68     . . . . . . . . . . R . . h h
000007c4    00  4e  00  51  4b  44  00  00  00  00  00  00  00  00  00  00     h . N . Q K D . . . . . . . . .
000007d4    00  00  66  00  00  00  00  00  00  00  73  6b  75  00  00  48     . . . f . . . . . . s k u . . H
000007e4    . 66  00  6f  00  76  00  00  00  00  64  59  6b  00  00  00  00     H f . o . v . . . . d Y k . . . .
000007f4    00  65  00  00  00  74  6c  00  00  00  00  00  58  6a  74  00     . . e . . . t l . . . . X j t .
00000804    00  00  63  00  00  00  00  00  56  00  00  00  00  5a  00  00     . . . c . . . . V . . . . Z . .

Found: moonrocks At Address:   00000e10
Offset      00  01  02  03  04  05  06  07  08  09  0A  0B  0C  0D  0E  0F       ASCII
---------------------------------------------------------------------------
00000df9    63  6f  6d  00  68  61  76  65  00  79  6f  75  00  73  65  65     . c o m . h a v e . y o u . s e e
00000e09    6e  00  61  6e  79  00  6d  6f  6f  6e  72  6f  63  6b  73  00     e n . a n y . m o o n r o c k s .
00000e19    00  00  00  00  00  00  00  00  00  00  4f  00  00  00  4f  00     . . . . . . . . . . O . . . O .
00000e29    00  00  63  00  00  00  00  00  5a  00  00  00  57  00  00  00     . . . c . . . . Z . . . W . . .
00000e39    00  00  00  00  00  00  00  00  00  00  59  00  00  00  00  00     . . . . . . . . . . Y . . . . .
00000e49    00  00  00  00  00  00  58  00  00  00  00  00  00  53  6d  00     . . . . . . X . . . . . . S m .
00000e59    00  00  4e  00  00  00  00  00  00  00  00  6e  00  00  00  00     . . . N . . . . . . . n . . . .
00000e69    00  72  5a  00  00  00  00  00  45  00  00  00  00  00  00  00     . . r Z . . . . E . . . . . . .

Index of All Words
----------------------
['adobe', 470]
['adobe', 494]
['adobe', 10042]
['adobe', 10066]
['aogij', 46360]
['colour', 7624]
['colour', 7681]
['company', 7257]
['condition', 7752]
['condition', 7807]
['copyright', 7222]
['default', 7612]
['default', 7669]
['gmail', 3572]
['hewlett', 7241]
```

FIGURE 4.11

Execution of p-search running on iMac.

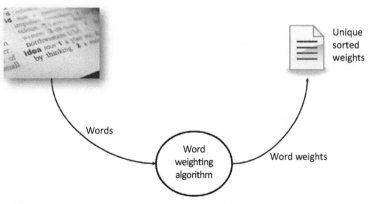

FIGURE 4.12

Diagram of word weighting approach.

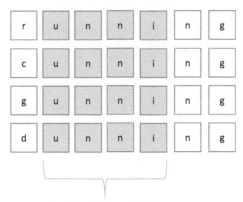

Used in weighting calculation

FIGURE 4.13

Weighted characteristics illustration.

of weights that can be used to compare strings found in raw data (using the same weighting algorithm used to create the original matrix) to the matrix. If the calculated weight matches one found in the matrix, I consider this a possible word, if not the string is discarded. Figure 4.13 provides an illustration of how this works. Each of the core letters contained in the word (ignoring the leading character) are used in the weighted calculation.

Since many words, at least in the English language, are derived from other words, this eliminates the need for having an all-encompassing dictionary of every possible word. In addition, if words are misspelled or newly created or derived, it is likely the weighting system vs. a direct match will provide a more liberal interpretation of a word being probable.

The importance of approximate searches and indexes can be vital. In the Casey Anthony case, for example, investigators missed probative Internet search history data because they looked for various search terms which *they* spelled correctly. She, however, had misspelled several search terms; while Google corrected the spelling during the search, it did not fix the misspelling in the Internet search history.

CODING isWordProbable

In order to create a method isWordProbable(word), I created a class named Matrix; let us take our typical deep dive into this new class.

```
class class_Matrix:
```

I start out by declaring a new set object named the weighted matrix.

```
weightedMatrix = set()
```

When the class is instantiated, the object will load the values contained in the matrix into the weighted matrix set. To handle this I simply added a new command line argument -m or --theMatrix to allow the user to specify a matrix file. I take the same precautions as you have seen before to trap any errors that might occur during the file handling operations.

```python
def __init__(self):
    try:
            fileTheMatrix = open(gl_args.theMatrix, 'rb')
            for line in fileTheMatrix:
                    value = line.strip()
                    self.weightedMatrix.add(int(value,16))
    except:
        log.error('Matrix File Error: '+ gl_args.theMatrix)
        sys.exit()
    finally:
        fileTheMatrix.close()

    return
```

Next I define the method isWordProbable which will calculate the weight of the passed string and perform a lookup in the weightedMatrix to determine if we have a match. Note I first check to see if theWord passed is of minimum size.

```python
def isWordProbable(self, theWord):
    if (len(theWord) < MIN_WORD):
        return False
    else:
        BASE = 96
        wordWeight = 0
```

This is the core weight calculation and produces an unsigned long integer value name wordWeight.

```python
        for i in range(4,0,-1):
            charValue = (ord(theWord[i]) - BASE)
            shiftValue = (i-1)*8
            charWeight = charValue << shiftValue
            wordWeight = (wordWeight | charWeight)
```

Once I have calculated the word weight I just check to see if the weight exists in the weighted matrix.

```python
        if ( wordWeight in self.weightedMatrix):
            return True
        else:
            return False
```

To properly incorporate this into the program the following code is all that is needed.

The initialization is simple, I create an object named wordCheck (which executes the initialization code of the Matrix to load in the weighed values. I also, create a list named indexOfWords where I will store the probable words that we find.

```
wordCheck = class_Matrix()
indexOfWords = []
...
...
```

Next, I embed the following code within the existing search loop to evaluate each string as a probable word. If wordCheck returns True, then I add the word to the indexOfWords list. Note that this list has two elements per entry: 1) the string new-Word and 2) the offset from the beginning of the target object where it was found.

```
if wordCheck.isWordProbable(newWord):
    indexOfWords.append([newWord, i-cnt])
```

Finally, I added a method to print the indexOfWords list at the end of the search that includes both the word and offset. I also sorted the list prior to print in order to make it alphabetical.

```
def PrintAllWordsFound(wordList):

    print "Index of All Words"
    print "——————————————————"

    wordList.sort()

    for entry in nfList:
        print entry

    print "——————————————————"
    print

    return
```

From an execution perspective you can see the results of the combined search and index program in Figure 4.14.

P-SEARCH COMPLETE CODE LISTINGS
p-search.py

```
#
# p-search : Python Word Search
# Author: C. Hosmer
# August 2013
# Version 1.0
#
# Simple p-search Python program
#
```

```
Found: moonrocks At Address:  00000e10
Offset    00  01  02  03   04  05  06   07  08  09  0A  0B  0C  0D  0E  0F      ASCII
-----------------------------------------------------------------------------
00000df9   63  6f  6d  00   68  61  76   65  00  79  6f  75  00  73  65  65     . c o m . h a v e . y o u . s e e
00000e09   6e  00  61  6e   79  00  6d   6f  6f  6e  72  6f  63  6b  73  00     e n . a n y . m o o n r o c k s .
00000e19   00  00  00  00   00  00  00   00  00  00  4f  00  00  00  4f  00     . . . . . . . . . . . O . . . O .
00000e29   00  00  63  00   00  00  00   00  5a  00  00  00  57  00  00  00     . . c . . . . . Z . . . W . . .
00000e39   00  00  00  00   00  00  00   00  59  00  00  00  00  00  00  00     . . . . . . . . Y . . . . . . .
00000e49   00  00  00  00   00  00  58   00  00  00  00  00  53  6d  00  00     . . . . . . X . . . . . S m . .
00000e59   00  00  4e  00   00  00  00   00  00  00  00  6e  00  00  00  00     . . N . . . . . . . . n . . . .
00000e69   00  72  5a  00   00  00  00   45  00  00  00  00  00  00  00  00     . . r Z . . . E . . . . . . . .
Index of All words
--------------------
['adobe', 470]
['adobe', 494]
['adobe', 10042]
['adobe', 10066]
['aogij', 46360]
['colour', 7624]
['colour', 7681]
['company', 7257]
['condition', 7752]
['condition', 7807]
['copyright', 7222]
['default', 7612]
['default', 7669]
['gmail', 3572]
['hewlett', 7241]
['hlino', 6881]
['johnny', 1936]
['julio', 1008]
['moonrocks', 3600]
['packard', 7249]
['photoshop', 24]
['photoshop', 476]
['photoshop', 10048]
['profile', 6868]
['qyzod', 11694]
['reference', 7734]
['reference', 7789]
['roren', 51038]
['space', 7631]
['space', 7688]
['sspahe', 22967]
['sugar', 1030]
['tornado', 1965]
['viewing', 7744]
['viewing', 7799]
['written', 459]
['written', 10031]
['yahoo', 1014]
--------------------
```

FIGURE 4.14

p-search execution with indexing capability.

```
# Read in a list of search words
# Read a binary file into a bytearray
# Search the bytearray for occurrences of any specified search words
# Print a HEX/ASCII display localizing the matching words
# Print out a list of possible words identified that didn't match
#
# Definition of a word. a word for this example is an uninterrupted
  sequence of
# 4 to 12 alpha characters
#

import logging
import time
import _psearch

if __name__ == '__main__':

    PSEARCH_VERSION = '1.0'

    # Turn on Logging
```

```
logging.basicConfig(filename='pSearchLog.log',level=logging.DEBUG,
format='%(asctime)s %(message)s')

    # Process the Command Line Arguments
    _psearch.ParseCommandLine()

    log = logging.getLogger('main._psearch')
    log.info("p-search started")

    # Record the Starting Time
    startTime = time.time()

    # Perform Keyword Search
    _psearch.SearchWords()

    # Record the Ending Time
    endTime = time.time()
    duration = endTime - startTime

    logging.info('Elapsed Time: ' + str(duration) +' seconds')
    logging.info(")

    logging.info('Program Terminated Normally')
```

_p-search.py

```
    #
    # psearch support functions, where all the real work gets done
    #
    # Display Message()                    ParseCommandLine()
    # ValidateFileRead()                    ValidateFileWrite()
    # Matrix (class)
    #
    import argparse                        # Python Standard Library -
                                           Parser for command-line
                                           options, arguments
    import os                                  # Standard Library OS
                                               functions
    import logging                         # Standard Library Logging
                                           functions

    log = logging.getLogger('main._psearch')

    #Constants
    MIN_WORD = 5                           # Minimum word size in bytes
    MAX_WORD = 15                          # Maximum word size in bytes
    PREDECESSOR_SIZE = 32              # Values to print before match found
    WINDOW_SIZE = 128                  # Total values to dump when match found

    # Name: ParseCommand() Function
    #
    # Desc:  Process and Validate the command line arguments
    #               use Python Standard Library module argparse
```

```
#
# Input: none
#
# Actions:
#                  Uses the standard library argparse to process the command
                   line
#
def ParseCommandLine():

    parser = argparse.ArgumentParser('Python Search')

    parser.add_argument('-v', '--verbose', help="enables printing of
    additional program messages", action='store_true')
    parser.add_argument('-k', '--keyWords', type= ValidateFileRead,
    required=True, help="specify the file containing search words")
    parser.add_argument('-t', '--srchTarget', type= ValidateFileRead,
    required=True, help="specify the target file to search")
    parser.add_argument('-m', '--theMatrix', type= ValidateFileRead,
    required=True, help="specify the weighted matrix file")

    global gl_args

    gl_args = parser.parse_args()

    DisplayMessage("Command line processed: Successfully")

    return

# End Parse Command Line

#
# Name: ValidateFileRead Function
#
# Desc: Function that will validate that a file exists and is readable
#
# Input: A file name with full path
#
# Actions:
#                  if valid will return path
#
#                  if invalid it will raise an ArgumentTypeError within
                   argparse
#                  which will inturn be reported by argparse to the user
#
def ValidateFileRead(theFile):

    # Validate the path is a valid
    if not os.path.exists(theFile):
        raise argparse.ArgumentTypeError('File does not exist')

    # Validate the path is readable
    if os.access(theFile, os.R_OK):
```

```
                    return theFile
            else:
                raise argparse.ArgumentTypeError('File is not readable')

    #End ValidateFileRead ====================================


    #
    # Name: DisplayMessage() Function
    #
    # Desc: Displays the message if the verbose command line option is present
    #
    # Input: message type string
    #
    # Actions:
    #                   Uses the standard library print function to display the
    #                   message
    #
    def DisplayMessage(msg):

        if gl_args.verbose:
            print(msg)

        return

    #End DisplayMessage====================================


    #
    # Name SearchWords()
    #
    # Uses command line arguments
    #
    # Searches the target file for keywords
    #

    def SearchWords():

        # Create an empty set of search words
        searchWords = set()

        # Attempt to open and read search words
        try:
            fileWords = open(gl_args.keyWords)
            for line in fileWords:
                searchWords.add(line.strip())
        except:
            log.error('Keyword File Failure: '+ gl_args.keyWords)
            sys.exit()
        finally:
            fileWords.close()
        # Create Log Entry Words to Search For
```

```python
log.info('Search Words')
log.info('Input File: '+gl_args.keyWords)
log.info(searchWords)

# Attempt to open and read the target file
# and directly load into a bytearray

try:
    targetFile = open(gl_args.srchTarget, 'rb')
    baTarget = bytearray(targetFile.read())
except:
    log.error('Target File Failure: '+ gl_args.srchTarget)
    sys.exit()
finally:
    targetFile.close()

sizeOfTarget= len(baTarget)

# Post to log

log.info('Target of Search: '+ gl_args.srchTarget)
log.info('File Size: '+str(sizeOfTarget))

baTargetCopy = baTarget

wordCheck = class_Matrix()

# Search Loop
# step one, replace all non characters with zero's

for i in range(0, sizeOfTarget):
    character = chr(baTarget[i])
    if not character.isalpha():
        baTarget[i] = 0

# step # 2 extract possible words from the bytearray
# and then inspect the search word list
# create an empty list of probable not found items

indexOfWords = []

cnt = 0
for i in range(0, sizeOfTarget):
    character = chr(baTarget[i])
    if character.isalpha():
        cnt += 1
    else:
        if (cnt >= MIN_WORD and cnt <= MAX_WORD):
            newWord = ""
            for z in range(i-cnt, i):
                newWord = newWord + chr(baTarget[z])
            newWord = newWord.lower()
```

```
                    if (newWord in searchWords):
                        PrintBuffer(newWord, i-cnt, baTargetCopy,
                        i-PREDECESSOR_SIZE, WINDOW_SIZE)
                        indexOfWords.append([newWord, i-cnt])
                        cnt = 0
                        print
                    else:
                        if wordCheck.isWordProbable(newWord):
                            indexOfWords.append([newWord, i-cnt])
                        cnt = 0
                else:
                    cnt = 0

    PrintAllWordsFound(indexOfWords)

    return

# End of SearchWords Function

#
# Print Hexidecimal / ASCII Page Heading
#
def PrintHeading():

    print("Offset  00 01 02 03 04 05 06 07 08 09 0A 0B 0C 0D 0E
    0F       ASCII")
    print("---------------------------------------------------
    ------------------")

    return
# End PrintHeading

#
# Print Buffer
#
# Prints Buffer contents for words that are discovered
# parameters
# 1) Word found
# 2) Direct Offset to beginning of the word
# 3 buff The bytearray holding the target
# 4) offset starting position in the buffer for printing
# 5) hexSize, size of hex display windows to print
#
def PrintBuffer(word, directOffset, buff, offset, hexSize):

    print "Found: "+ word + " At Address: ",
    print "%08x      " % (directOffset)

    PrintHeading()

    for i in range(offset, offset+hexSize, 16):
        for j in range(0,16):
```

```
                if (j == 0):
                    print "%08x " % i,
                else:
                    byteValue = buff[i+j]
                    print "%02x " % byteValue,
            print " ",
            for j in range (0,16):
                byteValue = buff[i+j]
                if (byteValue >= 0x20 and byteValue <= 0x7f):
                    print "%c" % byteValue,
                else:
                    print'.',
            print
    return

# End Print Buffer

#
# PrintAllWordsFound
#

def PrintAllWordsFound(wordList):

    print "Index of All Words"
    print "--------------------"

    wordList.sort()

    for entry in wordList:
        print entry

    print "--------------------"
    print

    return

#End PrintAllWordsFound


#
# Class Matrix
#
# init method, loads the matrix into the set
# weightedMatrix
#
# isWordProbable method
#    1) Calculates the weight of the provided word
#    2) Verifies the minimum length
#    3) Calculates the weight for the word
#    4) Tests the word for existence in the matrix
#    5) Returns true or false
#
```

```python
class class_Matrix:

    weightedMatrix = set()

    def __init__(self):
        try:
                fileTheMatrix = open(gl_args.theMatrix, 'rb')
                for line in fileTheMatrix:
                        value = line.strip()
                        self.weightedMatrix.add(int(value,16))
        except:
            log.error('Matrix File Error: '+ gl_args.theMatrix)
            sys.exit()
        finally:
            fileTheMatrix.close()

        return

    def isWordProbable(self, theWord):

        if (len(theWord) < MIN_WORD):
            return False
        else:
            BASE = 96
            wordWeight = 0

            for i in range(4,0,-1):
                charValue = (ord(theWord[i]) - BASE)
                shiftValue = (i-1)*8
                charWeight = charValue << shiftValue
                wordWeight = (wordWeight | charWeight)

            if ( wordWeight in self.weightedMatrix):
                    return True
            else:
                    return False

## End Class Matrix
```

CHAPTER REVIEW

In this chapter, I put to use new Python language elements including *sets* and *bytearrays* and I expanded the use of lists and classes. I also provided examples of how to open and read files containing a diverse set of values such as keywords, raw binary, and hexadecimal values and work with those directly within Python bytearrays, lists, and sets. I demonstrated how leveraging the right language elements can lead to simple, readable code that accomplishes our objectives. As a result, p-search is a useable application that provides investigators with the capability to search for keywords and generate an index of words found in documents, disk images, memory snapshots, and even network traces.

In addition, I once again demonstrated the interoperability of Python code by running the sample unaltered code on Windows, Linux, and Mac producing the same results.

SUMMARY QUESTIONS

1. What are the advantages and disadvantages of the built-in language types (lists, sets, and dictionary).
2. Explain the advantages of using a set to hold a list of keywords.
3. How does Python's ability to deal with a broad set of data (binary, text, and integers) differ from other languages?
4. Many modern files, disk images, memory snapshots, and network traces are going to contain Unicode data not only simple ASCII. Modify p-search to provide the ability to search and index data that contains a mixture of simple ASCII and Unicode.
5. Expand the matrix to include a broader set of weighted values that include foreign language, proper names, places, and vocabulary from other domains such as medical terminology.

Additional Resources

The Complete Sherlock Holmes: All 4 Novels and 56 Short Stories. Deluxe edition. Bantam Classics; October 1, 1986.
Python Programming Language—Official Website, Python.org. http://www.python.org.
The Python Standard Library. http://docs.python.org/2/library/.

Forensic Evidence Extraction (JPEG and TIFF)

5

CHAPTER CONTENTS

INTRODUCTION

Simple and complex digital data structures offer significant opportunities to collect and extract valuable evidence. Files have simple metadata that define modified, access, and created times along with file ownership, file size, and other attributes that label the file as read-only, system, or archive. This information is easy to retrieve and examine with common desktop tools. Memory snapshots contain both structured and unstructured data that can be carved and reconstructed to reveal running processes and threads, recent user activity, network data, and even user typed passwords and cryptographic keying material.

Other complex files structures, such as the JPEG files that include EXIF data (The Exchangeable Image File Format), contain a plethora of potentially valuable information about the image itself. This can include the camera type used to take the photograph, the time and date the photo was taken, and literally hundreds of individual data elements associated with the photograph. With the advent of Facebook, Instagram, Twitter, Flickr, and other social media services, the sharing of digital photographs has been weaved into the fabric of our culture. Today, over a billion people carry smart phones and tablets that have built-in cameras capable of taking high-quality photographs and movies that can be shared instantly across the globe using the aforementioned social network applications, text messaging, or good old-fashioned e-mail.

In addition, everyone from the Weather Channel to law enforcement investigators use digital photography to provide insight and understanding of physical events. The Federal Communications Commission (FCC) has adopted new rules that include mandatory improvements to the accuracy of the location information transmitted when cell phone-based 911 calls are made. Specifically, E911 rules require wireless service providers to deliver the latitude and longitude of the caller within 50-300 m [FCC]. These requirements have driven smart phone manufactures to include Global Positioning System (GPS) chips in their handsets along with high-quality cameras that can automatically embed location and time data directly into digital photographs. Consequently these innovations have delivered potentially valuable evidence including "what: the content of the photo," "when: the photo was snapped," and "where: the photo was taken."

Based on this, I wanted to delve deeper into the extraction of evidence from digital photographs, specifically those photos taken with smart phones that include EXIF data. I will focus most of my attention on the EXIF data associated with JPEG and TIFF images, mainly because the preponderance of photos generated today from smart phones support EXIF embedding.

Many of you may have already examined the contents of digital photographs and the EXIF information using Hex editors and other primitive tools, and as a result require an upgraded prescription from the optometrist afterword. To help us in peeling back the onion-like layers of digital photographs, I will be adding a new library that will do most of the heavy lifting for us—namely the *Python Image Library* (PIL). The PIL provides a great deal of capabilities to not only extract information from images but also provides capabilities to manipulate them. I am going to focus only on the data extraction of EXIF data using the PIL, but once you learn how to properly use the library you can use the PIL for other image processing activities [Python Image Library].

The Python Image Library

The first step in using the PIL is to install the library. If you are running Python on Windows platform, you are in luck as a simple installer is available as shown in Figure 5.1.

Python Imaging Library (PIL)

The **Python Imaging Library (PIL)** adds image processing capabilities to your Python interpreter. This library supports many file formats, and provides powerful image processing and graphics capabilities.

Status

The current free version is PIL 1.1.7. This release supports Python 1.5.2 and newer, including 2.5 and 2.6. A version for 3.X will be released later.

Support

Free Support: If you don't have a support contract, please send your question to the Python Image SIG mailing list. The same applies for bug reports and patches.

You can join the Image SIG via python.org's subscription page, or by sending a mail to image-sig-request@python.org. Put *subscribe* in the message body to automatically subscribe to the list, or *help* to get additional information.

You can also ask on the Python mailing list, *python-list@python.org*, or the newsgroup *comp.lang.python*. **Please don't send support questions to PythonWare addresses.**

Downloads

The following downloads are currently available:

PIL 1.1.7

- Python Imaging Library 1.1.7 Source Kit (all platforms) (November 15, 2009)
- Python Imaging Library 1.1.7 for Python 2.4 (Windows only)
- Python Imaging Library 1.1.7 for Python 2.5 (Windows only)
- Python Imaging Library 1.1.7 for Python 2.6 (Windows only)
- Python Imaging Library 1.1.7 for Python 2.7 (Windows only)

Additional downloads may be found here.

FIGURE 5.1

Downloading Python Image Library for Windows.

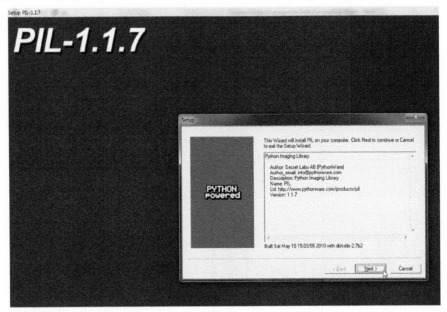

FIGURE 5.2

Windows installation Wizard for the Python Image Library.

Once you have successfully downloaded the proper version for your Python installation (I am using PIL version 1.1.7 for Python 2.7), you simply execute the downloaded file and accept the defaults provided by the Wizard as shown in Figure 5.2. (This is a great example of why I choose to utilize Python 2.x for the book, as you can see the PIL library has not yet been converted to work with Python 3.x. Once this is done, the programs in this chapter can be easily updated to work with Python 3.x.)

If you are working with Linux or Mac, the steps for library installation are readily available on the Web. Here is one excellent example for Ubuntu 12.04 LTS: https://gist.github.com/dwayne/3353083 (Figure 5.3).

Before diving straight in

Before I dive right into the PIL, I need to introduce the built-in Python Dictionary type. Up to this point we have used the *lists* and *sets* structures within Python in several examples. In some cases, structures with a bit more flexibility and capability are required. More specifically, since the PIL uses dictionaries, we need to better understand their operation.

As you can see in Code Script 5.1, each entry in the dictionary has two parts, first the key which is followed by the value. For example, the key "fast" has an associated value of "Porsche."

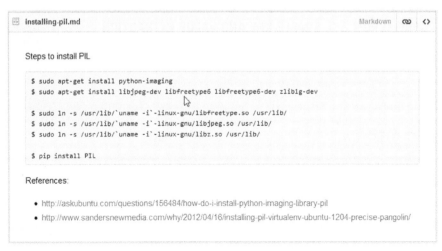

FIGURE 5.3

Installing Python Image Library on Ubuntu 12.04 LTS.

CODE SCRIPT 5.1 CREATING A DICTIONARY

```
>>> dCars = {"fast": "Porsche", "clean": "Prius", "expensive":
"Rolls"}
>>> print dCars
{'expensive': 'Rolls', 'clean': 'Prius', 'fast': 'Porsche'}
```

You might have noticed that when I printed the contents of the dictionary, the order has changed. This is due to the fact that the key is converted to a hash value when stored in order to both save space and to improve performance when searching or indexing the dictionary. If you want the dictionary printed in a specific order you can use the following code, which extracts the dictionary items and then sorts the items by the key.

CODE SCRIPT 5.2 PRINTING A SORTED DICTIONARY

```
>>> dCarsItems = dCars.items()
>>> dCarsItems.sort()
>>> print dCarsItems
[('clean', 'Prius'), ('expensive', 'Rolls'), ('fast', 'Porsche')]
```

What if the dictionary is large and you wish to find all the keys? Or once you find the keys you wish to extract the value of a specific key?

CODE SCRIPT 5.3 SIMPLE KEY AND VALUE EXTRACTION

```
>>> # what keys are available?
>>> dCars.keys()
['expensive', 'clean', 'fast']
>>> # what is the value associated with the key "clean"?
>>> dCars.get("clean")"
'Prius'
```

Finally, you might want to iterate over a dictionary and extract and display all the key, value pairs.

CODE SCRIPT 5.4 ITERATING OVER A DICTIONARY

```
>>> for key, value in dCars.items():
...        print key, value
expensive Rolls
clean Prius
fast Porsche
```

If you are not familiar with Python but have familiarity with other programming environments, Script 5.4 may seem a bit odd for several reasons.

1. We did not need to declare the variables' key and value, as Python takes care of that automatically. In this simple case both key and value are strings, but they are not required to be.
2. Since we know that dCars is a dictionary, the method *items* automatically returns both key and values. The keys are "clean," "expensive," and "fast" in this example and the values are the string names of the cars "Porsche," "Prius," and "Rolls."

Since Python will automatically handle the data typing for you, let us take a look at something a bit more complicated.

CODE SCRIPT 5.5 A MORE COMPLEX DICTIONARY EXAMPLE

```
>>> dTemp = {"2013:12:31":[22.0,"F","High"],
"2013:11:28":[24.5,"C","Low"], "2013:12:27":[32.7,"F","High"]}
>>> dTempItems = dTemp.items()
>>> dTempItems.sort()
>>> for key, value in dTempItems:
```

```
...  print key, value
...
2013:11:28 [24.5, 'C', 'Low']
2013:12:27 [32.7, 'F', 'High']
2013:12:31 [22.0, 'F', 'High']
```

As you can see in Code Script 5.5, the *keys* are strings that represent a date while *value* is actually a Python *list* that contains the time, the time reference, the temperature, and the units of the temperature.

Now that you have a good general understanding of the dictionaries, go create some of your own and experiment with the available methods. From this example, I hope you see the power of the Dictionary type and it has you thinking about other ways to apply this structure.

PIL test-before code

As with other modules and libraries, the best way to become comfortable with the library is to experiment with it. Remember our adage test-then code, this is especially true for PIL, mainly because the PIL uses a new Python language structure, the *Dictionary* data structure. In addition, the EXIF module of the PIL requires a solid understanding before you can put it to work for you. I will use the Python Shell and short scripts to demonstrate.

Determining the available EXIF TAGS

The PIL has two important sets of TAGS that provide *keys* that are used to access dictionary elements. They are EXIFTAGS and GPSTAGS. I developed a script to determine which EXIF TAGS are available by using the following method:

(1) Import the EXIFTAGS from the PIL library.
(2) Extract the dictionary items (the key, value pairs) from TAGS.
(3) Sort them to make it easier later to identify them.
(4) Print the sorted dictionary of key, value pairs.

CODE SCRIPT 5.6 EXTRACTING EXIF TAGS

```
>>> from PIL.EXIFTags import TAGS
>>> EXIFTAGS = TAGS.items()
>>> EXIFTAGS.sort()
>>> print EXIFTags
```

This produces the following printed list of available tags. Note this is not the data, just the global list of EXIF TAGS:

```
[(256, 'ImageWidth'), (257, 'ImageLength'), (258,'BitsPerSample'), (259,
'Compression'), (262, 'PhotometricInterpretation'), (270,
'ImageDescription'), (271,'Make'), (272,'Model'), (273,'StripOffsets'), (274,
'Orientation'), (277,'SamplesPerPixel'), (278, 'RowsPerStrip'), (279,
'StripByteConunts'), (282,'XResolution'), (283,'YResolution'), (284,
'PlanarConfiguration'), (296, 'ResolutionUnit'), (301, 'TransferFunction'),
(305,'Software'), (306,'DateTime'), (315,'Artist'), (318,'WhitePoint'), (319,
'PrimaryChromaticities'), (513, 'JpegIFOffset'), (514, 'JpegIFByteCount'),
(529, 'YCbCrCoefficients'), (530, 'YCbCrSubSampling'), (531,
'YCbCrPositioning'), (532, 'ReferenceBlackWhite'), (4096,
'RelatedImageFileFormat'), (4097, 'RelatedImageWidth'), (33421,
'CFARepeatPatternDim'), (33422, 'CFAPattern'), (33423, 'BatteryLevel'),
(33432, 'Copyright'), (33434, 'ExposureTime'), (33437, 'FNumber'), (34665,
'EXIFOffset'), (34675, 'InterColorProfile'), (34850, 'ExposureProgram'),
(34852, 'SpectralSensitivity'), (34853, 'GPSInfo'), (34855,
'ISOSpeedRatings'), (34856, 'OECF'), (34857, 'Interlace'), (34858,
'TimeZoneOffset'), (34859, 'SelfTimerMode'), (36864, 'EXIFVersion'), (36867,
'DateTimeOriginal'), (36868, 'DateTimeDigitized'), (37121,
'ComponentsConfiguration'), (37122, 'CompressedBitsPerPixel'), (37377,
'ShutterSpeedValue'), (37378, 'ApertureValue'), (37379, 'BrightnessValue'),
(37380, 'ExposureBiasValue'), (37381, 'MaxApertureValue'), (37382,
'SubjectDistance'), (37383, 'MeteringMode'), (37384, 'LightSource'), (37385,
'Flash'), (37386, 'FocalLength'), (37387, 'FlashEnergy'), (37388,
'SpatialFrequencyResponse'), (37389, 'Noise'), (37393, 'ImageNumber'),
(37394,'SecurityClassification'), (37395, 'ImageHistory'), (37396,
'SubjectLocation'), (37397, 'ExposureIndex'), (37398, 'TIFF/EPStandardID'),
(37500, 'MakerNote'), (37510, 'UserComment'), (37520, 'SubsecTime'), (37521,
'SubsecTimeOriginal'), (37522, 'SubsecTimeDigitized'), (40960,
'FlashPixVersion'), (40961,'ColorSpace'), (40962,'EXIFImageWidth'), (40963,
'EXIFImageHeight'), (40964, 'RelatedSoundFile'), (40965,
'EXIFInteroperabilityOffset'), (41483, 'FlashEnergy'), (41484,
'SpatialFrequencyResponse'), (41486, 'FocalPlaneXResolution'), (41487,
'FocalPlaneYResolution'), (41488, 'FocalPlaneResolutionUnit'), (41492,
'SubjectLocation'), (41493, 'ExposureIndex'), (41495, 'SensingMethod'),
(41728, 'FileSource'), (41729, 'SceneType'), (41730, 'CFAPattern')]
```

Time is a concept that allows society to function in an orderly fashion where all parties are able to easily understand the representation of time and agree on the sequence of events. Since 1972, the International standard for time is Coordinated Universal Time (UTC). UTC forms the basis for the official time source in most nations around the globe; it is governed by a diplomatic treaty adopted by the world community that designates National Metrology Institutes (NMIs) as UTC time sources. The National Institute of Standards and Technology in the United States and the National Physical Laboratory (NPL) in England are two examples of NMIs. There are about 50 similar metrology centers that are responsible for official time throughout the world. In addition, time zones can play a key role when examining digital evidence; they provide localization of events and actions based upon the computer's time zone setting. For example, if the computer's time zone is set to New York, the local time is −5 hours from UTC (or 5 hours behind). Finally, many U.S. States and foreign countries observe day light savings time, most modern operating systems automatically adjust for this observance which causes additional differences and calculations between UTC or when attempting to synchronize events across time zones.

Within the printed list, I have highlighted TAGS that are of immediate interest including GPSInfo, TimeZoneOffset, and DateTimeOriginal.

It is important to note that it is not guaranteed that all of these TAGS will be available for every image; rather this is the broad set of key value pairs that are potentially within an image. Each manufacturer independently determines which values will be included. Thus you must process the key value pairs for each target image to determine which TAGS are in fact available. I will show you how this is done shortly.

As you scan the list, you may find other TAGS that are of interest in your investigative activities and you can utilize the same approach defined here to experiment with those values.

Determining the available EXIF GPSTAGS

Next, I want to drill a bit deeper into the GPSInfo TAG, as our objective in this chapter is to extract GPS-based location data of specific images. I take a similar approach to determine what GPSTAGS are available at the next level by writing the following lines of code.

CODE SCRIPT 5.7 EXTRACTING GPS TAGS

```
>>> from PIL.EXIFTags import GPSTAGS
>>> gps = GPSTAGS.items()
>>> gps.sort()
>>> print gps
```

[(0, 'GPSVersionID'), (1, 'GPSLatitudeRef'), (2, 'GPSLatitude'), (3, 'GPSLongitudeRef'), (4, 'GPSLongitude'), (5, 'GPSAltitudeRef'), (6, 'GPSAltitude'), (7, 'GPSTimeStamp'), (8, 'GPSSatellites'), (9, 'GPSStatus'), (10, 'GPSMeasureMode'), (11, 'GPSDOP'), (12, 'GPSSpeedRef'), (13, 'GPSSpeed'), (14, 'GPSTrackRef'), (15, 'GPSTrack'), (16, 'GPSImgDirectionRef'), (17, 'GPSImgDirection'), (18, 'GPSMapDatum'), (19, 'GPSDestLatitudeRef'), (20, 'GPSDestLatitude'), (21, 'GPSDestLongitudeRef'), (22, 'GPSDestLongitude'), (23, 'GPSDestBearingRef'), (24, 'GPSDestBearing'), (25, 'GPSDestDistanceRef'), (26, 'GPSDestDistance')]

I have highlighted a few GPSTAGS that we need in order to pinpoint the location and time of the photograph. Again pointing out that there is no guarantee that any or all of these tags will be available within the subject image.

Longitude and latitude locations provide the ability to pinpoint a specific location on the earth. The Global Position System and GPS receivers built into smart phones and cameras can deliver very accurate geolocation information in the form of longitude and latitude coordinates. If so configured, this geolocation information can be directly embedded in photographs, movies, and other digital objects when certain events occur. Extracting this geolocation information from these digital objects and then entering that data into online services such as Mapquest, Google Maps, Google earth, etc., can provide evidence of where and when that digital object was created.

If we plan to utilize the TAGS to pinpoint the location, we need a better definition and understanding of the TAGS of interest, their meaning, and usage.

GPSLatitudeRef: Latitude is specified by either the North or South position in degrees from the equator. Those points that are north of the equator range from 0 to 90 degrees. Those points that are south of the equator range from 0 to −90 degrees. Thus this reference value is used to define where the latitude is in relationship to the equator. Since the value latitude is specified in EXIF as a positive integer, if the Latitude Reference is "S" or South, the integer value must be converted to a negative value.

GPSLatitude: Indicates the latitude measured in degrees. The EXIF data specify these as whole degrees, followed by minutes and then followed by seconds.

GPSLongitudeRef: Longitude is specified by either the east or west position in degrees. The convention is based on the Prime Meridian which runs through the Royal Observatory in Greenwich, England, which is defined as longitude zero degrees. Those points that are west of the Prime Meridian range from 0 to −180 degrees. Those points that are east of the Prime Meridian range from 0 to 180 degrees. Thus this reference value is used to define where the longitude value is in relationship to Greenwich. Since the value of longitude is specified in EXIF as a positive integer, if the Longitude Reference is west or "W," the integer value must be converted to a negative value.

GPSLongitude: Indicates the longitude measured in degrees. The EXIF data specify these as whole degrees, followed by minutes and then followed by seconds.

GPSTimeStamp: Specifies the time as Universal Coordinated Time that the photo was taken.

Since the data contained within the EXIF structure are digital values, they are subject to manipulation and forgery. Thus, securing the images or obtaining them directly from the Smart Mobile device makes fraudulent modification less likely and much more difficult to accomplish.

Now that we have a basic understanding of what TAGS are potentially available within a photograph, let us examine an actual photograph. Figure 5.4 depicts an image downloaded from the Internet and will be the subject of this experiment.

FIGURE 5.4

Internet Photo Cat.jpg.

CODE SCRIPT 5.8 EXTRACT EXIF TAGS OF A SAMPLE IMAGE

```
>>> from PIL import Image
>>> from PIL.EXIFTags import TAGS, GPSTAGS
>>>
>>> pilImage = Image.open("c:\\pictures\\cat.jpg)"
... EXIFData = pilImage._getEXIF()
...
>>> catEXIF = EXIFData.items()
>>> catEXIF.sort()
>>> print catEXIF
```

This script imports the PIL Image module that allows me to open the specific image for processing and to create the object *pilImage*. I can then use the object *pilImage* to acquire the EXIF data by using the *._getEXIF()* method. As we did when extracting the EXIFTAGS and GPSTAGS, in this example I am extracting the dictionary items and then sorting them. Note, in this example I am extracting the actual EXIF data (or potential evidence) not the TAG references.

The output from the Code Script 5.3 is shown here.

[(271, 'Canon'), (272, 'Canon EOS 400D DIGITAL'), (282, (300, 1)), (283, (300, 1)), (296, 2), (306, '2008:08:05 23:48:04'), (315, 'unknown'), (33432, 'Eirik Solheim - www.eirikso. com'), (33434, (1, 100)), (33437, (22, 10)), (34665, 240), (34850, 2), **(34853, {0: (2, 2, 0, 0), 1: 'N', 2: ((59, 1), (55, 1), (37417, 1285)), 3: 'E', 4: ((10, 1), (41, 1), (55324, 1253)), 5: 0, 6: (81, 1)}),** (34855, 400), (36864, '0221'), (36867, '2008:08:05 20:59:32'), (36868, '2008:08:05 20:59:32'), (37378, (2275007, 1000000)), (37381, (96875, 100000)), (37383, 1), (37385, 16), (37386, (50, 1)), (41486, (3888000, 877)), (41487, (2592000, 582)), (41488, 2), (41985, 0), (41986, 0), (41987, 0), (41990, 0)]

I have highlighted the GPSInfo data associated with this photograph. I was able to identify the GPSInfo TAG based on the output of the previous Code Script 5.1, whereby the output showed that the GPSInfo TAG had a key value of 34853. Therefore, this camera, the Canon EOS 400D DIGITAL, provides the GPS data highlighted between the curly braces. Closer examination of the GPS data reveals the specific key value pairs that are available. As you can see, the key value pairs embedded in the GPSInfo data dictionary are 0, 1, 2, 3, 4, 5, and 6. These TAGS refer to the standard GPS TAGS. In Code Script 5.2, I printed out all the possible GPS Tags, by referring to that output we discover the following GPS TAGS that were provided by the Cannon EOS 400D. They include:

```
0 GPSVersionID
1 GPSLatitudeRef
2 GPSLatitude
3 GPSLongitudeRef
4 GPSLongitude
5 GPSAltitudeRef
6 GPSAltitude
```

With this information I can calculate the longitude and latitude provided by the EXIF data within the photograph using the following process. But, first, I need to extract the latitude from the key value pair **GPSTag 2:**

((59, 1), (55, 1), (37417, 1285))

Each latitude and longitude value contains three sets of values. They are:

Degrees: **(59, 1)**
Minutes: **(55, 1)**
Seconds: **(37,417, 1285)**

You might be wondering why they are represented like this. The answer is the EXIF data does not hold floating point numbers (only whole integers). In order to provide more precise latitude and longitude data, each pair represents a ratio.

Next, I need to perform the ratio calculation to obtain a precise factional value, yielding:

Degrees: $59/1 = 59.0$
Minutes: $55/1 = 55.0$
Seconds: $37,417/1285 = 29.1182879$
Or more properly stated 59 degrees, 55 minutes, 29.1182879 seconds.

Note: **GPSTag 1:** "N" the Latitude Reference key value pair is a north reference from the equator and does not require us to convert this to a negative value, if it were "S" we would have make this additional conversion.

Next, most online mapping programs (i.e., Google Maps) require data to be provided as a fractional value. This is accomplished by using the following formula.

Degrees $+$ (minutes/60.0) $+$ (seconds/3600.0)

Note: the denominators of 60.0 and 3600.0 represent the number minutes (60.0) and seconds (3600.0) in each hour, respectively.

Thus this latitude value represented as floating point number would be:

Latitude = 39.0 + (55/60.0) + (29.1182879/3600.0)
Latitude = 39.0 + .91666667 + .00808841 = **59.9247551**

Performing the same calculation on the longitude value extracted from **GPSTag 4**:

((10, 1), (41, 1), (55324, 1253))
With a **GPSTag 3**: **"E"**
Yields a longitude value of **10.6955981201**
Giving us a latitude/longitude value of **59.924755, 10.6955981201**

Using Google Maps, I can now plot the **59.924755, 10.6955981201** yielding a point just north and west of Oslo, Norway as shown in Figure 5.5. Noting that Oslo, Norway is in fact East of the Prime Meridian in Greenwich, England.

One final note, this camera did not include other GPSTAGS such as the GPSTimestamp, which could have given us the time as reported by GPS.

p-ImageEvidenceExtractor fundamental requirements

Now that I have experimented with the PIL, discovered how to extract the EXIF TAGS, the GPS tags, and the EXIF data from a target image, I want to define our first full extraction application.

Design considerations

Now that I have defined the basic approach, Table 5.1 and Table 5.2 define the program requirements and design considerations for the p-ImageEvidenceExtractor.

Next, I want to define the overall design of the p-gpsExtractor as depicted in Figure 5.6. I will again be using the command line parser to convey selections from the user. I will be directing output to *standard out*, *a CSV file*, and the *forensic log*. The user will specify a folder containing images to process. I have also created a class to handle forensic logging operations that I can reuse or expand in the future. Finally, I will be reusing a slightly modified version of the CVSWriter class I created in Chapter 3 for the pFish application.

CODE WALK-THROUGH

In order to get a feel for the program take a look at Figure 5.7, which is a screenshot of the WingIDE project. You notice on the far right this program contains five Python source files:

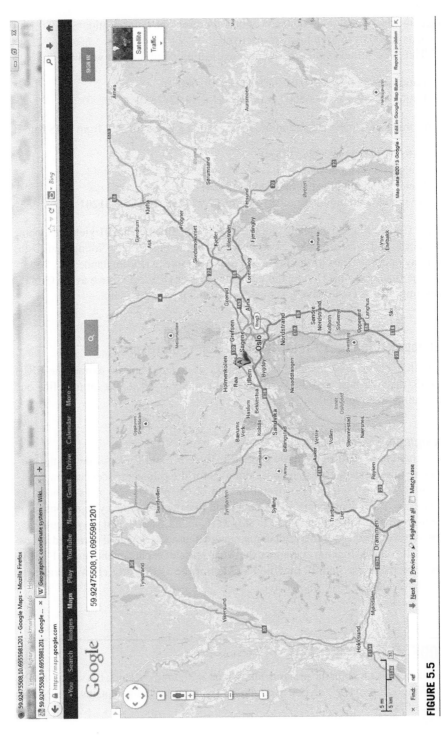

FIGURE 5.5

Map of GPS coordinates extracted From Cat.jpg.

Table 5.1 Basic Requirements for GPS/EXIF Extraction

Requirement number	Requirement name	Short description
GPS-001	Command Line Arguments	Allow the user to specify a directory that contains sample images to attempt to extract GPS information from
GPS-002	Log	The program must produce a forensic audit log
GPS-003	Output	The program should produce a list of latitude and longitude values from the GPS information found. The format must be simple lat, lon values in order to be pasted into online mapping applications
GPS-004	Error Handling	The application must support error handling and logging of all operations performed. This will include a textual description and a timestamp

Table 5.2 Design Consideration and Library Mapping

Requirement	Design considerations	Library selection
User Input (001)	User input for keyword and target file	I will be using `argparse` from the Standard Library module to obtain input from the user
Output (003)	The extracted GPS location will be printed out using simple built-in print commands	I will be using the Python Image Library and the standard Python language to extract and format the output in order to cut and paste directly into the Web page: http://www.darrinward.com/lat-long/
(Additional)	Extract additional EXIF and GPS values and record the data for each file encountered in a CSV file	Use the Python Image Library and Python CVS Library
(002 and 004) Logging and Error Handling	Errors may occur during the processing of the files and EXIF data. Therefore, handling these potential errors must be rigorous	The Python Standard Library includes a `logging` facility which I can leverage to report any events or errors that occur during processing. Note for this application I will create a reuseable logging class

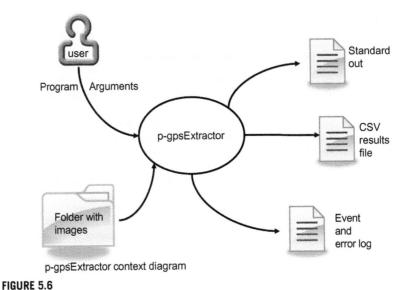

p-gpsExtractor context diagram

FIGURE 5.6

p-gpsExtractor context diagram.

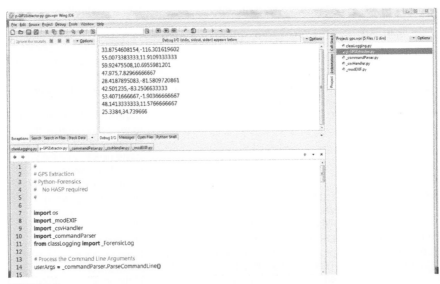

FIGURE 5.7

WingIDE Project Overview.

Main Program

p-gpsExtractor.py: This is the Main Program for this application handling the overall program flow and the processing of each potential image file contained in a folder specified by the user via the command line. Main writes data to standard out in order to make it easy to cut and paste that data into a Web page for map viewing. Main also handles output to the CSV file that provides the results for each of the files processed, as well as any forensic log entries.

Class Logging

classLogging.py: The new class logger abstracts the logging function in a Python class for handling Forensic Logging functions. This will allow for log object passing for future applications to any module or function eliminating any need for global variables.

cvsHandler

csvHandler.py: This modified class for handling CSV File Creation and Writing provides a single point interface to writing output files in CVS format, once again to abstract the functions and make interface simpler. More work will be done on this class in the future to abstract this further.

Command line parser

commandParser.py: I separated out the commandParser.py into its own file for greater portability for this application and for future applications. This allows command line parser to be handled, modified, or enhanced and is more loosely coupled from the Main Program. Like the Logging functions this will eventually be turned into a Class-based module to allow cross-module access and interface.

EXIF and GPS Handler

_modEXIF.py: This module directly interfaces with the PIL to perform the needed operations to extract both EXIF and GPS data from image files that contain EXIF data.

Examining the code
Main Program

```
# GPS Extraction
# Python-Forensics
# No HASP required
#
```

```
import os
import _modEXIF
import _csvHandler
import _commandParser
from classLogging import ForensicLog
```

*For the main program we need to import **os** to handle folder processing, the command line processor, the cvsHandler and the new ForensicLog Class.*

```
# Process the Command Line Arguments
userArgs = _commandParser.ParseCommandLine()
```

As I typically do, I process the command line arguments to obtain the user specified values. If command parsing is successful we create a new logging object to handle any necessary forensic log events and write the first log event.

```
# create a log object
logPath = userArgs.logPath+"ForensicLog.txt"
oLog = _ForensicLog(logPath)

oLog.writeLog("INFO", "Scan Started)"
```

Next I create a CSV File Object that I will use to write data to the CSV results file that will contain the files processed and the resulting GPS data extracted

```
csvPath = userArgs.csvPath+"imageResults.csv"
oCSV = _csvHandler._CSVWriter(csvPath)
```

Needing to obtain the user specified target directory for our GPS extraction, I attempt to open and then process each of the files in the target directory. If any errors occur they are captured using the try except model and appropriate errors are written to the forensic log file.

```
# define a directory to scan

scanDir = userArgs.scanPath
try:
    picts = os.listdir(scanDir)
except:
    oLog.writeLog("ERROR", "Invalid Directory "+ scanDir)
    exit(0)

for aFile in picts:

    targetFile = scanDir+aFile

    if os.path.isfile(targetFile):
```

Once the preliminaries are out of the way, I can now utilize the _modEXIF module to process each target file, with the result being a gpsDictionary object if successful. This object will contain the EXIF data that is available for this file as embedded in the EXIF record. Before using the data, I check to ensure that the gpsDictionary object contains data.

```
gpsDictionary =
                  _modEXIF.ExtractGPSDictionary(targetFile)

    if (gpsDictionary):

        # Obtain the Lat Lon values from the gpsDictionary
        # converted to degrees
        # the return value is a dictionary key value pairs

        dCoor = _modEXIF.ExtractLatLon(gpsDictionary)
```

Next, I call another _modEXIF function to process further the gpsDictionary. This function as you will see, processes the GPS coordinates, and if successful returns the raw coordinate data. Then using the Dictionary methods you learned about earlier in this chapter, I extract the latitude and longitude data from the dictionary by using the get method.

```
            lat = dCoor.get("Lat)"
            latRef = dCoor.get("LatRef)"
            lon = dCoor.get("Lon)"
            lonRef = dCoor.get("LonRef)"

        if ( lat and lon and latRef and lonRef):
```

Upon successful extraction of the latitude and longitude values I print the results to standard out, write the data to the CSV file and update the forensic log accordingly. Or if unsuccessful, I report the appropriate data to the forensic log file.

```
            print str(lat)+','+str(lon)

            # write one row to the output csv file
            oCSV.writeCSVRow(targetFile, EXIFList[TS], EXIFList
                [MAKE], EXIFList[MODEL],latRef, lat, lonRef,
                lon)

            oLog.writeLog("INFO", "GPS Data Calculated for:" +
                targetFile)
        else:
            oLog.writeLog("WARNING", "No GPS EXIF Data for"+
                targetFile)
    else:
        oLog.writeLog("WARNING", "No GPS EXIF Data for
            "+ targetFile)
else:
    oLog.writeLog("WARNING", targetFile + " not a valid file)"
```

Finally before program exit I delete the forensic log and CSV objects which in turn closes the log and the associated CSV file.

```
# Clean up and Close Log and CSV File

del oLog
del oCSV
```

EXIF and GPS processing

The core data extraction elements of the p-gpsExtractor are contained within the _modEXIF.py module.

```
#
# Data Extraction - Python-Forensics
# Extract GPS Data from EXIF supported Images (jpg, tiff)
# Support Module
#
```

I start by importing the libraries and modules needed by _modEXIF.py. Important module of note is the Python Imaging Library and associated capabilities.

```
import os # Standard Library OS functions
from classLogging import _ForensicLog # Logging Class
```

From the PIL I import the Image Library and the EXIF and GPS Tags in order to index into the dictionary structures, much like I did in the script examples 5-6 thru 5-8.

```
# import the Python Image Library
# along with TAGS and GPS related TAGS

from PIL import Image
from PIL.EXIFTags import TAGS, GPSTAGS
```

Now let's take a look and breakdown the individual functions. I will start with the extraction of the GPS Dictionary. The function take the full path name of the target file that the extraction is to occur with.

```
#
# Extract EXIF Data
#
# Input: Full Pathname of the target image
#
# Return: gpsDictionary and extracted EXIFData list
#
def ExtractGPSDictionary(fileName):
```

Using the familiar try / except module I attempt to open the filename provided and if successful I then extract the EXIF data by using the PIL getEXIF() function.

```
    try:
        pilImage = Image.open(fileName)
        EXIFData = pilImage._getEXIF()

    except Exception:
        # If exception occurs from PIL processing
        # Report the
        return None, None

    # Iterate through the EXIFData
    # Searching for GPS Tags
```

Next, I'm going to iterate through the **EXIFData** *TAGS and collect some basic EXIF data and then obtain the GPSTags if they are included within the EXIF data of the specific image.*

```
imageTimeStamp = "NA"
CameraModel = "NA"
CameraMake = "NA"

if EXIFData:

    for tag, theValue in EXIFData.items():

        # obtain the tag
        tagValue = TAGS.get(tag, tag)

        # Collect basic image data if available
```

As I iterate through the tags that are present within this image, I check for the presence of the DataTimeOriginal along with the camera make and model in order to include them in the result file.

```
        if tagValue == 'DateTimeOriginal':
            imageTimeStamp = EXIFData.get(tag)

        if tagValue == "Make":
            cameraMake = EXIFData.get(tag)

        if tagValue == 'Model':
            cameraModel = EXIFData.get(tag)
```

I also check for the GPSInfo TAG, and if present I iterate through GPSInfo and extract the GPS Dictionary using the `GPSTAGS.get()` *functions.*

```
        # check the tag for GPS
        if tagValue == "GPSInfo":

            # Found it !
            # Now create a Dictionary to hold the GPS Data

            gpsDictionary = {}

            # Loop through the GPS Information

            for curTag in theValue:
                gpsTag = GPSTAGS.get(curTag, curTag)
                gpsDictionary[gpsTag] = theValue[curTag]
```

Next, I create a simple Python List to hold the EXIF Timestamp and Camera Make and Model. Then we return gpsDictionary and the basicEXIFData that was collected.

```
        basicEXIFData = [imageTimeStamp, cameraMake,
                         cameraModel]

        return gpsDictionary, basicEXIFData
    else:
```

*If the target file doesn't contain any EXIF data I return **None** in order to prevent any further processing of this file. Note **None** is a built in Python constant that is used to represent empty or missing data.*

```
     return None, None
# End ExtractGPSDictionary ==============================
```

The next support function is ExtractLatLon. As I covered in the narrative of this chapter, I need to convert the EXIF GPS data into floating point values in order to use them with online mapping applications.

```
#
# Extract the Latitude and Longitude Values
# from the gpsDictionary
#
```

The ExtractLatLon function takes as input a gps Dictionary structure.

```
def ExtractLatLon(gps):

    # to perform the calculation we need at least
    # lat, lon, latRef and lonRef
```

Before I attempt the conversion, I need to validate the gps Dictionary contains the proper key value pairs. This includes the latitude, longitude, latitude reference and longitude reference.

```
    if (gps.has_key("GPSLatitude)" and
        gps.has_key("GPSLongitude)"
        and gps.has_key("GPSLatitudeRef)"
        and gps.has_key("GPSLatitudeRef)"):
```

Once we have the minimum inputs I extract the individual values.

```
        latitude     = gps["GPSLatitude"]
        latitudeRef  = gps["GPSLatitudeRef"]
        longitude    = gps["GPSLongitude"]
        longitudeRef = gps["GPSLongitudeRef"]
```

I then call the conversion function for both latitude and longitude values.

```
        lat = ConvertToDegrees(latitude)
        lon = ConvertToDegrees(longitude)
```

Next I need to account for the latitude and longitude reference values and set the proper negative values if necessary.

```
        # Check Latitude Reference
        # If South of the Equator then lat value is negative

        if latitudeRef == "S":
            lat = 0 - lat

        # Check Longitude Reference
```

```
# If West of the Prime Meridian in
# Greenwich then the Longitude value is negative

if longitudeRef == "W":
    lon = 0 - lon
```

Once this has been accounted for, I create a new dictionary to hold the final values and return that to the caller. In this case the main program.

```
gpsCoor = {"Lat": lat, "LatRef":latitudeRef,
            "Lon": lon, "LonRef": longitudeRef}


    return gpsCoor
else:
```

Once again, if the minimum values are not present, I return the built in Python constant None to indicate and empty return.

```
    return None
```

The final support function is the ConvertToDegrees function that converts the GPS data into a floating point value. This code is very straightforward and follows the formula presented in the narrative of this chapter. The only important aspect to point out is the try/except model used whenever dividing two numbers, as a divide by zero would cause a failure to occur and the program to abort. As with any data coming from the wild, anything is possible and we need to account for possible zero division. I have seen this with EXIF data, when the value for seconds is zero the ratio is reported as 0:0. Since this is a legal value, I simply set the degrees, minutes, or seconds to zero when the exception occurs.

```
#
# Convert GPSCoordinates to Degrees
#
# Input gpsCoordinates value from in EXIF Format
#

def ConvertToDegrees(gpsCoordinate):
    d0 = gpsCoordinate[0][0]
    d1 = gpsCoordinate[0][1]

    try:
        degrees = float(d0) / float(d1)
    except:
        degrees = 0.0

    m0 = gpsCoordinate[1][0]
    m1 = gpsCoordinate[1][1]
    try:
        minutes = float(m0) / float(m1)
    except:
        minutes=0.0
```

```
s0 = gpsCoordinate[2][0]
s1 = gpsCoordinate[2][1]
try:
    seconds = float(s0) / float(s1)
except:
    seconds = 0.0

floatCoordinate = float (degrees + (minutes / 60.0) +
                     (seconds / 3600.0))
return floatCoordinate
```

Logging Class

For this application I have include a new class *logging* that abstracts and simplifies the handling of forensic logging events across modules.

```
import logging
#
# Class: _ForensicLog
#
# Desc: Handles Forensic Logging Operations
#
# Methods
#    constructor:      Initializes the Logger
#    writeLog:         Writes a record to the log
#    destructor:       Writes an information message
#                          and shuts down the logger

class _ForensicLog:
```

init is the constructor method that is called whenever a new ForensicLog object is created. The method initializes a new Python logging object using the Python Standard Library. The filename of the log is passed in as part of the object instantiation. If an exception is encountered a message is sent to standard output and the program is aborted.

```
def __init__(self, logName):
    try:
        # Turn on Logging
        logging.basicConfig(filename=logName,
            level=logging.DEBUG,format='%(asctime) s %(message)s')
    except:
        print "Forensic Log Initialization
                Failure ... Aborting"
        exit(0)
```

The next method is writeLog which takes two parameters (along with self), the first is the type or level of the log event (INFO, ERROR or WARNING) and then a string representing the message that will be written to the log.

```
def writeLog(self, logType, logMessage):
    if logType == "INFO":
        logging.info(logMessage)
    elif logType == "ERROR":
        logging.error(logMessage)
    elif logType == "WARNING":
        logging.warning(logMessage)
    else:
        logging.error(logMessage)
    return
```

Finally the del method is used to shutdown logging and to close the log file. The message Logging Shutdown is sent to the log as an information message just prior to shutdown of the log.

```
def __del__(self):
    logging.info("Logging Shutdown)"
    logging.shutdown()
```

Command line parser

Command line parser handles the user input, provides validation for the arguments passed, and reports error along with help text to assist the user.

```
import argparse      # Python Standard Library - Parser for
command-line options, arguments
import os            # Standard Library OS functions
# Name: ParseCommand() Function
#
# Desc: Process and Validate the command line arguments
#           use Python Standard Library module argparse
#
# Input: none
#
# Actions:
#               Uses the standard library argparse
#               to process the command line
#

def ParseCommandLine():
```

gpsExtractor requires three inputs 1) the directory path for the forensic log, 2) the directory path to be scanned and 3) the directory path for the CSV result file. All these directory paths must exist and be writable in order for parsing to succeed.

```
parser = argparse.ArgumentParser('Python gpsExtractor)
parser.add_argument('-v', '--verbose', help="enables
                    printing of additional program
                    messages", action='store_true')
```

```
parser.add_argument('-l', '--logPath',
                     type= ValidateDirectory, required=True,
                     help="specify the directory
                     for forensic log output file")

parser.add_argument('-c', '--csvPath',
                     type= ValidateDirectory, required=True,
                     help="specify the output directory for
                     the csv file)"

parser.add_argument('-d', '-scanPath',
                     type=ValidateDirectory, required=True,
                     help="specify the directory to scan)"

theArgs = parser.parse_args()

return theArgs

# End Parse Command Line ===============================
```

The ValidateDirectory function verifies that value passed is a bona fide directory and the path is in fact writable. I use the os.path.isdir() method to verify the existence and the os.access() method to verify the writing.

```
def ValidateDirectory(theDir):

    # Validate the path is a directory
    if not os.path.isdir(theDir):
        raise argparse.ArgumentTypeError('Directory does not exist')

    # Validate the path is writable
    if os.access(theDir, os.W_OK):
        return theDir
    else:
        raise argparse.ArgumentTypeError
            ('Directory is not writable')

#End ValidateDirectory ===================================
```

Comma separated value (CSV) Writer class

The _CSVWriter class provides object-based abstraction for writing headings and data to a standard CSV file.

```
import csv #Python Standard Library - for csv files

#
# Class: _CSVWriter
#
# Desc: Handles all methods related to
#       comma separated value operations
#
# Methods
```

```
#    constructor:      Initializes the CSV File
#    writeCVSRow:      Writes a single row to the csv file
#    writerClose:      Closes the CSV File

class _CSVWriter:
```

The constructor opens the filename provided as a csvFile and then writes the header to the csv File.

```
def __init__(self, fileName):
    try:
        # create a writer object and then write the header row

        self.csvFile = open(fileName, 'wb')

        self.writer = csv.writer(self.csvFile,
                        delimiter=',',
                        quoting=csv.QUOTE_ALL)

        self.writer.writerow( ('Image Path', 'TimeStamp',
                            'Camera Make',
                            'Camera Model',
                            'Lat Ref', 'Latitude',
                            'Lon Ref','Longitude' ) )
    except:
        log.error('CSV File Failure')
```

The actual writeCSVRow method takes as input the individual columns defined and writes them to the file. In addition, the function converts the floating point latitude and longitude values to properly formatted strings.

```
def writeCSVRow(self, fileName, timeStamp, CameraMake,
                    CameraModel,latRef, latValue, lonRef,
                    lonValue):

    latStr = '%.8f' % latValue
    lonStr = '%.8f' % lonValue

    self.writer.writerow( (fileName, timeStamp, CameraMake,
                        CameraModel, latRef, latStr,
                        lonRef, lonStr))
```

Finally the del method closes the csvFile for proper deconstruction of the object.

```
def __del__(self):
    self.csvFile.close()
```

Full code listings

```
#
# GPS Extraction
# Python-Forensics
#     No HASP required
```

```
#

import os
import _modEXIF
import _csvHandler
import _commandParser
from classLogging import _ForensicLog

# Offsets into the return EXIFData for
# TimeStamp, Camera Make and Model

TS = 0
MAKE = 1
MODEL = 2

# Process the Command Line Arguments
userArgs = _commandParser.ParseCommandLine()

# create a log object
logPath = userArgs.logPath+"ForensicLog.txt"
oLog = _ForensicLog(logPath)

oLog.writeLog("INFO", "Scan Started")

csvPath = userArgs.csvPath+"imageResults.csv"
oCSV = _csvHandler._CSVWriter(csvPath)

# define a directory to scan
scanDir = userArgs.scanPath
try:
    picts = os.listdir(scanDir)
except:
    oLog.writeLog("ERROR", "Invalid Directory "+ scanDir)
    exit(0)

print "Program Start"
print

for aFile in picts:

    targetFile = scanDir+aFile

    if os.path.isfile(targetFile):

        gpsDictionary, EXIFList = _modEXIF.ExtractGPSDictionary
        (targetFile)

        if (gpsDictionary):

            # Obtain the Lat Lon values from the gpsDictionary
            # Converted to degrees
            # The return value is a dictionary key value pairs

            dCoor = _modEXIF.ExtractLatLon(gpsDictionary)

            lat = dCoor.get("Lat")
```

```
            latRef = dCoor.get("LatRef")
            lon = dCoor.get("Lon")
            lonRef = dCoor.get("LonRef")

            if ( lat and lon and latRef and lonRef):
                print str(lat)+','+str(lon)

                # write one row to the output file
                oCSV.writeCSVRow(targetFile, EXIFList[TS], EXIFList
                [MAKE], EXIFList[MODEL],latRef, lat, lonRef, lon)
                oLog.writeLog("INFO", "GPS Data Calculated for :" +
                targetFile)
            else:
                oLog.writeLog("WARNING", "No GPS EXIF Data for "+
                targetFile)
        else:
            oLog.writeLog("WARNING", "No GPS EXIF Data for "+
            targetFile)
    else:
        oLog.writeLog("WARNING", targetFile + " not a valid file")

# Clean up and Close Log and CSV File
del oLog
del oCSV
import argparse                    # Python Standard Library - Parser
for command-line options, arguments
import os                         # Standard Library OS functions

# Name: ParseCommand() Function
#
# Desc: Process and Validate the command line arguments
#          use Python Standard Library module argparse
#
# Input: none
#
# Actions:
#             Uses the standard library argparse to process the command
line
#
def ParseCommandLine():

    parser = argparse.ArgumentParser('Python gpsExtractor')

    parser.add_argument('-v', '--verbose',    help="enables printing of
    additional program messages", action='store_true')
    parser.add_argument('-l', '--logPath',     type= ValidateDirectory,
    required=True, help="specify the directory for forensic log output
    file")
    parser.add_argument('-c', '--csvPath',     type= ValidateDirectory,
    required=True, help="specify the output directory for the csv
    file")
```

```python
        parser.add_argument('-d', '--scanPath',    type= ValidateDirectory,
        required=True, help="specify the directory to scan")

        theArgs = parser.parse_args()

        return theArgs

# End Parse Command Line ==============================

def ValidateDirectory(theDir):

    # Validate the path is a directory
    if not os.path.isdir(theDir):
        raise argparse.ArgumentTypeError('Directory does not exist')

    # Validate the path is writable
    if os.access(theDir, os.W_OK):
        return theDir
    else:
        raise argparse.ArgumentTypeError('Directory is not writable')

#End ValidateDirectory ====================================

import logging
#
# Class: _ForensicLog
#
# Desc: Handles Forensic Logging Operations
#
# Methods constructor:        Initializes the Logger
#                writeLog:            Writes a record to the log
#                destructor:          Writes an information message and
                                      shuts down the logger

class _ForensicLog:

    def __init__(self, logName):
        try:
            # Turn on Logging

logging.basicConfig(filename=logName,level=logging.DEBUG,
format='%(asctime)s %(message)s')
        except:
            print "Forensic Log Initialization Failure... Aborting"
            exit(0)

    def writeLog(self, logType, logMessage):
        if logType == "INFO":
            logging.info(logMessage)
        elif logType == "ERROR":
            logging.error(logMessage)
        elif logType == "WARNING":
            logging.warning(logMessage)
        else:
```

```python
            logging.error(logMessage)
        return

    def __del__(self):
        logging.info("Logging Shutdown")
        logging.shutdown()
#
# Data Extraction - Python-Forensics
# Extract GPS Data from EXIF supported Images (jpg, tiff)
# Support Module
#
import os                            # Standard Library OS functions
from classLogging import _ForensicLog    # Abstracted Forensic Logging
                                         # Class

# import the Python Image Library
# along with TAGS and GPS related TAGS

from PIL import Image
from PIL.EXIFTags import TAGS, GPSTAGS

#
# Extract EXIF Data
#
# Input: Full Pathname of the target image
#
# Return: gps Dictionary and selected EXIFData list
#

def ExtractGPSDictionary(fileName):

    try:
        pilImage = Image.open(fileName)
        EXIFData = pilImage._getEXIF()

    except Exception:
        # If exception occurs from PIL processing
        # Report the
        return None, None

    # Iterate through the EXIFData
    # Searching for GPS Tags

    imageTimeStamp = "NA"
    CameraModel = "NA"
    CameraMake = "NA"

    if EXIFData:

        for tag, theValue in EXIFData.items():

            # obtain the tag
            tagValue = TAGS.get(tag, tag)
```

```
        # Collect basic image data if available

        if tagValue == 'DateTimeOriginal':
            imageTimeStamp = EXIFData.get(tag)

        if tagValue == "Make":
            cameraMake = EXIFData.get(tag)

        if tagValue == 'Model':
            cameraModel = EXIFData.get(tag)

        # check the tag for GPS
        if tagValue == "GPSInfo":

            # Found it !
            # Now create a Dictionary to hold the GPS Data

            gpsDictionary = {}

            # Loop through the GPS Information
            for curTag in theValue:
                gpsTag = GPSTAGS.get(curTag, curTag)
                gpsDictionary[gpsTag] = theValue[curTag]

            basicEXIFData = [imageTimeStamp, cameraMake,
                            cameraModel]
            return gpsDictionary, basicEXIFData

    else:
        return None, None

# End ExtractGPSDictionary ==============================

#
# Extract the Latitude and Longitude Values
# From the gpsDictionary
#

def ExtractLatLon(gps):

    # to perform the calculation we need at least
    # lat, lon, latRef and lonRef

    if (gps.has_key("GPSLatitude") and gps.has_key("GPSLongitude")
    and gps.has_key("GPSLatitudeRef") and gps.has_key
    ("GPSLatitudeRef")):

        latitude     = gps["GPSLatitude"]
        latitudeRef  = gps["GPSLatitudeRef"]
        longitude    = gps["GPSLongitude"]
        longitudeRef = gps["GPSLongitudeRef"]

        lat = ConvertToDegrees(latitude)
        lon = ConvertToDegrees(longitude)
        # Check Latitude Reference
```

```
        # If South of the Equator then lat value is negative

        if latitudeRef == "S":
            lat = 0 - lat

        # Check Longitude Reference
        # If West of the Prime Meridian in
        # Greenwich then the Longitude value is negative

        if longitudeRef == "W":
            lon = 0- lon

        gpsCoor = {"Lat": lat, "LatRef":latitudeRef, "Lon": lon,
        "LonRef": longitudeRef}

        return gpsCoor

    else:
        return None

# End Extract Lat Lon ===================================
#
# Convert GPSCoordinates to Degrees
#
# Input gpsCoordinates value from in EXIF Format
#
def ConvertToDegrees(gpsCoordinate):
    d0 = gpsCoordinate[0][0]
    d1 = gpsCoordinate[0][1]
    try:
        degrees = float(d0) / float(d1)
    except:
        degrees = 0.0

    m0 = gpsCoordinate[1][0]
    m1 = gpsCoordinate[1][1]
    try:
        minutes = float(m0) / float(m1)
    except:
        minutes=0.0

    s0 = gpsCoordinate[2][0]
    s1 = gpsCoordinate[2][1]
    try:
        seconds = float(s0) / float(s1)
    except:
        seconds = 0.0

    floatCoordinate = float (degrees + (minutes / 60.0) + (seconds /
    3600.0))
    return floatCoordinate
```

```
import csv      #Python Standard Library - reader and writer for csv files
#
# Class: _CSVWriter
#
# Desc: Handles all methods related to comma separated value operations
#
# Methods constructor: Initializes the CSV File
#               writeCVSRow:   Writes a single row to the csv file
#               writerClose:      Closes the CSV File

class _CSVWriter:

    def __init__(self, fileName):
        try:
            # create a writer object and then write the header row
            self.csvFile = open(fileName, 'wb')
            self.writer = csv.writer(self.csvFile, delimiter=',',
            quoting=csv.QUOTE_ALL)
            self.writer.writerow( ('Image Path', 'Make', 'Model', 'UTC Time',
'Lat Ref', 'Latitude', 'Lon Ref','Longitude', 'Alt Ref', 'Altitude') )
        except:
            log.error('CSV File Failure')

    def writeCSVRow(self, fileName, cameraMake, cameraModel, utc,
        latRef, latValue, lonRef, lonValue, altRef, altValue):
        latStr = '%.8f' % latValue
        lonStr= '%.8f' % lonValue
        altStr = '%.8f' % altValue
        self.writer.writerow(fileName, cameraMake, cameraModel, utc,
        latRef, latStr, lonRef, lonStr, altRef, AltStr)

    def __del__(self):
        self.csvFile.close()
```

Program execution

The p-gpsExtractor produces three separate results: (1) The standard output rendering of the latitude and longitude values extracted from the target files. (2) The CSV file that contains the details of each EXIF and GPS extraction. (3) The forensic log file that contains the log of program execution. Execution of the program is accomplished by using the following command and line options.

```
C:\pictures\Program>Python p-GPSExtractor.py -d c:\pictures\ -c
   c:\pictures\Results\ -l c:\pictures\Log\
```

Figure 5.8 depicts the results of program execution. I have selected the output results and copied them into the paste buffer in order to plot all the points within an online mapping program.

Figure 5.8 contains a screenshot of a Windows execution of p-gpsExtractor.

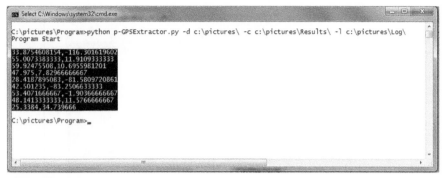

FIGURE 5.8

p-gpsExtractor.py execution.

In Figure 5.9, I paste the selected coordinates from the program execution into the online Web site, http://www.darrinward.com/lat-long/ [Ward] and submit the values. The page plots each of the points on the map as a push pin. Figures 5.10 and 5.11 illustrate the zoom into the locations in Germany.

In addition to the mapped data, I also generated a .csv result file for the scan. Figure 5.12 shows the resulting .csv file.

Finally, I also create a Forensic Log file associated with program execution. This file contains the forensic log results shown in Figure 5.13.

CHAPTER REVIEW

In this chapter, I put to use new Python language elements including the dictionary in order to handle more complex data types and to interface with the PIL. I also utilized the PIL to systematically extract EXIF data from photographs including GPS data when available with photographs. I demonstrated not only how to extract the GPS raw data but also how to calculate the lon and lat positions and then later integrated the output of the program into an online mapping program to plot the locations of the photographs. In addition, I demonstrated how to extract data from the EXIF data structure and included some of those values in a resulting .csv file that contains information about the file, camera, timestamp, and location information.

SUMMARY QUESTIONS

1. Based on the experimentation with the Python built-in data type dictionary, what limitations for key and value do you see?
2. Choose five additional fields from the EXIF structure, develop the additional code to extract them, locate several photographs that contain this additional data, and add them to the .csv output.

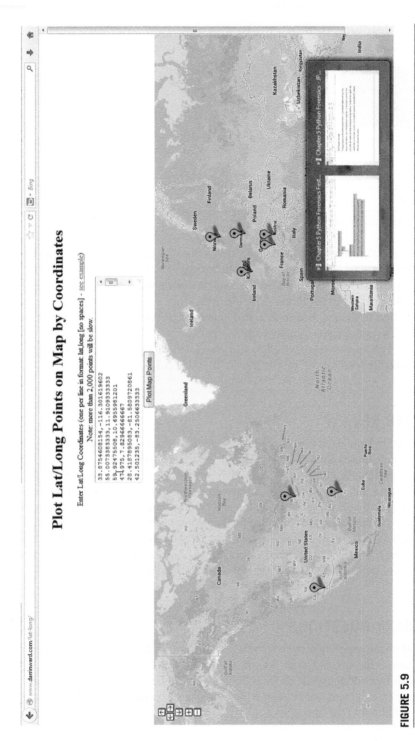

FIGURE 5.9

Mapping the coordinates extracted from photos.

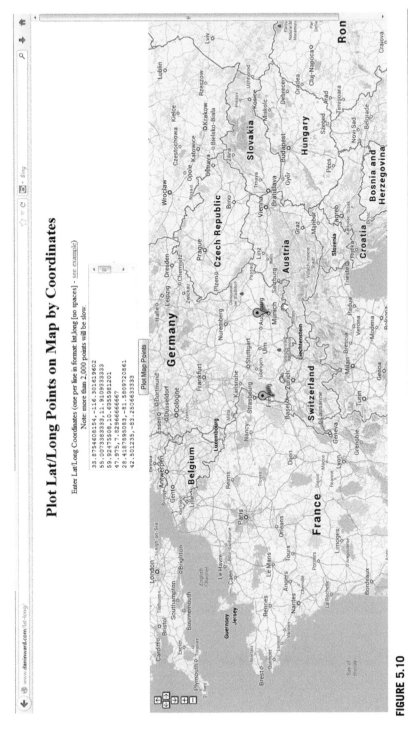

FIGURE 5.10

Map zoom into Western Europe.

FIGURE 5.11

Map zoom to street level in Germany.

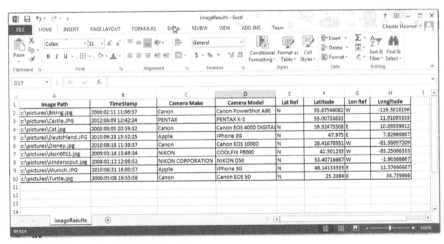

FIGURE 5.12

Snapshot of Results.csv file.

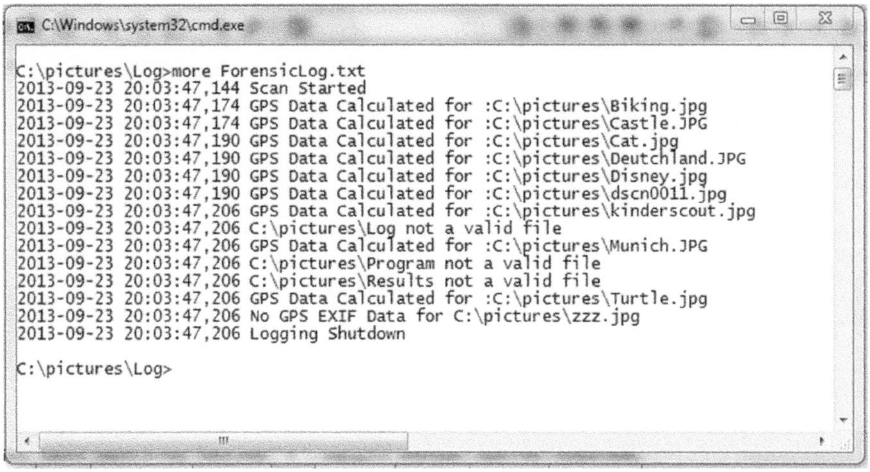

FIGURE 5.13

Snapshot of the Forensic Log file.

3. Locate other online mapping resources (for example, ones that would allow you to tag the photo, for example, with a filename) and then use the mapping function to render the additional data.
4. Using the PIL, develop a program that will maliciously modify the latitude, longitude, and/or timestamp values of an existing photograph.
5. Expand the extraction method to include altitude and then find a mapping program that would allow you to map latitude, longitude, and altitude. Then locate photos with varying altitudes, for example, photos taken from hot air balloons.

Additional Resources

FCC 911 Wireless Service Guide. http://www.fcc.gov/guides/wireless-911-services.
Python Imaging Library. https://pypi.python.org/pypi/PIL.
The Python Standard Library. http://docs.python.org/2/library/.
Web Based multiple coordinate mapping website. http://www.darrinward.com/lat-long/.

Forensic Time

CHAPTER CONTENTS

INTRODUCTION

Before we can even consider time from an evidentiary point of view, we need to better understand what time is. I will start with an excerpt from one of my favorite books "Longitude" by Dava Sobel:

> *"Anyone alive in the eighteenth century would have known that the **longitude problem** was the thorniest scientific dilemma of the day and had been for centuries. Lacking the ability to measure their longitude, sailors throughout the great ages of the exploration had been literally lost at sea as soon as they lost sight of land.*
>
> *The quest for a solution had occupied scientists and their patrons for the better part of two centuries when, in 1714, England's Parliament upped the ante by offering a king's ransom (£20,000, approximately $12 million in today's currency) to anyone whose method or device proved successful. The scientific establishment throughout Europe from Galileo to Sir Isaac Newton had mapped the heavens in the both hemispheres in its certain pursuit of a celestial answer. In stark contrast, one man, John Harrison, dared to imagine a mechanical solution – a clock that would keep precise time at sea, something no clock had every been able to do on land. Mr. Harrison's invention resulted in a solution to the greatest scientific problem of this time." [Sobel, 1995]*

The basis of Harrison's clock and solution still guide navigation today as the use of time within GPS and other navigation systems remains the key underlying

FIGURE 6.1

John Harrison H1 clock

component that allows us to calculate where we are. Figure 6.1 depicts the first Harrison sea clock H1.

Mr. Harrison's lifetime work was the impetus for the formation of Greenwich Mean Time or GMT. In today's high-speed global economy and communication infrastructure, precise, accurate, reliable, nonforgeable, and nonreputable time is almost as elusive as it was in the eighteenth century. Of course, atomic, rubidium, and cesium clocks are guaranteed to deliver accurate time—and without missing a beat—for over a 1000 years. But, delivering that accuracy to digital evidence is elusive. My favorite saying is, "*anyone* can tell you what time it is, *proving* what time it *was* is the still the challenge" [Hosmer 2002].

Time is a concept that allows society to function in an orderly fashion where all parties are able to easily understand the representation of time and agree on a sequence of events. Since 1972, the international standard for time is Coordinated Universal Time or UTC. UTC forms the basis for the official time source in most nations around the globe; it is governed by a diplomatic treaty adopted by the world community that designates National Measurement (or Metrology) Institutes (NMIs) as UTC time sources. The National Institute of Standards and Technology (NIST) in the United States, the Communications Research Laboratory (CRL) in Japan, and the National Physical Laboratory (NPL) in the United Kingdom are examples of NMIs. There are about 50 similar metrology centers that are responsible for official time throughout the world.

Time has been a critical element in business for hundreds of years. The time—via a mechanical record—established and provided evidence as to the "when" of business transactions and events. (Usually recorded on paper, these time records provided an evidentiary trail due to a number of unique attributes—the distinctiveness of the ink embedded in the paper, the style and method of type, whether mechanical or hand written, the paper and its characteristics, and the detectability of modifications, insertions, or deletions). In the electronic world where documents and timestamps are simply bits and bytes, authoritative proof of the time of an event has been hard to nail down. Since the security of time is absolutely linked to its origination from an official source, the reliance on easily manipulated time sources (e.g., typical computer system clocks) is problematic.

Precision and reliability have long been the major factors driving the design of electronic timing technology. The next technology wave adds the dimensions of authenticity, security, and auditability to digital timestamps. These three attributes, when applied to documents, transactions, or any other digital entity, provide the following advantages over traditional computer clock-based timestamps:

Assurance that the time came from an official source
Assurance that time has not been manipulated
An evidentiary trail for auditing and nonrepudiation

Authentication (knowledge of the originator's identity) and integrity (protection against content modification) are essential elements in trusted transactions. But if one cannot trust the time, can the transaction really be trusted? Secure timestamps add the missing link in the trusted transaction equation: "when" did it happen? However, for the timestamp to provide a reliable answer to that question, the time upon which it is based must be derived from a trusted source.

ADDING TIME TO THE EQUATION

Using the best practices afforded to us, today digital signatures are able to successfully bind "who" (the signer) with the "what" (the digital data). However, digital signatures have shortcomings that leave two critical questions unanswered:

1. When did the signing of the digital evidence occur?
2. How long can we prove the integrity of the digital evidence that we signed?

For both of these questions, time becomes a critical factor in proving the integrity of digital evidence. Through the work of the Internet Engineering Task Force (IETF) and private companies, timestamping has advanced to a realistic deployment stage.

To understand this, we must first understand a little about time itself and what is necessary if we choose to utilize time as a digital evidence trust mechanism. From ancient societies to the present day, time has been interpreted in many ways. Time is essentially an agreement that allows society to function in an orderly fashion—where all parties are easily able to understand the representation. Some examples of time measurement are included in Figure 6.2.

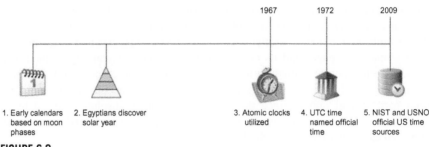

FIGURE 6.2

A very brief history of time.

As shown in Figure 6.2, the first calendars known to man were based upon the moon because everyone could easily agree on this as a universal measure of time. Moving forward, the Egyptians were the first to understand the solar year and they were able to develop a calendar based on the rotation of the earth around the sun. In 1967, an international agreement defined the unit of time as the second, measured by the decay of Cesium using precision instruments known as atomic clocks. And in 1972, the Treaty of the Meter (also known as the Convention of the Metre, established in 1875) was expanded to include the current time reference known as UTC, which replaced GMT as the world's official time.

Today, more than 50 national laboratories operate over 300 atomic clocks in order to provide a consistent and accurate UTC. Thus, in order to create a trusted source of time, you must first reference an official time source. In the United States, we have two official sources of time; the National Institute of Standards and Technology (NIST) in Boulder, CO for commercial time and the United States Naval Observatory (USNO) for military time.

Despite the broad accessibility of accurate time (watches, computer clocks, time servers, etc.), the incorporation of trusted time within a system requires a *secure, auditable digital date/timestamp.* Unless you have direct connection to the NMIs, most trusted sources today utilize GPS as a source of time. When used properly to tune Rubidium timeservers, the accuracy provided by GPS signals provides the exactness and precision that are required for most transactions and record keeping. This is true if and only if these requirements, standards, and processes are followed:

> *Accuracy*: The time presented is from an authoritative source and is accurate to the precision required by the transaction, whether day, hour, or millisecond.
> *Authentication:* The source of time is authenticated to a trusted source of time, such as an NMI timing lab, GPS signal, or the NIST long-wave standard time signal (WWVB in the United States).
> *Integrity:* The time should be secure and not be subject to corruption during normal "handling." If it is corrupted, either inadvertently or deliberately, the corruption should be apparent to a third party.

Nonrepudiation: An event or document should be bound to its time so that the association between event or document and the time cannot be later denied. *Accountability:* The process of acquiring time, adding authentication and integrity, and binding it to the subject event should be accountable so that a third party can determine that due process was applied, and that no corruption transpired.

Most people reading this book will quickly recognize that from a practical perspective the timestamps that we collect during digital investigations rarely meet the standards set forth above. However, the knowledge of the standards we are striving for is vital. This should cause you to question everything—especially anything that is related to time. To get started, let us take a deep dive into the Python Standard Library examining the *time, datetime*, and *calendar* modules.

THE *TIME* MODULE

The *time* module has many attributes and methods that assist in processing time-related information. To get started, I will use the proven technique of "test before code" to experiment with the *time* module.

The first issue we encounter is the definition of "the epoch." An epoch is defined as a notable event that marks the beginning of a period in time. Modern digital computers reference specific points in history, for example, most Unix-based systems select midnight on January 1, 1970, whereas Windows uses January 1, 1601; and Macintosh systems typically reference January 1, 1904.

The original Unix Epoch was actually defined on January 1, 1971 and was later revised to January 1, 1970. This epoch allows for a 32-bit unsigned integer to represent approximately 136 years, if each increment since the epoch is equivalent to 1 second. Thus by specifying a 32-bit unsigned integer as the number of seconds since January 1, 1970, you can mark any moment in time until February 7, 2106. If you are limited to signed 32-bit numbers, the maximum date is January 19, 2038.

As stated *most* system epochs start on January 1, 1970. The question is, how would you know? The simple answer is to ask the Python *time* module to tell us using the *gmtime()* method, *gmtime* converts the number of seconds (provided as a parameter to the *gmtime()* method) into the equivalent GMT. To illustrate, let us pass 0 (zero) as the parameter and see what epoch date the method returns.

```
>>> import time
>>> print time.gmtime(0)
time.struct_time(tm_year=1970, tm_mon=1, tm_mday=1, tm_hour=0,
tm_min=0, tm_sec=0, tm_wday=3, tm_yday=1, tm_isdst=0)
```

Similarly, if I wish to know the maximum time value (based upon a maximum limit of an unsigned 32-bit number), I would execute the following code.

```
>>> import time
>>> time.gmtime(0xffffffff)
time.struct_time(tm_year=2106, tm_mon=2, tm_mday=7, tm_hour=6,
tm_min=28, tm_sec=15, tm_wday=6, tm_yday=38, tm_isdst=0)
```

Additionally, you might be wondering, how many seconds have passed since the epoch right now? To determine this, I use the *time()* method provided by the *time* module. This method calculates the number of seconds since the epoch.

```
>>> time.time()
1381601236.189
```

As you can see, when executing this command under the Windows version of the time() method, the time() method returns a floating point number not a simple integer, providing subsecond precision.

```
>>> secondsSinceEpoch=time.time()
>>> secondsSinceEpoch
1381601264.237
```

I can then use this time (converted to an integer first) as input to the gmtime() method to determine the date and time in Greenwich.

```
>>> time.gmtime(int(secondsSinceEpoch))
time.struct_time(tm_year=2013, tm_mon=10, tm_mday=12, tm_hour=18,
tm_min=7, tm_sec=44, tm_wday=5, tm_yday=285, tm_isdst=0)
```

The result is October 12, 2013 at 18 hours, 7 minutes, 44 seconds; the weekday is 5 (assuming that the week begins with 0=Monday, this value would indicate Saturday); this is the 285th day of 2013; and we are not currently observing daylight savings time. It should be further noted for complete clarity that this time represents UTC/GMT time *not* local time. Also, it is important to note that the *time* module is using the computer's system time and timezone settings to calculate the number of seconds since the epoch, not some magical time god. Therefore, if I wish to change what the *now* is I could do that by simply changing my system clock and then I rerun the previous script.

```
>>> secondsSinceEpoch=time.time()
>>> secondsSinceEpoch
1381580629.793
>>> time.gmtime(int(secondsSinceEpoch))
time.struct_time(tm_year=2013, tm_mon=10, tm_mday=12, tm_hour=12,
tm_min=23, tm_sec=49, tm_wday=5, tm_yday=285, tm_isdst=0)
```

This results in our first successful forgery of time.

Now, if I compare GMT/UTC with local time I utilize both the *gmtime()* and *localtime()* methods.

```
>>> import time
>>> now = time.time()
>>> now
1381670992.539
>>> time.gmtime(int(now))
time.struct_time(tm_year=2013, tm_mon=10, tm_mday=13, tm_hour=13,
tm_min=29, tm_sec=52, tm_wday=6, tm_yday=286, tm_isdst=0)
>>> time.localtime(int(now))
time.struct_time(tm_year=2013, tm_mon=10, tm_mday=13, tm_hour=9,
tm_min=29, tm_sec=52, tm_wday=6, tm_yday=286, tm_isdst=1)
```

As you can see this yields:

Local Time: Sunday October 13, 2013 **09:29:52**
GMT Time: Sunday October 13, 2013 **13:29:52**

Both the localtime() and gmtime() take into consideration many factors to determine the date and time, one important consideration is the timezone that my system is currently configured to:

I can use Python to provide me with the current timezone setting of my system, by using the following script. Note *time.timezone* is an attribute rather than a method so it can be read directly.

```
>>> import time
>>> time.timezone
18000
```

Ok, what does 18,000 mean? We tend to think of timezones being a specific area or zone, which they are. We also tend to think each timezone is exactly 1 hour apart. This is not always true.

For example, some locations around the globe utilize 30-minute offsets from UTC/GMT.

Afghanistan
Australia (both Northern and Southern Territories)
India
Iran
Burma
Sri Lanka

Other locations use 15-minute offsets values related to UTC/GMT. Examples include:

Nepal
Chatham Island in New Zealand
Parts of Western Australia

The 18,000 represents the number of seconds west of UTC and points that are east of UTC are recorded in negative seconds. Since 18,000 represents the number of seconds west of UTC, I can easily calculate the number of hours west of UTC by dividing 18,000 seconds by 60 (seconds in a minute) and then again by 60 (minutes in an hour):

$$18,000/60/60 = 5\,hours$$

This means that my local time is 5 hours west of UTC/GMT. Going back to our comparison then, there should be 5 hours difference between localtime and GMT correct?

Local Time: Sunday October 13, 2013 **09:29:52**
GMT Time: Sunday October 13, 2013 **13:29:52**

Not quite! The difference between *localtime()* and *gmtime()* in this example only depicts 4 hours difference. It turns out that Sunday October 13, 2013 falls within daylight savings time here in the Eastern U.S. timezone as noted by `tm_isdst=1` found in the local time example, therefore the time difference on this particular date is 4 hours from GMT/UTC correctly reported by the two methods.

Next, you might be wondering how one determines the name of the current time zone set for my system. The *time* module provides an additional attribute specifically *time.tzname* that provides a tuple. The first value is the standard time zone designation while the second value is local daylight savings time zone designation.

Here is the example using my local time.

```
>>>import time
>>>time.tzname
('Eastern Standard Time', 'Eastern Daylight Time')
```

Note, this information is based upon the local operating system internal representation. For example, on a Mac, this returns ("EST,", "EDT").

Therefore, if we wish to print the current time zone designation of a local system, the following code will provide that for you.

```
import time

# Get the current local time

now=time.localtime()

# if we are observing daylight savings time
# tm_isdst is an attribute that can be examined,
# if the value is 0 the current local time is in
# standard time observations and if tm_isdst is 1
# then daylight savings time is being observed

if now.tm_isdst:

    # print the daylight savings time string

    print time.tzname[1]
```

```
else:
    # Otherwise print the standard time string
    print time.tzname[0]
```

```
Eastern Daylight Time
```

Another very useful method within the *time* module is the `strftime()`. This method provides great flexibility in generating custom strings from the base time structure provided. This allows us to format output without having to extract individual time attributes manually.

For example:

```
import time
print time.strftime("%a, %d %b %Y %H:%M:%S %p",time.localtime())
time.sleep(5)
print time.strftime("%a, %d %b %Y %H:%M:%S %p",time.localtime())
```

This short script prints out the local time value using the `strftime` method and uses the `sleep()` method to delay (in this example 5 seconds) and then prints another time string. The result produces the following output:

```
Sun, 13 Oct 2013 10:38:44 AM
Sun, 13 Oct 2013 10:38:49 AM
```

The `strftime` method has great flexibility in the available options, which are shown in Table 6.1.

As you can see the *time* module has a plethora of methods and attributes and is straightforward to use. For more information on the *time* module, you can check out the Python Standard Library [PYLIB].

THE NETWORK TIME PROTOCOL

Today, the most widely accepted practice for synchronizing time is to employ the Network Time Protocol (NTP). NTP utilizes the User Datagram Protocol (UDP) to communicate minimalistic timing packets communicated between a server (containing a highly accurate source of time) and a client wishing to synchronize with that time source. (The default server port for the NTP protocol is 123.) The NTP model includes not one, but many easily accessible time servers synchronized to national laboratories. The point of NTP is to convey or distribute time from these servers to clients via the Internet. The NTP protocol standard is governed by the IETF and the Proposed Standard is RFC 5905, titled "Network Time Protocol Version 4: Protocol and Algorithms Specification" [NTP RFC]. Many programs, operating systems, and applications have been developed to utilize this protocol to synchronize time. As you have probably guessed we are going to develop a simple time synchronization Python program and use this to synchronize forensic operations. Instead of implementing the protocol from scratch I am going to leverage a third-party Python Library *ntplib* to handle the heavy lifting and then compare the results to my local system clock.

Table 6.1 `strftime` Output Specification

Parameter	Definition
%a	Abbreviation of weekday string
%A	Complete weekday string
%b	Abbreviation of month string
%B	Complete month name
%c	Appropriate date and time representation based on locale
%d	Day of the month as a decimal number 01-31
%H	Hour (24-hour clock) as a decimal number 00-24
%I	Hour (12-hour clock) as a decimal number 00-12
%j	Day of the year as a decimal number 001-356
%m	Month as a decimal number 01-12
%M	Minute as a decimal number 00-59
%p	AM or PM representation based on locale
%S	Second as a decimal number 00-59
%U	Week number of the year 00-53 (assumes week begins on Sunday)
%w	Weekday 0-6 Sunday is 0
%W	Week number of the year 00-53 (assumes week begins on Monday)
%x	Date representation based on locale
%X	Time representation based on locale
%y	Year without century as a decimal number 00-99
%Y	Year with century as a decimal number
%Z	Time zone name

OBTAINING AND INSTALLING THE NTP LIBRARY *ntplib*

The ntplib is available for download at https://pypi.python.org/pypi/ntplib/ as shown in Figure 6.3 and as of this writing it is currently version 0.3.1. The library provides a simple interface to NTP servers along with methods that can translate NTP protocol fields to text allowing easy access to other key values such as leap seconds and special indicators.

FIGURE 6.3

Python ntplib download page.

Installing the current library is a manual process, but still straightforward and because ntplib is written completely in native Python the library is compatible across platforms (Windows, Linux, and Mac OS X).

The first installation step is to download the installation package in this case a tar.gz file as shown in Figure 6.4.

Once download you must decompress the tar.gz into a local directory. I have unzipped the archive into c:\Python27\Lib\ntplib-0.3.1 (Figure 6.5). Since I am utilizing Python 2.75, decompressing the download in this directory organizes the library with the other installed libs for easy access and update in the future.

The installation process for manually installed libraries like ntplib is accomplished by executing the included setup program *setup.py* that is included in the directory. To perform the installation you simply open a command window as shown in Figure 6.6 and enter the command:

Python setup.py install

The setup.py program performs all the necessary installation steps. Next, I always like to verify the installation of the new library by opening a Python Shell and importing the library and then by simply typing the name of the library. Python provides basic information regarding the library confirming it is available for use (see Figure 6.7).

As with any module you can always enter the *dir(objName)* built-in function to obtain details about the properties, classes, and methods that are available for the

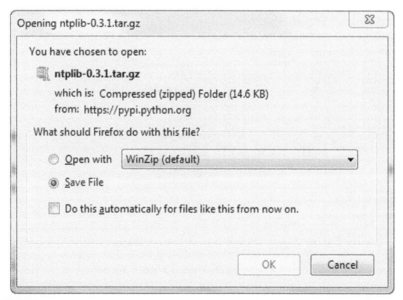

FIGURE 6.4

Download of ntplib-0.3.1.tar.gz.

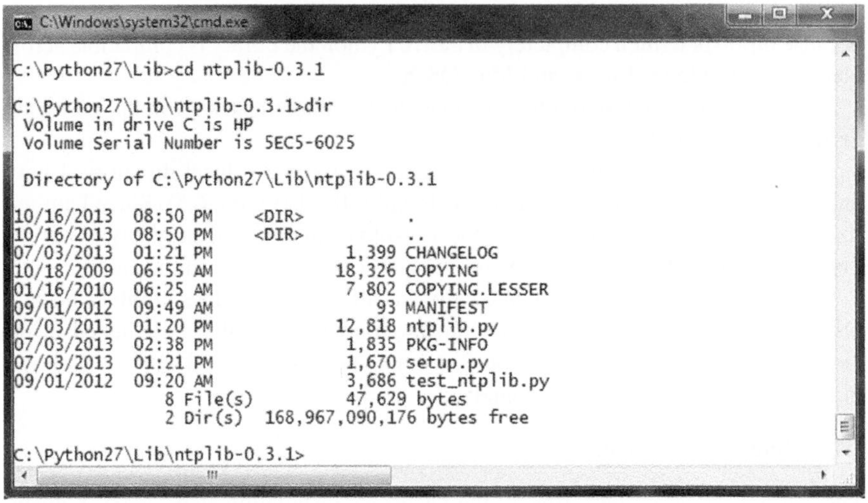

```
C:\Windows\system32\cmd.exe

C:\Python27\Lib>cd ntplib-0.3.1

C:\Python27\Lib\ntplib-0.3.1>dir
 Volume in drive C is HP
 Volume Serial Number is 5EC5-6025

 Directory of C:\Python27\Lib\ntplib-0.3.1

10/16/2013  08:50 PM    <DIR>          .
10/16/2013  08:50 PM    <DIR>          ..
07/03/2013  01:21 PM             1,399 CHANGELOG
10/18/2009  06:55 AM            18,326 COPYING
01/16/2010  06:25 AM             7,802 COPYING.LESSER
09/01/2012  09:49 AM                93 MANIFEST
07/03/2013  01:20 PM            12,818 ntplib.py
07/03/2013  02:38 PM             1,835 PKG-INFO
07/03/2013  01:21 PM             1,670 setup.py
09/01/2012  09:20 AM             3,686 test_ntplib.py
               8 File(s)         47,629 bytes
               2 Dir(s)  168,967,090,176 bytes free

C:\Python27\Lib\ntplib-0.3.1>
```

FIGURE 6.5

Decompressed ntplib-0.3.1.

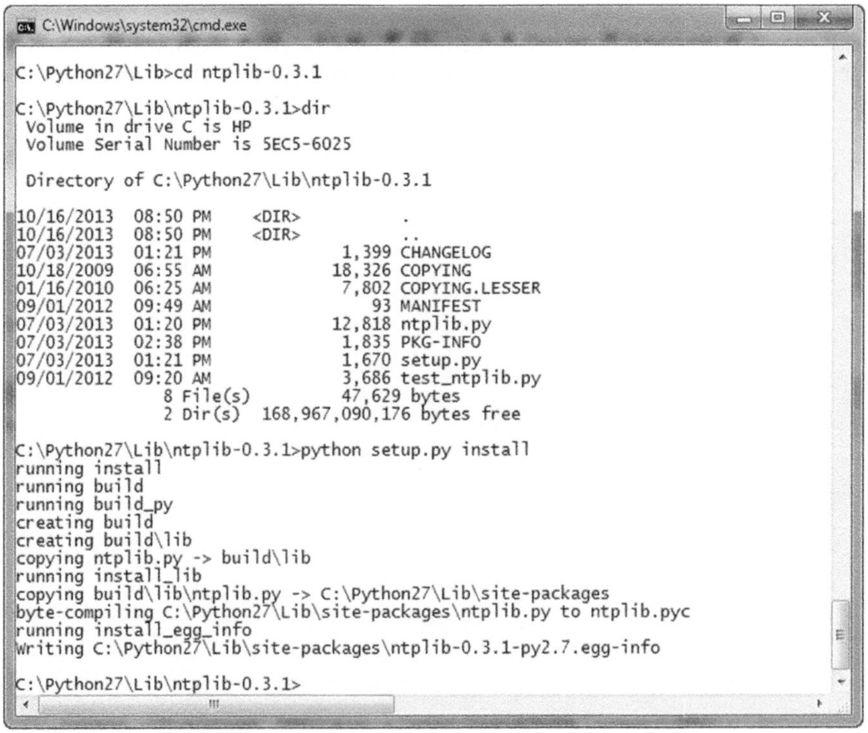

```
C:\Windows\system32\cmd.exe

C:\Python27\Lib>cd ntplib-0.3.1

C:\Python27\Lib\ntplib-0.3.1>dir
 Volume in drive C is HP
 Volume Serial Number is 5EC5-6025

 Directory of C:\Python27\Lib\ntplib-0.3.1

10/16/2013  08:50 PM    <DIR>          .
10/16/2013  08:50 PM    <DIR>          ..
07/03/2013  01:21 PM             1,399 CHANGELOG
10/18/2009  06:55 AM            18,326 COPYING
01/16/2010  06:25 AM             7,802 COPYING.LESSER
09/01/2012  09:49 AM                93 MANIFEST
07/03/2013  01:20 PM            12,818 ntplib.py
07/03/2013  02:38 PM             1,835 PKG-INFO
07/03/2013  01:21 PM             1,670 setup.py
09/01/2012  09:20 AM             3,686 test_ntplib.py
               8 File(s)         47,629 bytes
               2 Dir(s)  168,967,090,176 bytes free

C:\Python27\Lib\ntplib-0.3.1>python setup.py install
running install
running build
running build_py
creating build
creating build\lib
copying ntplib.py -> build\lib
running install_lib
copying build\lib\ntplib.py -> C:\Python27\Lib\site-packages
byte-compiling C:\Python27\Lib\site-packages\ntplib.py to ntplib.pyc
running install_egg_info
Writing C:\Python27\Lib\site-packages\ntplib-0.3.1-py2.7.egg-info

C:\Python27\Lib\ntplib-0.3.1>
```

FIGURE 6.6

Install ntplib.

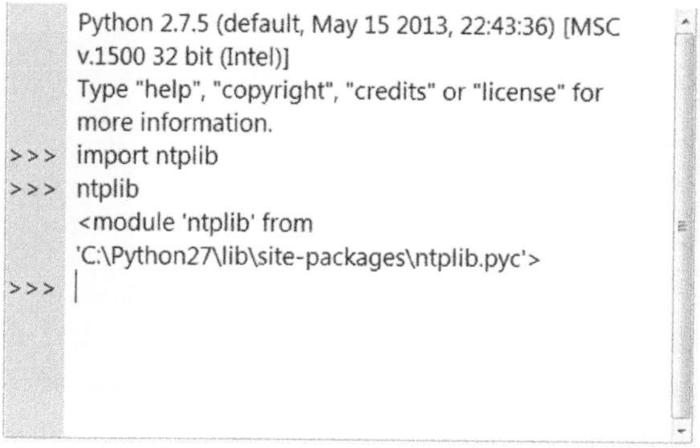

FIGURE 6.7

Verifying the installation.

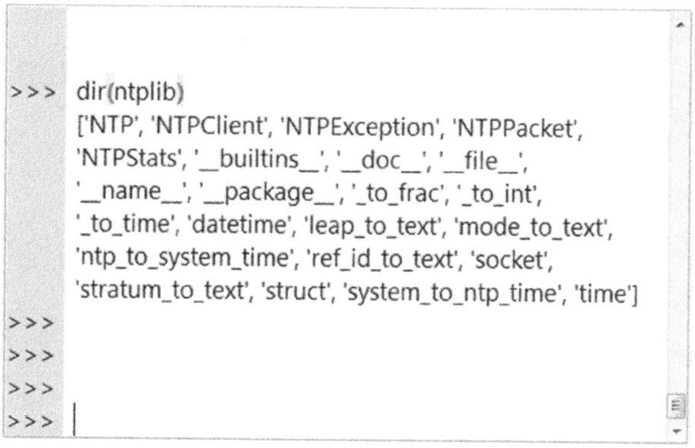

FIGURE 6.8

dir(ntplib) results.

object (see Figure 6.8). For even more information, you can use the *help(objName)* built-in function.

WORLD NTP SERVERS

Examining the methods and properties may seem a bit confusing at first; however, using the library module is in fact quite simple. Simply put we want to create an ntp client capable of accessing a specified ntp server to obtain a third-party source of time. In the United States, NIST manages a list of time servers that can be accessed to obtain "root" time (Figure 6.9).

Updated lists can be found at: http://tf.nist.gov/tf-cgi/servers.cgi.

In Europe, you can find an active list of NTP servers at the NTP Pool Project. Figure 6.10 shows a screenshot from their home page at http://www.pool.ntp.org/zone/europe.

Name	IP Address	Location	Status
nist1-ny.ustiming.org	64.90.182.55	New York City, NY	
nist1-nj.ustiming.org	96.47.67.105	Bridgewater, NJ	all services available
nist1-nj2.ustiming.org	165.193.126.229	Weehawken, NJ	all services available
nist1-ny2.ustiming.org	216.171.112.36	New York City, NY	All services available
nist1-pa.ustiming.org	206.246.122.250	Hatfield, PA	All services available
time-a.nist.gov	129.6.15.28	NIST, Gaithersburg, Maryland	All services busy, not recommended
time-b.nist.gov	129.6.15.29	NIST, Gaithersburg, Maryland	All services busy, not recommended
time-c.nist.gov	129.6.15.30	NIST, Gaithersburg, Maryland	All services available
time-d.nist.gov	2610:20:6F15:15::27	NIST, Gaithersburg, Maryland	All services via IPV6
nist1.aol-va.symmetricom.com	64.236.96.53	Reston, Virginia	All services available
nist1.macon.macon.ga.us	98.175.203.200	Macon, Georgia	All services available
nist1-atl.ustiming.org	64.250.177.145	Atlanta, Georgia	All services available
wolfnisttime.com	207.223.123.18	Birmingham, Alabama	All services available
nist1-chi.ustiming.org	216.171.120.36	Chicago, Illinois	All services available

FIGURE 6.9

Partial list of NIST time servers.

  JOIN THE POOL USE THE POOL MANAGE SERVERS

NTP POOL PROJECT

Europe — europe.pool.ntp.org

To use this pool zone, add the following to your ntp.conf file:

```
server 0.europe.pool.ntp.org
server 1.europe.pool.ntp.org
server 2.europe.pool.ntp.org
server 3.europe.pool.ntp.org
```

News

How do I *use* pool.ntp.org?

How do I *join* pool.ntp.org?

Information for vendors

The mailing lists

Additional links

Translations

Deutsch
English
Español
Suomi
Français
日本語
한국어
Nederlands
Português
русский
Svenska

IPv4
There are 2084 active servers in this zone.

2092 (-8) active 1 day ago
2089 (-5) active 7 days ago
2101 (-17) active 14 days ago
2080 (+4) active 60 days ago
1992 (+92) active 1 year ago
1342 (+742) active 3 years ago
829 (+1255) active 6 years ago

See all zones in Global.

Austria — at.pool.ntp.org (78)
Switzerland — ch.pool.ntp.org (119)
Germany — de.pool.ntp.org (702)
Denmark — dk.pool.ntp.org (52)
Spain — es.pool.ntp.org (22)
France — fr.pool.ntp.org (297)
Italy — it.pool.ntp.org (40)
Luxembourg — lu.pool.ntp.org (25)
Netherlands — nl.pool.ntp.org (225)

IPv6
There are 617 active servers in this zone.

619 (-2) active 1 day ago
613 (+4) active 7 days ago
637 (-20) active 14 days ago
606 (+11) active 60 days ago
468 (+149) active 1 year ago

FIGURE 6.10

European NTP Pool Project.

For those of you wishing to obtain your time from the U.S. Naval Observatory or USNO, you might be interested to know that for many years, the USNO has provided access to NTP servers' aptly named tick and tock. For more information on the U.S. Naval Observatory you can visit: http://www.usno.navy.mil/USNO.

NTP CLIENT SETUP SCRIPT

To setup a Python ntp client using the ntplib is a simple process:

```python
import ntplib        # import the ntplib
import time          # import the Python time module

# url of the closest NIST certified NTP server

NIST='nist1-macon.macon.ga.us'

# Create NTP client object using the ntplib

ntp=ntplib.NTPClient()

# initiate an NTP client request for time

ntpResponse=ntp.request(NIST)

# Check that we received a response

if ntpResponse:
    # obtain the seconds since the epoch from response
    nistUTC=ntpResponse.tx_time
    print 'NIST reported seconds since the Epoch :',
    print nistUTC
else:
    print 'NTP Request Failed'
```

Program Output
```
NIST reported seconds since the Epoch : 1382132161.96
```
Now that we can obtain the seconds since the epoch, we can use the Python Standard Library *time* module to display the time in either local or GMT/UTC time, and can even compare the current NTP time to our own local system clock as shown below.

CODE LISTING 6.1

```python
import ntplib
import time

NIST='nist1-macon.macon.ga.us'

ntp=ntplib.NTPClient()

ntpResponse=ntp.request(NIST)

if (ntpResponse):
    now=time.time()
    diff=now-ntpResponse.tx_time
    print 'Difference :',
```

Continued

```
        print diff,
        print 'seconds'

        print 'Network Delay: ',
        print ntpResponse.delay

        print 'UTC: NIST :'+time.strftime("%a, %d %b %Y %H:%M:%S +0000",
        time.gmtime(int(ntpResponse.tx_time)))

        print 'UTC: SYSTEM : '+time.strftime("%a, %d %b %Y %H:%M:%S
        +0000", time.gmtime(int(now)))

    else:
        print 'No Response from Time Service'
```

Program Output
```
Difference    : 3.09969758987 seconds
Network Delay : 0.0309739112854
UTC NIST      : Fri, 18 Oct 2013 21:48:48 +0000
UTC SYSTEM    : Fri, 18 Oct 2013 21:48:51 +0000
```

Notable observations:

(1) It is important that you obtain the local system time immediately after obtaining the time from the time server (in my case from NIST):

```
ntpResponse=ntp.request(NIST)
if (ntpResponse):
    now=time.time()
```

This ensures that our comparison with the local time maintained by our system clock is influenced by the smallest amount of processing.

(2) It is also important to consider the network delay reported by the NTP client. In this example, the delay was a little over 30 milliseconds (specifically 0.0309739112854 seconds), however, in certain situations the delay can be much longer based on the time of day, your network connection speed, and other network latency issues.

(3) In this example, I calculated a difference of 3.09969758987 seconds. This means that my local system clock is running 3 + seconds faster than that of the NIST server.

```
diff=now-ntpResponse.tx_time
```

If the resulting value was negative instead of positive, I can conclude that my system clock is running behind that reported by NIST.

(4) Finally, the ntplib client operations are synchronous. In other words, once I make the request:

```
ntpResponse=ntp.request(NIST)
```

the code does not continue processing until the request is fulfilled or fails just like any method or function call.

CHAPTER REVIEW

In this chapter, I explained the basics of time and computing. This includes a better understanding of the *epoch*, the origins of modern time keeping along with a bit of history on time. I then took a deep dive into the Standard Library module *time* and I explained and demonstrated many methods and properties associated with the module. I developed several short Python scripts to give you a feel for how to apply and interpret the results of time processing.

I then provided an overview of the NTP that provides us with the ability to synchronize time with National Measurement sources. Next, I walked you through the installation and setup of a Python NTP Library *ntplib*. I then experimented with the module to setup a NTP client that interfaces with a network-based time source. I wrote a script that would compare and calculate the difference between my local system clock and that of a NIST time server.

SUMMARY QUESTIONS

1. Back in Chapter 3, I developed a program that walked the files system, hashed the files, and recorded the modified, access, and created (MAC) times of each file. Modify that program using the *time* module to convert the MAC times from local time to GMT/UTC time values.
2. Expanding on Code Listing 6.1, choose five additional time servers throughout the world and devise a method to compare and contrast the time reported by each in relationship to your local system clock. Also, record the network delay values from each. Note, you should execute multiple runs and average the results.
3. What other time sources should be carefully examined and/or normalized during a forensic investigation?

Additional Resources

Proving the integrity of digital evidence with time. Int J Digital Evid 2002;1(1) 1–7.

The Python Standard Library. http://docs.python.org/2/library/time.html?highlight= time#time.

The Network Time Protocol Version 4: Protocol and Algorithms Specification. http://tools. ietf.org/html/rfc5905.

Longitude. Longitude: the true story of a Lone Genius who solved the greatest scientific problem of his time. New York, NY: Walker & Co.; 1995.

Using Natural Language Tools in Forensics

CHAPTER CONTENTS

WHAT IS NATURAL LANGUAGE PROCESSING?

Before I begin, Natural Language needs to be defined. Back in 1987, I read the book *Introduction to Natural Language Processing* as part of a research project I was working on with Dr. James Cook at the Illinois Institute of Technology Research Institute (IITRI). My wife Janet was also working on Natural Language projects at IITRI with Dr. Larry Jones. Her work employed Natural Language as part of a decision engine that could diagnose and better understand the behaviors of cattle. The book we referenced had the best definitions that I have seen for Natural Language, therefore I will share that excerpt with you here.

> *"Natural Language is any language that humans learn from their environment and use to communicate with each other. Whatever the form of the communication, Natural Languages are used to express our knowledge and emotions and to convey our responses to other people and to our surroundings."* [Harris]

Obviously, like all good definitions they stand the test of time. Since the Internet really did not materialize into a recognizable form until the late 1980s, the concept of expressing emotion and knowledge digitally did not include Facebook, Twitter, Emoticons, Blogging, Texting, Sexting, BitStrips, or even Internet-based e-mail! However, the definition certainly provides coverage for these latest forms of Natural Language expression. Extracting meaning (semantics) from Natural Language is quite a bit more difficult than it looks.

Judging the effectiveness of Natural Language systems that attempt to interpret, understand, and respond accordingly falls to the Turing Test, named after Alan Turing based on his 1950 paper *"Computing Machinery and Intelligence."* In his paper, Turing asks the proactive question, "Can machines think?" [Turing]

Dialog-based systems

The goal of dialog-based systems is to respond to a user input naturally, meaning that we cannot distinguish between human or machine-based responses. Some may be familiar with systems that are moving toward this capability. For example, here is a dialog between me and the Sync system in my car:

> Me: I'm hungry.
> Sync: Ok, Where would you like to search nearby, along your route or in a city?
> Me: Nearby.
> Sync: How would you like to search—by name or by category?
> Me: By category.
> Sync: Ok, what category?
> Me: Italian.
> Sync: Ok, please select from the list on your screen, for example say Line 1.
> Me: Line 4.
> Sync: Ok, Rossi's Restaurant. Would you like to make a call or set as destination?
> Me: Make a call.
> Sync: Ok: Calling Rossi's Restaurant. . . . .

Although useful, it certainly does not meet the Turing standard because I know that I am talking to a computer not a human. However, Sync does translate the spoken word into text and then responds in a timely fashion and as a result the system usually gets me where I want to go or provides me the information I am seeking.

Corpus

One of the key elements needed to perform Natural Language Processing (NLP) is a corpus. A corpus is a large volume of linguistic samples that is relevant to a specific genre. For example, the Guttenberg Project [Gutenberg] that is available at http://www.gutenberg.org/ contains over 40,000 books in electronic form.

One of the challenges in creating meaningful examples in this chapter was establishing a corpus. Then I needed to demonstrate the use of the corpus to create these examples that will serve as a catalyst for the development of new applications of NLP within the field of forensic science. Bear in mind, depending on the application you intend for NLP, more than one genre may be necessary.

INSTALLING THE NATURAL LANGUAGE TOOLKIT AND ASSOCIATED LIBRARIES

As with other third-party libraries and modules, installation is available for Windows, Linux, and Mac. The Natural Language Toolkit (NLTK) library is free and can be easily obtained online, from *nltk.org*. Installation of NLTK does require the installation of other dependency libraries including Numpy and PyYAML. Figure 7.1 depicts the nltk.org installation page with easy to follow instructions. Once you have installed everything, you can verify the installation through your favorite Python Shell by typing:

Import NLTK

WORKING WITH A CORPUS

The first step in working with a corpus is to either load an existing corpus that is included with NLTK or create your own from local files or the Internet. Once this is done, there are a variety of powerful operations you can perform on the corpus,

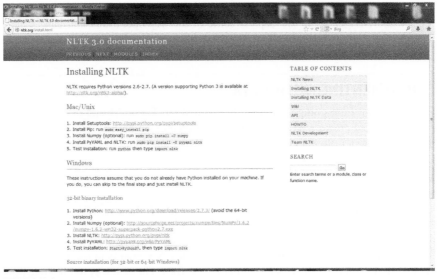

FIGURE 7.1

nltk.org Installation url.

Table 7.1 Introductory List of NLTK Operations

Method	Description
raw()	Extracts the raw contents of the corpus. The method returns the type: Python "*str*"
word_tokenize()	Removes white space and punctuation and then creates a list of the individual tokens (basically words). The method returns the type: Python "list"
collocations()	Words often appear consecutively within a text and these provide useful information to investigators. In addition, once detected they can be used to find associations between word occurrences. This is accomplished by calculating the frequencies of words and their connections with other words. The collocations method performs all of this in a single method
concordance()	This method provides the ability to generate every occurrence of a specific word along with the context (how the word was used in a specific sentence, for example)
findall(search)	This method can be used for simple and even regular expression searches of the corpus text
index(word)	This method provides an index to the first occurrence of the word provided
similar(word)	Note this is *not* synonyms, rather the method provides *distribution similarities*, stated simply it identifies other words which appear in the same "context" as the specified word
vocab()	Produces a comprehensive vocabulary list of the text submitted

operations that would be both complicated and time-consuming without the aid of a toolset like NLTK. Table 7.1 depicts some of the key operations that can be performed on a corpus, I will be demonstrating these in code later in this chapter.

EXPERIMENTING WITH NLTK

In this section, I am going to invoke the methods in Table 7.1 and create a simple program to first create a new text corpus, and then examine that corpus with these methods. First, a little background on the corpus I am going to create.

Jack Walraven maintains the web site http://simpson.walraven.org/. At that site, Jack has organized the transcripts of the O.J. Simpson trial. For this experiment, I downloaded the Trial Transcripts for January 1995 (you can of course download as many months and excerpts as you like). There are nine Trial Transcript text files stored there for the January 1995 proceedings, and they represent transcripts for the dates of January 11-13, 23-26, 30, and 31. I created a directory on my Windows system, c:\simpson\, to hold each of the separate files. My goal is to use these files to create a new text corpus that includes all of these files. The best way to illustrate how this works is to walk you through some sample code that deals with each aspect. I have annotated the code to make sure you understand each step of the process.

NLTK Experimentation

This first section imports the modules necessary for the experiment. The most important is the newly installed NLTK module.

```
from __future__ import division
```

```
import nltk
```

Next, I'm going to import the PlaintextCorpusReader from the NLTK module. This method will allow me to read in and ultimately create a text corpus that I can work with.

```
from nltk.corpus import PlaintextCorpusReader
```

The first thing I need to specify is the location of the files that will be included in the corpus. I have placed those files in c:\simpson\. Each of the 9 files are stored there and each is a text document.

```
rootOfCorpus = "c:\\simpson\\"
```

Now I'm going to use the PlainTextCorpusReader method to collect all the files in the directory I specified in the variable rootOfCorpus. I specify all the files by the second parameter '.*'. If you have directories that had multiple file types and you only wanted to include the text documents you could have specified '.txt'. The result of this call will be an NLTK Corpus Object named newCorpus.

```
newCorpus = PlaintextCorpusReader(rootOfCorpus, '.*')
```

```
print type(newCorpus)
```

The print type(newCorpus) produces the following output providing me with the NLTK type of the newCorpus.

```
<class 'nltk.corpus.reader.plaintext.PlaintextCorpusReader'>
```

I can also print the file identification of each file that makes up the new corpus by using the fileids() method.

```
print newCorpus.fileids()
```

```
['Trial-January-11.txt', 'Trial-January-12.txt', 'Trial-January-13.txt',
'Trial-January-23.txt', 'Trial-January-24.txt', 'Trial-January-25.txt',
'Trial-January-26.txt', 'Trial-January-30.txt', 'Trial-January-31.txt']
```

I can also, determine the absolute paths of the individual documents contained in the new corpus, by using the abspaths() method.

```
print newCorpus.abspaths()
```

```
[FileSystemPathPointer('c:\\simpson\\Trial-January-11.txt'),
FileSystemPathPointer('c:\\simpson\\Trial-January-12.txt'),
FileSystemPathPointer('c:\\simpson\\Trial-January-13.txt'),
```

```
FileSystemPathPointer('c:\\simpson\\Trial-January-23.txt'),
FileSystemPathPointer('c:\\simpson\\Trial-January-24.txt'),
FileSystemPathPointer('c:\\simpson\\Trial-January-25.txt'),
FileSystemPathPointer('c:\\simpson\\Trial-January-26.txt'),
FileSystemPathPointer('c:\\simpson\\Trial-January-30.txt'),
FileSystemPathPointer('c:\\simpson\\Trial-January-31.txt')]
```

Now I can leverage the newCorpus object to extract the raw text which represents the complete collection of files contained in the rootOfCorpus directory specified. I can then determine the length or size of the combination of the 9 trial transcript files.

```
rawText = newCorpus.raw()
```

```
print len(rawText)
```

This produces the output:

2008024

I can now apply the nltk.Text module methods in order to better understand and interpret the content of the corpus. I start this process by tokenizing the rawText of the corpus. This produces tokens (mainly words, but also includes numbers and recognized special character sequences).

```
tokens = nltk.word_tokenize(rawText)
```

Tokenization creates a standard Python list that I can now work with using both standard Python language operations and of course any methods associated with list objects. For example I can use len (tokens) to determine the number of tokens that were extracted from the text.

```
print len(tokens)
```

Which produces the result for this corpus of 401,032 tokens.

401032

Since this is now a simple list, I can display some or a portion of the contents. In this example I print out the first 100 list elements representing the first 100 tokens returned from the tokenization process.

```
print tokens[0:100]
```

['*LOS', 'ANGELES', ',', 'CALIFORNIA', ';', 'WEDNESDAY', ',','JANUARY', '11', ',', '1995', '9:05', 'A.M.*', 'DEPARTMENT', 'NO.', '103', 'HON.', 'LANCE', 'A.', 'ITO', ',', 'JUDGE', 'APPEARANCES', ':', '(', 'APPEARANCES', 'AS', 'HERETOFORE', 'NOTED', ',', 'DEPUTY', 'DISTRICT', 'ATTORNEY', 'HANK', ';', 'ALSO', 'PRESENT', 'ON', 'BEHALF', 'OF', 'SOJOURN', ',', 'MS.', 'PAMELA', 'W.', 'WITHEY', ',', 'ATTORNEY-AT-LAW.', ')', '(', 'JANET', 'M.', 'MOXHAM', ',', 'CSR', 'NO.', '4855', ',', 'OFFICIAL', 'REPORTER.', ')', '(', 'CHRISTINE',

'M.', 'OLSON', ',', 'CSR', 'NO.', '2378', ',', 'OFFICIAL', 'REPORTER.', ')', '(', 'THE',
'FOLLOWING', 'PROCEEDINGS', 'WERE', 'HELD', 'IN', 'OPEN', 'COURT', ',', 'OUT', 'OF', 'THE',
'PRESENCE', 'OF', 'THE', 'JURY', ':', ')', '*THE', 'COURT', ':', '*', 'ALL', 'RIGHT.', 'THE',
'SIMPSON']

Next, I want to create a text that I can apply the NLTK text methods to. I do this by creating NLTK Text Object textSimpson using the Text method to the tokens extracted by the tokenization process.

```
textSimpson = nltk.Text(tokens)
```

```
print type(textSimpson)
```

As expected the object type is nltk.text.Text

```
<class 'nltk.text.Text'>
```

I would like to know the size of the vocabulary used across the corpus. I know the number of tokens, but there are of course duplicates. Therefore, I use the Python set method to obtain the unique set of vocabulary present in the text in the trial transcript.

```
vocabularyUsed = set(textSimpson)
```

```
print len(vocabularyUsed)
```

```
12604
```

Which produces 12,604 unique tokens from the total of 401,032 a much more manageable number. From this I would like to see all the unique tokens, and I can accomplish that by sorting the set.

```
print sorted(set(textSimpson))
```

'ABERRANT', 'ABIDE', 'ABIDING', 'ABILITIES', 'ABILITIES.', 'ABILITY', 'ABILITY.',
'ABLAZE', 'ABLE', 'ABOUT', 'ABOUT.', 'ABOVE', 'ABRAHAM', 'ABROGATE', 'ABROGATED',
'ABRUPT', 'ABRUPTLY', 'ABSENCE', 'ABSENCE.', 'ABSENT', 'ABSOLUTE', 'ABSOLUTELY',
'ABSOLUTELY.', 'ABSORB', 'ABSTRACT', 'ABSTRACT.', 'ABSURD.', 'ABSURDITY', 'ABUDRAHM',
'ABUDRAHM.', 'ABUNDANCE', 'ABUNDANT', 'ABUNDANTLY', 'ABUSE', 'ABUSE.', 'ABUSE/
BATTERED', 'ABUSED', 'ABUSER', 'ABUSER.', 'ABUSES', 'ABUSES.', 'ABUSING', 'ABUSIVE',
'ABUSIVE.',

```
    . . .
```
. . . skipping about 10,000 tokens
```
    . . .
```

'WRITTEN', 'WRITTEN.', 'WRONG', 'WRONG.', 'WRONGFULLY', 'WRONGLY', 'WROTE', 'X', 'X-
RAYS', 'XANAX', 'XEROX', 'XEROXED', 'XEROXED.', 'XEROXING', 'XEROXING.', 'Y',
'YAMAUCHI', 'YAMAUCHI.', 'YARD', 'YARD.', 'YARDS', 'YEAGEN', 'YEAH', 'YEAH.', 'YEAR',
'YEAR.', 'YEARS', 'YEARS.', 'YELL', 'YELLED', 'YELLING', 'YELLING.', 'YELLOW', 'YEP.',
'YES', 'YES.', 'YESTERDAY', 'YESTERDAY.', 'YET', 'YET.', 'YIELD', 'YORK', 'YORK.', 'YOU',

"YOU'LL", "YOU'RE", "YOU'VE", 'YOU.', 'YOUNG', 'YOUNGER', 'YOUNGSTERS', 'YOUR', 'YOURS.', 'YOURSELF', 'YOURSELF.', 'YOURSELVES', 'YOUTH', 'YUDOWITZ', 'YUDOWITZ.', 'Z', 'ZACK', 'ZACK.', 'ZEIGLER', 'ZERO', 'ZLOMSOWITCH', "ZLOMSOWITCH'S", 'ZLOMSOWITCH.', 'ZOOM'

> *Next, I can determine how many times a particular word appears in the Trial Transcript. I accomplish using the count() method of the nltk.Text object type.*

```
myWord = "KILL"
```

```
textSimpson.count(myWord)
```

84

> *This produces a count of the 84 times that the word KILL appeared in the Trial Transcription for the 9 days included in this corpus, during the month of January 1995.*
> *Up to this point all of this is pretty straight-forward. Let's take a look at a couple of the more advanced methods included in the nltk.Text Module. I'm going to start with the collocations method. This will provide me with a list of words that occur together statistically often in the text.*

```
print textSimpson.collocations()
```

```
Building collocations list
*THE COURT; *MS. CLARK; *MR. COCHRAN; MR. SIMPSON; NICOLE BROWN;
*MR. DARDEN; OPENING STATEMENT; LOS ANGELES; MR. COCHRAN; DETECTIVE FUHRMAN;
DISCUSSION HELD; WOULD LIKE; *MR. DOUGLAS; BROWN SIMPSON; THANK YOU.;
MR. DARDEN; DEPUTY DISTRICT; FOLLOWING PROCEEDINGS; DISTRICT ATTORNEYS.;
MISS CLARK
```

> *As you can see, the collocation list generated makes a great deal of sense. These pairings would naturally occur more often that others during the proceedings.*
> *Next, I want to generate a concordance from the transcript for specific words that might be of interest. NLTK will produce each occurrence of the word along with context (in other words the sentence surrounding the concordance word). A second optional parameter indicates the size of the window of surrounding words you would like to see. I will demonstrate a couple examples.*
> *I will start with the word "KILL", this produces 84 matches and I have included the first 6.*

```
myWord = "KILL"
```

```
print textSimpson.concordance(myWord)
```

```
Displaying 6 of 84 matches:
```

WAS IN EMINENT DANGER AND NEEDED TO KILL IN SELF-DEFENSE. BUT THE ARIS COURT

R OCCURRED. '' I KNOW HE 'S GOING TO KILL ME. I WISH HE WOULD HURRY UP AND GET

FLICTED HARM WAY BEYOND NECESSARY TO KILL THE VICTIM. AND THIS IS A QUOTE FROM

'M GOING TO HURT YOU , I 'M GOING TO KILL YOU , I 'M GOING TO BEAT YOU. '' THO

HAVE HER AND NO ONE ELSE WILL IS TO KILL HER. THAT IS CLEAR IN THE RESEARCH.

WAS A FIXED PURPOSE , FULL INTENT TO KILL , WHERE THE DEFENDANT LITERALLY WENT

If I use the word "GLOVE", the code produces 92 matches; I have included the first 6:

```
myWord = "GLOVE"

print textSimpson.concordance(myWord)
```

Displaying 6 of 92 matches:

CE DEPARTMENT PLANTED EVIDENCE , THE GLOVE AT ROCKINGHAM. NOW , THAT OF COURSE

HAT A POLICE DETECTIVE WOULD PLANT A GLOVE , AND IT MADE HOT NEWS AND THE DEFEN

R THIS POLICE DETECTIVE PLANTED THIS GLOVE AT ROCKINGHAM. NOW , YOUR HONOR , BE

DETECTIVE FUHRMAN 'S RECOVERY OF THE GLOVE AND AS - INSOFAR AS IT RELATES TO T

HEY SAW THE LEFT-HANDED BULKY MAN 'S GLOVE THERE AT THE FEET OF RONALD GOLDMAN.

E BUNDY CRIME SCENE. THEY SAW A LONE GLOVE , A SINGLE GLOVE AT THE FEET OF RONA

NLTK also provides more sophisticated methods that can operate on text corpus. For example the ability to identify similarities of word usage. The method identifies words that are used within similar contexts.

```
myWord = "intent"

print textSimpson.similar(myWord)
```

Building word-context index...
time cochran court evidence and house it blood defense motive that jury other people the this witnesses case defendant discovery

if I change the word to "victim" the results are as follows:

```
Building word-context index...
court defendant jury defense prosecution case evidence and people record
police time relationship house question statement tape way crime glove
```

*I can also utilize NLTK to produce a comprehensive vocabulary list and frequency distribution that covers all the tokens in the corpus. By using this method across documents, one can derive tendencies of the writer or creator of a document. The vocab method returns an object based on the class **nltk.probability.FreqDist** as shown here.*

```
simpsonVocab = textSimpson.vocab()
```

```
type(simpsonVocab)
```

```
<class 'nltk.probability.FreqDist'>
```

Thus the simpsonVocab object can now be utilized to examine the frequency distribution of any and all tokens within the text. By using just one of the methods, for example, simpsonVocab.items(), I can obtain a sorted usage list (most used first) of each vocabulary item.

```
simpsonVocab.items()
```

```
<bound method FreqDist.items of <FreqDist with 12604 samples and 401032
outcomes>>
```

[('THE', 19386), (',', 18677), ('TO', 11634), ('THAT', 10777), ('AND', 8938), (':', 8369), ('OF', 8198), ('', 7850), ('IS', 6322), ('I', 6244), ('A', 5590), ('IN', 5456), ('YOU', 4879), ('WE', 4385), ('THIS', 4264), ('IT', 3815), ('COURT', 3763), ('WAS', 3255), ('HAVE', 2816), ('–', 2797), ('?', 2738), ('HE', 2734), ("'S", 2677), ('NOT', 2417), ('ON', 2414), ('THEY', 2287), ('*THE', 2275), ('BE', 2240), ('ARE', 2207), ('YOUR', 2200), ('WHAT', 2122), ('AT', 2112), ('WITH', 2110),*

...

... Skipping to the bottom of the output for brevity

...

('WRENCHING', 1), ('WRESTLING.', 1), ('WRISTS.', 1), ('WRITERS', 1), ('WRONGLY', 1), ('X-RAYS', 1), ('XANAX', 1), ('XEROXED.', 1), ('XEROX-ING.', 1), ('YAMAUCHI.', 1), ('YARD.', 1), ('YARDS', 1), ('YEAGEN', 1), ('YELL', 1), ('YELLING.', 1), ('YEP.', 1), ('YIELD', 1), ('YOUNGSTERS', 1), ('YOURS.', 1), ('YUDOWITZ', 1), ('YUDOWITZ.', 1), ('Z', 1), ('ZEIGLER', 1), ('ZERO', 1), ("ZLOMSOWITCH'S", 1)]

Note: A nice by-product of the vocab method is when different vocabulary items have the same number of occurrences, they are sorted alphabetically.

CREATING A CORPUS FROM THE INTERNET

In many cases, the text that we wish to examine is found on the Internet. By combining Python, the Python Standard Library *urllib*, and NLTK we can perform the same types of analysis of online documents. I will start with a simple text document downloaded from the Guttenberg Project to illustrate.

I start by importing the necessary modules in this case NLTK and the urlopen module from the urllib. Note: As you can see, I can selectively bring in specific modules from a library instead of loading the entire library.

```
>>> import nltk

>>> from urllib import urlopen
```

Next, I specify the URL I wish to access and call the urlopen.read method.

```
>>> url = "http://www.gutenberg.org/files/2760/2760.txt"

>>> raw = urlopen(url).read()
```

As expected this returns the type 'str'.
   Note: since I'm entering these commands from the Python Shell and interrogating the output directly, I'm not using the same try/except care that I would use if this example was actual program execution. You can of course add that if you'd like.

```
>>> type(raw)

<type 'str'>
```

Now that I have confirmed that the result is a string, I check the length that was returned. In this case 3.6 MB

```
>>> len(raw)

3608901
```

To get a feel for what is contained in this online source, I simply use the standard Python string capabilities to print out the first 200 characters, this produces the following output.

```
>>> raw[:200]
```

'CELEBRATED CRIMES, COMPLETE\r\n\r\n\r\n\r\nThis eBook is for the use of anyone anywhere at no cost and with almost\r\nno restrictions whatsoever. You may copy it, give it away or re-use it\r\n'

Now I can perform any of the NLTK module capabilities, I have included a couple here to give you a feel for the text that I downloaded.

```
>>> tokenList = nltk.word_tokenize(raw)

>>> type(tokenList)

<type 'list'>

>>> len(tokenList)

707397

>>> tokenList[:40]

['CELEBRATED', 'CRIMES', ',', 'COMPLETE', 'This', 'eBook', 'is', 'for', 'the', 'use', 'of',
'anyone', 'anywhere', 'at', 'no', 'cost', 'and', 'with', 'almost', 'no', 'restrictions',
'whatsoever.', 'You', 'may', 'copy', 'it', ',', 'give', 'it', 'away', 'or', 're-use', 'it',
'under', 'the', 'terms', 'of', 'the', 'Project', 'Gutenberg']
```

Many other NLTK methods, objects, and functions exist to allow the exploration of Natural Language. For now, you have learned the basics using the test-then code method. Now I will create a simple application that will make it much easier to both access NLTK capabilities using these same methods and provide a baseline for you to extend the capability.

NLTKQuery APPLICATION

In order to make the interface with NLTK both easier and extensible, I have built the NLTKQuery application. The application has three source files:

Source File	Description
NLTKQuery.py	Serves as the main program loop for interfacing with NLTK
_classNLTKQuery.py	This module defines a new class that when instantiated and used properly will allow access to NLTK methods in a controlled manner
_NLTKQuery.py	This module provides support functions for the NLTKQuery main program loop, mainly to handle user input and menu display

The program provides a simplified user interface access to NLTK methods without forcing the user to understand how the NLTK library works. All the user needs to do is setup a directory that contains the file or files that they wish to include in a corpus. The application will create the corpus based on the directory path provided and then allow the user to interact, or better stated, query the corpus.

The contents of the three source files are listed here:

NLTKQuery.py

```
#
#  NLTK QUERY FRONT END
#  Python-Forensics
#      No HASP required
#

import sys
import _NLTKQuery

print "Welcome to the NLTK Query Experimentation"
print "Please wait loading NLTK ... "

import _classNLTKQuery

oNLTK = _classNLTKQuery.classNLTKQuery()

print
print "Input full path name where intended corpus file or files are stored"
print "Note: you must enter a quoted string e.g. c:\\simpson\\ "
print
userSpecifiedPath = raw_input("Path: ")

# Attempt to create a text Corpus
result = oNLTK.textCorpusInit(userSpecifiedPath)

if result == "Success":

    menuSelection = -1

    while menuSelection != 0:

        if menuSelection != -1:
            print
            s = raw_input('Press Enter to continue...')

        menuSelection = _NLTKQuery.getUserSelection()

        if menuSelection == 1:
            oNLTK.printCorpusLength()

        elif menuSelection == 2:
            oNLTK.printTokensFound()

        elif menuSelection == 3:
            oNLTK.printVocabSize()

        elif menuSelection == 4:
            oNLTK.printSortedVocab()
```

```
            elif menuSelection == 5:
                oNLTK.printCollocation()

            elif menuSelection == 6:
                oNLTK.searchWordOccurence()
            elif menuSelection == 7:
                oNLTK.generateConcordance()

            elif menuSelection == 8:
                oNLTK.generateSimiliarities()

            elif menuSelection == 9:
                oNLTK.printWordIndex()

            elif menuSelection == 10:
                oNLTK.printVocabulary()

            elif menuSelection == 0:
                print "Goodbye"
                print

            elif menuSelection == -1:
                continue

            else:
                print "unexpected error condition"
                menuSelection = 0

    else:
            print "Closing NLTK Query Experimentation"
```

_classNLTKQuery.py

```
#
# NLTK QUERY CLASS MODULE
# Python-Forensics
#      No HASP required
#

import os                              #Standard Library OS functions
import sys
import logging                         # Standard Library Logging functions
import nltk                            # Import the Natural Language Toolkit
from nltk.corpus import PlaintextCorpusReader    #Import the PlainText
                                                 CorpusReader Module

# NLTKQuery Class

class classNLTKQuery:

            def textCorpusInit(self, thePath):
                    # Validate the path is a directory
                    if not os.path.isdir(thePath):
                            return "Path is not a Directory"
```

```
                    # Validate the path is readable
                    if not os.access(thePath, os.R_OK):
                                return "Directory is not Readable"
                    # Attempt to Create a corpus with all .txt files
                    found in the directory
                    try:

                                self.Corpus   =   PlaintextCorpus
                                Reader(thePath, '.*')
                                print "Processing Files : "
                                print self.Corpus.fileids()
                                print "Please wait ..."
                                self.rawText = self.Corpus.raw()
                                self.tokens = nltk.word_tokenize
                                (self.rawText)
                                self.TextCorpus = nltk.Text(self.
                                tokens)
            except:
                                return "Corpus Creation Failed"

            self.ActiveTextCorpus = True

            return "Success"

    def printCorpusLength(self):
            print "Corpus Text Length: ",
            print len(self.rawText)

    def printTokensFound(self):
            print "Tokens Found: ",
            print len(self.tokens)

    def printVocabSize(self):
            print "Calculating ..."
            print "Vocabulary Size: ",
            vocabularyUsed = set(self.TextCorpus)
            vocabularySize = len(vocabularyUsed)
            print vocabularySize

    def printSortedVocab(self):
            print "Compiling ..."
            print "Sorted Vocabulary ",
            print sorted(set(self.TextCorpus))

    def printCollocation(self):
            print "Compiling Collocations ..."
            self.TextCorpus.collocations()

    def searchWordOccurence(self):
            myWord = raw_input("Enter Search Word : ")
            if myWord:
                        wordCount = self.TextCorpus.count
                        (myWord)
```

```
                                    print myWord+" occured: ",
                                    print wordCount,
                                    print " times"
                        else:
                                    print "Word Entry is Invalid"

        def generateConcordance(self):
                    myWord = raw_input("Enter word to Concord : ")
                    if myWord:
                                self.TextCorpus.concordance
                                (myWord)
                    else:
                                print "Word Entry is Invalid"

        def generateSimiliarities(self):
                    myWord = raw_input("Enter seed word : ")
                    if myWord:
                                self.TextCorpus.similar(myWord)
                    else:
                                print "Word Entry is Invalid"

        def printWordIndex(self):
                    myWord = raw_input("Find first occurrence of
                    what Word? : ")
                    if myWord:
                                wordIndex = self.TextCorpus.index
                                (myWord)
                                print "First Occurrence of: " +
                                myWord + "is at offset: ",
                                print wordIndex
                    else:
                                print "Word Entry is Invalid"

        def printVocabulary(self):
                    print "Compiling Vocabulary Frequencies",
                    vocabFreqList = self.TextCorpus.vocab()
                    print vocabFreqList.items()
```

_NLTKQuery.py

```
#
# NLTK Query Support Methods
# Python-Forensics
#     No HASP required
#

# Function to print the NLTK Query Option Menu
def printMenu():
```

```
        print "==========NLTK Query Options ========="
        print "[1] Print Length of Corpus"
        print "[2] Print Number of Token Found"
        print "[3] Print Vocabulary Size"
        print "[4] Print Sorted Vocabulary"
        print "[5] Print Collocation"
        print "[6] Search for Word Occurrence"
        print "[7] Generate Concordance"
        print "[8] Generate Similarities"
        print "[9] Print Word Index"
        print "[10] Print Vocabulary"
        print
        print "[0] Exit NLTK Experimentation"
        print

    # Function to obtain user input

def getUserSelection ():
    printMenu ()

    try:
        menuSelection = int(input('Enter Selection (0-10) >>'))
    except ValueError:
        print 'Invalid input. Enter a value between 0 -10 .'
        return -1

    if not menuSelection in range(0, 11):
        print 'Invalid input. Enter a value between 0 - 10.'
        return -1

    return menuSelection
```

NLTKQuery example execution

Executing NLTKQuery from the command line for Windows, Linux, or MAC is the same. Simply use the command Python NLTKQuery.py and then follow the onscreen instructions and menu prompts.

NLTK execution trace

Note for brevity some of the output was edited where noted. I also left out the redisplay of the menu options.

```
C:\Users\app\Python NLTKQuery.py
Welcome to the NLTK Query Experimentation
Please wait loading NLTK ...
Input full path name where the intended corpus file or files are stored
Format for Windows e.g. c:\simpson\
Path: c:\simpson\
```

```
Processing Files:
['Trial-January-11.txt', 'Trial-January-12.txt', 'Trial-January-13.txt',
'Trial-January-23.txt', 'Trial-January-24.txt', 'Trial-January-25.txt',
'Trial-January-26.txt', 'Trial
-January-30.txt', 'Trial-January-31.txt']


=========NLTK Query Options =====
[1]     Print Length of Corpus
[2]     Print Number of Token Found
[3]     Print Vocabulary Size
[4]     Print Sorted Vocabulary
[5]     Print Collocation
[6]     Search for Word Occurrence
[7]     Generate Concordance
[8]     Generate Similarities
[9]     Print Word Index
[10]    Print Vocabulary

[0] Exit NLTK Experimentation

Enter Selection (0-10) >> 1
Corpus Text Length: 2008024

Enter Selection (0-10) >> 2
Tokens Found: 401032


Enter Selection (0-10) >> 3
Calculating...
Vocabulary Size: 12604


Enter Selection (0-10) >> 4
Compiling ... Sorted Vocabulary
'ABYSMALLY', 'ACADEMY', 'ACCENT', 'ACCEPT', 'ACCEPTABLE', 'ACCEPTED', 'ACCEPTING',
'ACCESS', 'ACCESSIBLE', 'ACCIDENT', 'ACCIDENT.', 'ACCIDENTAL', 'ACCIDENTALLY',
'ACCOMMODATE',
.
. Edited for brevity
.
'YOUNGER', 'YOUNGSTERS', 'YOUR', 'YOURS.', 'YOURSELF', 'YOURSELF.', 'YOURSELVES',
'YOUTH', 'YUDOWITZ', 'YUDOWITZ.', 'Z', 'ZACK', 'ZACK.',
"ZLOMSOWITCH'S" , 'ZLOMSOWITCH.', 'ZOOM', '''']

Enter Selection (0-10) >> 5
Compiling Collocations...
Building collocations list
*THE COURT; *MS. CLARK; *MR. COCHRAN; MR. SIMPSON; NICOLE BROWN; *MR.
DARDEN; OPENING STATEMENT; LOS ANGELES; MR. COCHRAN; DETECTIVE FUHRMAN;
DISCUSSION HELD; WOULD LIKE; *MR. DOUGLAS; BROWN SIMPSON; THANK YOU. ;
```

MR. DARDEN; DEPUTY DISTRICT; FOLLOWING PROCEEDINGS; DISTRICT
ATTORNEYS.; MISS CLARK

Enter Selection (0-10) >> 6
Enter Search Word: MURDER
MURDER occurred: 125 times

Enter Selection (0-10) >> 7
Enter word to Concord: KILL
Building index...
Displaying 15 of 84 matches:
WAS IN EMINENT DANGER AND NEEDED TO KILL IN SELF-DEFENSE. BUT THE ARIS
COURT
R OCCURRED. " I KNOW HE 'S GOING TO KILL ME. I WISH HE WOULD HURRY UP AND GET
FLICTED HARM WAY BEYOND NECESSARY TO KILL THE VICTIM. AND THIS IS
A QUOTE FROM
'M GOING TO HURT YOU , I 'M GOING TO KILL YOU , I 'M GOING TO BEAT YOU. " THO
HAVE HER AND NO ONE ELSE WILL IS TO KILL HER. THAT IS CLEAR IN THE RESEARCH.
ELLED OUT TO HIM , " HE 'S GOING TO KILL ME. " IT WAS CLEAR TO OFFICER EDWAR
NNING OUT SAYING , " HE 'S GOING TO KILL ME , " THEN THE DEFENDANT ARRIVES I
NS OUT AND SAYS , " HE 'S TRYING TO KILL ME. " SHE 'S LITERALLY IN FLIGHT. S
HER DURING THE BEATING THAT HE WOULD KILL HER , AND THE DEFENDANT CONTINUED TH
TATEMENT OF THE DEFENDANT , " I 'LL KILL YOU , " CONSTITUTES COMPOUND HEARSA
FFICER SCREAMING , " HE 'S GOING TO KILL ME. " I CA N'T IMAGINE A STRONGER C
'' HE 'S GOING CRAZY. HE IS GOING TO KILL ME. " THIS IS VERY SIMILAR TO THE S
NNER THAT SHE BELIEVED THAT HE WOULD KILL HER. NOW , MR. UELMEN HAS TALKED
ABO
OF A DOMESTIC VIOLENCE , A MOTIVE TO KILL , THE FINAL ACT OF CONTROL. THERE IS
CTIM THAT THE DEFENDANT HAD TRIED TO KILL HER PREVIOUSLY WAS USED TO SHOW THAT

Enter Selection (0-10) >> 8
Enter seed word: MURDER
Building word-context index...
court and case evidence defendant time jury crime motion relationship
statement witness issue so that trial blood defense person problem

Enter Selection (0-10) >> 9
Find first occurrence of what Word? : GLOVE
First Occurrence of: GLOVE is at offset: 93811

Enter Selection (0-10) >> 10
Compiling Vocabulary Frequencies Building vocabulary index...
[('THE', 19386), (',', 18677), ('TO', 11634), ('THAT', 10777), ('AND', 8938),
(':', 8369), ('OF', 8198), ('*', 7850), ('IS', 6322), ('I', 6244), ('A', 5590),
('IN', 5456), ('YOU', 4879), ('WE', 4385), ('THIS', 4264), ('IT', 3815), ('COURT',
3763), ('WAS', 3255), ('HAVE', 2816), ('-', 2797), ('?', 2738),

.
. Edited for brevity
.

('WORLDWIDE', 1), ('WORRYING', 1), ('WORSE.', 1), ('WORTHWHILE', 1), ('WOULD-BE', 1), ("WOULDN'T", 1), ('WOUNDS.', 1), ('WRECKED.', 1), ('WRENCHING', 1), ('WRESTLING.', 1), ('WRISTS.', 1), ('WRITERS', 1), ('WRONGLY', 1), ('X-RAYS', 1), ('XANAX', 1), ('XEROXED.', 1), ('XEROXING.', 1), ('YAMAUCHI.', 1), ('YARD.', 1), ('YARDS', 1), ('YEAGEN', 1), ('YELL', 1), ('YELLING.', 1), ('YEP.', 1), ('YIELD', 1), ('YOUNGSTERS', 1), ('YOURS.', 1), ('YUDOWITZ', 1), ('YUDOWITZ.', 1), ('Z', 1), ('ZEIGLER', 1), ('ZERO', 1), ("ZLOMSOWITCH'S", 1)]

Now that you have a working example of NLTK, I suggest that you experiment with the application and start to add new NLTK operations to the classNLTKQuery in order to further explore the possibilities of Natural Language experimentation.

CHAPTER REVIEW

In this chapter, I introduced the concept of NLP in order to expand your thinking beyond simple acquire, format, and display forensic applications. I discussed some of the history of NLP and Alan Turing's intriguing question. I then introduced you to the NLTK that performs much of the heavy lifting and allows us to experiment with NLP in Python almost immediately. I also introduced you to the concept and application of a text-based corpus and used a small sample from the transcripts of the O.J. Simpson Trial to create a small corpus for experimentation. I walked through some of the basic NLTK methods and operations in detail in order to not only create but also query our corpus. Once comfortable with the basics, I created the NLTKQuery application that abstracted the NLTK functions through a menu driven interface. The heart of NLTKQuery is the classNLTKQuery. This class can easily be extended to perform more complex operations and dive deeper into NLTK and I challenge you to do so.

SUMMARY QUESTIONS

1. Expand the NLTKQuery class by adding the following capabilities:
   a. Create a new class method that generates a Frequency Distribution Graph for the Simpson Trial showing how the language in the transcripts shifts throughout the trial. (Hint: Experiment with the dispersion_plot method that can be applied to the self.textCorpus object.)
   b. Create a new method that will generate a list of unusual words. This may be words that are unusually long or are not found in the standards dictionary. (Hint: Download the NLTK Data found at http://nltk.org/data.html and leverage the "word list" corpus to filter out common words.)
   c. Create a new method that can identify names or places. (Hint: Leverage the "names" corpus match names found in the Simpson Corpus.)
2. From your own reference, collect a set of text files and create your own corpus for a domain or genre that will help the forensic field.

Additional Resources

Project Gutenberg. http://www.gutenberg.org/.

Harris MD. Introduction to Natural Language Processing. Reston, VA: A Prentice-Hall Company: Reston Publishing Company, Inc.; 1985.

Turing A. Computing machinery and intelligence. http://www.csee.umbc.edu/courses/471/papers/turing.pdf; October 1950.

Network Forensics: Part I

CHAPTER CONTENTS

NETWORK INVESTIGATION BASICS

Investigating modern network environments can be fraught with difficulties. This is true whether you are responding to a breach, investigating insider activities, performing vulnerability assessments, monitoring network traffic, or validating regulatory compliance.

Many professional tools and technologies exist from major vendors like McAfee, Symantec, IBM, Saint, Tenable, and many others. However, a deep understanding of what they do, how they do it, and whether the investigative value is complete can be somewhat of a mystery. There are also free tools like Wireshark that perform network packet capture and analysis.

In order to uncloak some of the underpinnings of these technologies, I will examine the basics of network investigation methods. I will be leveraging the Python Standard Library, along with a couple of third-party libraries to accomplish the cookbook examples. I will be walking through the examples in considerable detail, so if this is your first interaction with network programming you will have sufficient detail to expand upon the examples.

What are these sockets?

When interacting with a network, *sockets* are the fundamental building block allowing us to leverage the underlying operating system capabilities to interface with the network. Sockets provide an information channel for communicating between network endpoints, for example, between a client and server. You can think about sockets as the endpoint of the connection between a client and a server. Applications developed in languages like Python, Java, C++, and C# interface with network sockets utilizing an application programming interface (API). The sockets API on most systems today is based upon the Berkeley sockets. Berkeley sockets were originally provided with UNIX BSD Version 4.2 back in 1983. Later around 1990, Berkeley released a license-free version that is the basis of today's socket API across most operating systems (Linux, Mac OS, and Windows). This standardization provides consistency in implementation across platforms.

Figure 8.1 depicts a sample network where multiple hosts (endpoints) are connected to a network hub. Each host has a unique Internet Protocol (IP) address, and for this simple network we see that each host has a unique IP address.

These IP addresses are the most common that you will see in local area network setting. These specific addresses are based on the Internet Protocol Version 4 (IPv4) standard and represent a Class C network address. The Class C address is commonly written in a dotted notation such as 192.168.0.1. Breaking the address down into the component parts, the first three octets or the first 24 bits are considered the network address (aka the Network Identifier, or NETID). The fourth and final octet or 8 bits are considered the Local Host Address (aka the Host Identifier, or HOSTID).

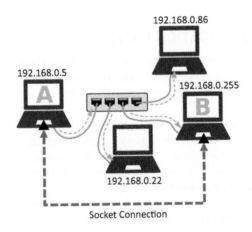

FIGURE 8.1

Simplest local area network.

Network Address   Local Host Address

In this example each host, network device, router, firewall, etc., on the local network would have the same network address portion of the IP address (192.168.0), but each will have a unique host address ranging from 0 to 255. This allows for 256 unique IP addresses within the local environment. Thus the range would be: 192.168.0.0-192.168.0.255. However, only 254 addresses are usable, this is because 192.168.0.0 is the network address and cannot be assigned to a local host, and 192.168.0.255 is dedicated as the broadcast address.

Based on this, I could use a few simple built-in Python language capabilities to create a list of IP addresses that represent the complete range. These language capabilities include a String, a List, the range function, and a "for loop."

```
# Specify the Base Network Address (the first 3 octets)
ipBase = '192.168.0.'

# Next Create an Empty List that will hold the completed
# List of IP Addresses
ipList = []
# Finally, loop through the possible list of local host
# addresses 0-255 using the range function
# Then append each complete address to the ipList
# Notice that I use the str(ip) function in order
# concatenate the string ipBase with list of numbers 0-255

for ip in range(0,256):
    ipList.append(ipBase+str(ip))
    print ipList.pop()
```

Program Output Abbreviated
192.168.0.0
192.168.0.1
192.168.0.2
192.168.0.3
..... skipped items
192.168.0.252
192.168.0.253
192.168.0.254
192.168.0.255

As you can see, manipulating IP addresses with standard Python language elements is straightforward. I will employ this technique in the Ping Sweep section later in this chapter.

127.0.0.1
Port 5555

FIGURE 8.2

Isolated *localhost* loopback.

The simplest network client server connect using sockets

As a way of an introduction to the sockets API provided by Python, I will create a simple network server and client. To do this I will use the same host (in other words the client and server will use the same IP address executing on the same machine), I will specifically use the special purpose and reserved *localhost* loopback IP address 127.0.0.1. This standard loopback IP is the same on virtually all systems and any messages sent to 127.0.0.1 never reach the outside world, and instead are automatically returned to the *localhost*. As you begin to experiment with network programming, use 127.0.0.1 as your IP address of choice until you perfect your code and are ready to operate on a real network (Figure 8.2).

In order to accomplish this, I will actually create two Python programs: (1) server. py and (2) client.py. In order to make this work, the two applications must agree on a port that will be used to support the communication channel. (We already have decided to use the *localhost* loopback IP address 127.0.0.1.) Port numbers range between 0 and 65,535 (basically, any unsigned 16-bit integer value). You should stay away from lower numbered ports <1024 as they are assigned to standard network services (actually the registered ports now range as high as 49,500 but none of those are on my current system). For this application I will use port 5555 as it is easy to remember. Now that I have defined the IP address and port number, I have all the information that I need to make a connection.

IP Address and Port: One way to think about this in more physical terms. Think of the IP Address as the street address of a post office and the Port as the specific post-office box within the post office that I wish to address.

---

server.py code

```
#
# Server Objective
# 1) Setup a Simple listening Socket
# 2) Wait for a connection request
```

```
# 3) Accept a connection on port 5555
# 4) Upon a successful connection send a message to the client
#

import socket          # Standard Library Socket Module

# Create Socket
myServerSocket = socket.socket()

# Get my local host address

localHost = socket.gethostname()

# Specify a local Port to accept connections on

localPort = 5555

# Bind myServerSocket to localHost and the specified Port
# Note the bind call requires one parameter, but that
# parameter is a tuple (notice the parenthesis usage)

myServerSocket.bind((localHost, localPort))

# Begin Listening for connections

myServerSocket.listen(1)

# Wait for a connection request
# Note this is a synchronous Call
# meaning the program will halt until
# a connection is received.
# Once a connection is received
# we will accept the connection and obtain the
# ipAddress of the connector

print 'Python-Forensics .... Waiting for Connection Request'

conn, clientInfo = myServerSocket.accept()

# Print a message to indicate we have received a connection

print 'Connection Received From: ', clientInfo

# Send a message to connector using the connection object 'conn'
# that was returned from the myServerSocket.accept() call
# Include the client IP Address and Port used in the response

conn.send('Connection Confirmed: '+'IP: '+ clientInfo[0] +' Port: '+ str
(clientInfo[1]))
```

client.py code

Next, the client code that will make a connection to the server

```
#
# Client Objective
```

```
# 1) Setup a Client Socket
# 2) Attempt a connection to the server on port 5555
# 3) Wait for a reply
# 4) Print out the message received from the server
#

import socket          # Standard Library Socket Module

MAX_BUFFER = 1024      # Set the maximum size to receive

# Create a Socket

myClientSocket = socket.socket()

# Get my local host address

localHost = socket.gethostname()

# Specify a local Port to attempt a connection

localPort = 5555

# Attempt a connection to my localHost and localPort

myClientSocket.connect((localHost, localPort))

# Wait for a reply
# This is a synchronous call, meaning
# that the program will halt until a response is received
# or the program is terminated

msg = myClientSocket.recv(MAX_BUFFER)
print msg

# Close the Socket, this will terminate the connection

myClientSocket.close()
```

server.py and client.py program execution

Figure 8.3 depicts the program execution. I created two terminal windows, the top is the execution of server.py (which I started first) and the bottom is the execution of client.py. Notice that the client communicated from the source port 59,714, this was chosen by the socket service and not specified in the client code. The server port 5555 in this example is the destination port.

I realize this does not provide any investigative value, however it does provide a good foundational understanding of how network sockets function and this is a prerequisite to understanding some of the probative or investigative programs.

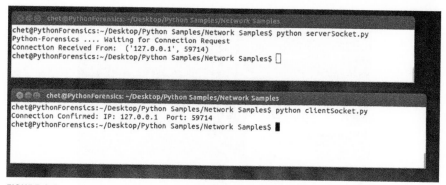

FIGURE 8.3

server.py/client.py program execution.

CAPTAIN RAMIUS: RE-VERIFY OUR RANGE TO TARGET... ONE PING ONLY

You probably remember this famous line from the book and then the movie "The Hunt for Red October" [CLANCY] spoken so eloquently by Sean Connery as the character Marko Ramius. Of course they were using a sonar wave to calculate the distance between the Red October and the USS Dallas (Figure 8.4).

Similar to submarine warfare, one of the key elements to network investigation is the discovery of all the hosts (or more generally referred to as endpoints) on a network. This is accomplished by sending a ping (using an Internet Control Message Protocol, or ICMP for short) to each possible IP address on a network. The IP addresses that respond provide us with two vital pieces of information: (1) if they respond we know they are there and responsive and (2) how long it took for the response to be returned. One special note, many modern firewalls block ICMP messages as these can be used by hackers to perform reconnaissance activities on networks. This is also true of modern operating systems, by default they will not respond to ICMP. However, inside the network they provide a valuable service to locate and detect endpoints on a network.

For this next cookbook example, I will develop a ping sweep application in Python to scan a local network for available IP addresses. I will be using a couple special modules for this section. First I will be using *wxPython* to build a simple graphical user interface (GUI) for the ping sweep application. Second, I will be using a third-party module, Ping.py which is completely written in Python that handles the heavy lifting of the ICMP protocol.

I choose to develop the applications in this chapter within a GUI environment for two reasons—first to give you exposure to a cross platform GUI environment *wxPython*, and second because the execution of ping sweeps by using command line options would be quite tedious and the GUI interface will simplify the interaction.

FIGURE 8.4

Photo of the actual USS Dallas Los Angeles-class nuclear-powered attack submarine.

wxPython

As you have seen throughout this book one of the advantages of Python is the out-of-the-box cross-platform capabilities that it provides. In the spirit of Python, wxPython provides GUI capabilities that are also cross platform (Windows, Linux, and Mac). This library allows us to build fully functional GUI-based applications that integrate directly in the standard Python language and structure. The simple GUI applications in this chapter are only a brief introduction to wxPython, as I am trying to keep the first GUI application as simple and easy to understand as possible. As I move forward I will be utilizing wxPython throughout the remaining chapters in the book.

To obtain more information about wxPython and to install the environment, visit the http://www.wxPython.org/ project page. Third-party libraries like wxPython have multiple versions that can support different versions of Python and different operating systems (i.e., Windows, Mac, and Linux). Make sure that you choose the installation that is compatible with your configuration.

ping.py

The ping.py module is available at http://www.g-loaded.eu/2009/10/30/Python-ping/ and is an open source Python module that handles the details of ICMP operations completely written in Python. Since this is an open source module, I am including the source here for your inspection, and including all the appropriate attributions and revisions.

[PYTHON PING]

```
#!/usr/bin/env Python
"""
    A pure Python ping implementation using raw socket.

    Note that ICMP messages can only be sent from processes running as root.

    Derived from ping.c distributed in Linux's netkit. That code is
    copyright (c) 1989 by The Regents of the University of California.
    That code is in turn derived from code written by Mike Muuss of the
    US Army Ballistic Research Laboratory in December, 1983 and
    placed in the public domain. They have my thanks.

    Bugs are naturally mine. I'd be glad to hear about them. There are
    certainly word-size dependencies here.

    Copyright (c) Matthew Dixon Cowles, <http://www.visi.com/~mdc/>.
    Distributable under the terms of the GNU General Public License
    version 2. Provided with no warranties of any sort.

    Original Version from Matthew Dixon Cowles:
      -> ftp://ftp.visi.com/users/mdc/ping.py

    Rewrite by Jens Diemer:
      -> http://www.Python-forum.de/post-69122.html#69122

    Rewrite by George Notaras:
      -> http://www.g-loaded.eu/2009/10/30/Python-ping/

    Revision history
    ~~~~~~~~~~~~~~~~~~~

    November 8, 2009
    - - - - - - - - - - - - -
    Improved compatibility with GNU/Linux systems.

    Fixes by:
     * George Notaras -- http://www.g-loaded.eu
    Reported by:
     * Chris Hallman -- http://cdhallman.blogspot.com
```

```
    Changes in this release:
    - Re-use time.time() instead of time.clock(). The 2007 implementation
      worked only under Microsoft Windows. Failed on GNU/Linux.
      time.clock() behaves differently under the two OSes[1].

    [1] http://docs.Python.org/library/time.html#time.clock

    May 30, 2007
    - - - - - - - - - -
    little rewrite by Jens Diemer:
    - change socket asterisk import to a normal import
    - replace time.time() with time.clock()
    - delete "return None" (or change to "return" only)
    - in checksum() rename "str" to "source_string"

    November 22, 1997
    - - - - - - - - - - - - -
    Initial hack. Doesn't do much, but rather than try to guess
    what features I (or others) will want in the future, I've only
    put in what I need now.

    December 16, 1997
    - - - - - - - - - - - - - -
    For some reason, the checksum bytes are in the wrong order when
    this is run under Solaris 2.X for SPARC but it works right under
    Linux x86. Since I don't know just what's wrong, I'll swap the
    bytes always and then do an htons().

    December 4, 2000
    - - - - - - - - - - - - -
    Changed the struct.pack() calls to pack the checksum and ID as
    unsigned. My thanks to Jerome Poincheval for the fix.

    Last commit info:
    ~~~~~~~~~~~~~~~~~~~~~
    $LastChangedDate: $
    $Rev: $
    $Author: $
    """


import os, sys, socket, struct, select, time

# From /usr/include/linux/icmp.h; your mileage may vary.
ICMP_ECHO_REQUEST = 8 # Seems to be the same on Solaris.

def checksum(source_string):
    """
```

```python
    I'm not too confident that this is right but testing seems
    to suggest that it gives the same answers as in_cksum in ping.c
    """
    sum = 0
    countTo = (len(source_string)/2)*2
    count = 0
    while count<countTo:
        thisVal = ord(source_string[count + 1])*256 + ord
        (source_string[count])
        sum = sum + thisVal
        sum = sum & 0xffffffff # Necessary?
        count = count + 2

    if countTo<len(source_string):
        sum = sum + ord(source_string[len(source_string) - 1])
        sum = sum & 0xffffffff # Necessary?

    sum = (sum >> 16) + (sum & 0xffff)
    sum = sum + (sum >> 16)
    answer = ~sum
    answer = answer & 0xffff

    # Swap bytes. Bugger me if I know why.
    answer = answer >> 8 | (answer << 8 & 0xff00)

    return answer

def receive_one_ping(my_socket, ID, timeout):
    """
    receive the ping from the socket.
    """
    timeLeft = timeout
    while True:
        startedSelect = time.time()
        whatReady = select.select([my_socket], [], [], timeLeft)
        howLongInSelect = (time.time() - startedSelect)
        if whatReady[0] == []: # Timeout
            return

        timeReceived = time.time()
        recPacket, addr = my_socket.recvfrom(1024)
        icmpHeader = recPacket[20:28]
        type, code, checksum, packetID, sequence = struct.unpack(
            "bbHHh", icmpHeader
        )
        if packetID == ID:
            bytesInDouble = struct.calcsize("d")
```

```
            timeSent = struct.unpack("d", recPacket[28:28 +
            bytesInDouble])[0]
            return timeReceived - timeSent
        timeLeft = timeLeft - howLongInSelect
        if timeLeft <= 0:
            return

def send_one_ping(my_socket, dest_addr, ID):
    """
    Send one ping to the given >dest_addr<.
    """
    dest_addr = socket.gethostbyname(dest_addr)

    # Header is type (8), code (8), checksum (16), id (16), sequence (16)
    my_checksum = 0

    # Make a dummy header with a 0 checksum.
    header = struct.pack("bbHHh", ICMP_ECHO_REQUEST, 0, my_checksum,
    ID, 1)
    bytesInDouble = struct.calcsize("d")
    data = (192 - bytesInDouble) * "Q"
    data = struct.pack("d", time.time()) + data

    # Calculate the checksum on the data and the dummy header.
    my_checksum = checksum(header + data)

    # Now that we have the right checksum, we put that in. It's just easier
    # to make up a new header than to stuff it into the dummy.
    header = struct.pack(
        "bbHHh", ICMP_ECHO_REQUEST, 0, socket.htons(my_checksum), ID, 1
    )
    packet = header + data
    my_socket.sendto(packet, (dest_addr, 1)) # Don't know about the 1

def do_one(dest_addr, timeout):
    """
    Returns either the delay (in seconds) or none on timeout.
    """
    icmp = socket.getprotobyname("icmp")
    try:
        my_socket = socket.socket(socket.AF_INET, socket.SOCK_RAW,
        icmp)
    except socket.error, (errno, msg):
        if errno == 1:
            # Operation not permitted
            msg = msg + (
                " - Note that ICMP messages can only be sent from
                processes"
```

```
                    " running as root."
                )
            raise socket.error(msg)
        raise # raise the original error

    my_ID = os.getpid() & 0xFFFF

    send_one_ping(my_socket, dest_addr, my_ID)
    delay = receive_one_ping(my_socket, my_ID, timeout)

    my_socket.close()
    return delay
def verbose_ping(dest_addr, timeout = 2, count = 4):
    """
    Send >count< ping to >dest_addr< with the given >timeout< and
    display the result.
    """
    for i in xrange(count):
        print "ping %s..." % dest_addr,
        try:
            delay = do_one(dest_addr, timeout)
        except socket.gaierror, e:
            print "failed. (socket error: '%s')" % e[1]
            break

        if delay == None:
            print "failed. (timeout within %ssec.)" % timeout
        else:
            delay = delay * 1000
            print "get ping in %0.4fms" % delay
    print
if __name__ == '__main__':
    verbose_ping("heise.de")
    verbose_ping("google.com")
    verbose_ping("a-test-url-taht-is-not-available.com")
    verbose_ping("192.168.1.1")
```

I have provided detailed documentation in line with the program so you can walk through the program reading the comments for clarity. Figures 8.5 and 8.6 depict the launch and startup GUI of Ping Sweep. Notice in Figure 8.5 that I launched the program from the command line with administrative privilege. This is necessary as administrator privilege is required to perform the ping operations. Before examining the code, take a look at the overall layout of the program. I recommend that you start by examining the "Setup the Application Windows" section a couple pages down in the code. Then, I would move back to the beginning of the code and examine the pingScan event handler starting with "def pingScan(event)":

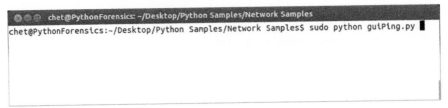

FIGURE 8.5

Command line launch of the guiPing.py as root.

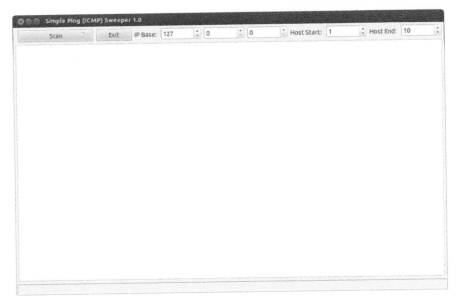

FIGURE 8.6

GUI interface for Ping Sweep.

I chose a simple GUI design with just two buttons, Scan and Exit, along with several spin controls to specify the base IP address and Local Host Range.

guiPing.py code

```
#
# Python Ping Sweep GUI Application
#

import wxversion          # Specify the proper version of wxPython
wxversion.select("2.8")
```

```python
# Import the necessary modules
import wx              # Import the GUI module wx
import sys             # Import the standard library module sys
import ping            # Import the ICMP Ping Module
import socket          # Import the standard library module socket

from time import gmtime, strftime # import time functions

#
# Event Handler for the pingScan Button Press
# This is executed each time the Scan Button is pressed on the GUI
#

def pingScan(event):

    # Since the user specifies a range of Hosts to Scan, I need to verify
    # that the startHost value is <= endHost value before scanning
    # this would indicate a valid range
    # If not I need to communicate the error with the user

    if hostEnd.GetValue() < hostStart.GetValue():

        # This is an improper setting
        # Notify the user using a wx.MessageDialog Box

        dlg = wx.MessageDialog(mainWin,"Invalid Local Host
            Selection","Confirm", wx.OK | wx.ICON_EXCLAMATION)

        result = dlg.ShowModal()
        dlg.Destroy()
        return

    # If we have a valid range update the Status Bar

    mainWin.StatusBar.SetStatusText('Executing Ping Sweep .... Please
Wait'

    # Record the Start Time and Update the results window

    utcStart = gmtime()
    utc = strftime("%a, %d %b %Y %X +0000", utcStart)
    results.AppendText("\n\nPing Sweep Started: "+ utc+ "\n\n")

    # Similar to the example script at the beginning of the chapter
    # I need to build the base IP Address String
    # Extract data from the ip Range and host name user selections
    # Build a Python List of IP Addresses to Sweep
```

```
baseIP = str(ipaRange.GetValue())+'.'+str(ipbRange.GetValue())+'.'
+str(ipcRange.GetValue())+'.'

ipRange = []

for i in range(hostStart.GetValue(), (hostEnd.GetValue()+1)):
    ipRange.append(baseIP+str(i))

# For each of the IP Addresses in the ipRange List, Attempt an PING

for ipAddress in ipRange:

  try:

        # Report the IP Address to the Window Status Bar
        # Prior to the attempt

        mainWin.StatusBar.SetStatusText('Pinging IP: '+ ipAddress)

        # Perform the Ping
        delay = ping.do_one(ipAddress, timeout=2)

        # Display the IP Address in the Main Window
        results.AppendText(ipAddress+'\t')

        if delay != None:
            # If Successful (i.e. no timeout) display
            # the result and response time

            results.AppendText(' Response Success')
            results.AppendText(' Response Time: '+str(delay)+'
            Seconds')
            results.AppendText("\n")
        else :
            # If delay == None, then the request timed out
            # Report the Response Timeout
            results.AppendText(' Response Timeout')
            results.AppendText("\n")

  except socket.error, e:

        # If any socket Errors occur Report the offending IP
        # along with any error information provided by the socket

        results.AppendText(ipAddress)
        results.AppendText(' Response Failed: ')
        results.AppendText(e.message)
```

```python
            results.AppendText("\n")

    # Once all ipAddresses are processed
    # Record and display the ending time of the sweep

    utcEnd = gmtime()
    utc = strftime("%a, %d %b %Y %X +0000", utcEnd)
    results.AppendText("\nPing Sweep Ended: "+ utc + "\n\n")

    # Clear the Status Bar
    mainWin.StatusBar.SetStatusText("")

    return

# End Scan Event Handler ============================


#
# Program Exit Event Handler
# This is executed when the user presses the exit button
# The program is terminated using the sys.exit() method
#

def programExit(event):
    sys.exit()

# End Program Exit Event Handler ==================


#
# Setup the Application Windows ====================
#
# This section of code sets up the GUI environment
#

# Instantiate a wx.App()objet
app = wx.App()

# define the main window including the size and title

mainWin = wx.Frame(None, title="Simple Ping (ICMP) Sweeper 1.0", size
=(1000,600))

# define the action panel, this is the area where the buttons and spinners
# are located

panelAction = wx.Panel(mainWin)
```

```python
# define action buttons
# I'm creating two buttons, one for Scan and one for Exit
# Notice that each button contains the name of the function that will
# handle the button press event -- pingScan and ProgramExit respectively

scanButton = wx.Button(panelAction, label='Scan')
scanButton.Bind(wx.EVT_BUTTON, pingScan)

exitButton = wx.Button(panelAction, label='Exit')
exitButton.Bind(wx.EVT_BUTTON, programExit)

# define a Text Area where I can display results

Results = wx.TextCtrl(panelAction, style = wx.TE_MULTILINE | wx.
HSCROLL)

# Base Network for Class C IP Addresses have 3 components
# For class C addresses, the first 3 octets (24 bits) define the network
# e.g., 127.0.0
# the last octet (8 bits) defines the host i.e., 0-255
# Thus I setup 3 spin controls one for each of the 3 network octets
# I also set the default value to 127.0.0 for convenience

ipaRange = wx.SpinCtrl(panelAction, -1, ")
ipaRange.SetRange(0, 255)
ipaRange.SetValue(127)

ipbRange = wx.SpinCtrl(panelAction, -1, ")
ipbRange.SetRange(0, 255)
ipbRange.SetValue(0)

ipcRange = wx.SpinCtrl(panelAction, -1, ")
ipcRange.SetRange(0, 255)
ipcRange.SetValue(0)

# Also, I'm adding a label for the user

ipLabel = wx.StaticText(panelAction, label="IP Base: ")

# Next, I want to provide the user with the ability to set the host range
# they wish to scan. Range is 0 - 255

hostStart = wx.SpinCtrl(panelAction, -1, ")
hostStart.SetRange(0, 255)
hostStart.SetValue(1)

hostEnd = wx.SpinCtrl(panelAction, -1, ")
```

```
hostEnd.SetRange(0, 255)
hostEnd.SetValue(10)

HostStartLabel    = wx.StaticText(panelAction, label="Host Start: ")
HostEndLabel      = wx.StaticText(panelAction, label="Host End: ")

# Now I create BoxSizer to automatically align the different components
# neatly within the panel
# First, I create a horizontal Box
# I'm adding the buttons, ip Range and Host Spin Controls

actionBox = wx.BoxSizer()
actionBox.Add(scanButton, proportion=1, flag=wx.LEFT, border=5)
actionBox.Add(exitButton, proportion=0, flag=wx.LEFT, border=5)

actionBox.Add(ipLabel, proportion=0, flag=wx.LEFT, border=5)

actionBox.Add(ipaRange, proportion=0, flag=wx.LEFT, border=5)
actionBox.Add(ipbRange, proportion=0, flag=wx.LEFT, border=5)
actionBox.Add(ipcRange, proportion=0, flag=wx.LEFT, border=5)

actionBox.Add(HostStartLabel, proportion=0, flag=wx.LEFT|wx.CENTER,
border=5)
actionBox.Add(hostStart, proportion=0, flag=wx.LEFT, border=5)

actionBox.Add(HostEndLabel, proportion=0, flag=wx.LEFT|wx.CENTER,
border=5)
actionBox.Add(hostEnd, proportion=0, flag=wx.LEFT, border=5)

# Next I create a Vertical Box that I place the Horizontal Box Inside
# Along with the results text area

vertBox = wx.BoxSizer(wx.VERTICAL)
vertBox.Add(actionBox, proportion=0, flag=wx.EXPAND | wx.ALL, border=5)
vertBox.Add(results, proportion=1, flag=wx.EXPAND | wx.LEFT | wx.
BOTTOM | wx.RIGHT, border=5)

# I'm adding a status bar to the main windows to display status messages

mainWin.CreateStatusBar()

# Finally, I use the SetSizer function to automatically size the windows
based on the definitions above

panelAction.SetSizer(vertBox)
```

```
# Display the main window

mainWin.Show()

# Enter the Applications Main Loop
# Awaiting User Actions

app.MainLoop()
```

Ping Sweep execution

Figure 8.7 provides a summary of two executions of the Ping Sweep program. In the first run, the base IP address 127.0.0. is utilized and hosts 1-5 are selected and the results are displayed. In the second run I chose my local network 192.168.0. base address and I scanned hosts 1-7 and the results of each ping is recorded. For both runs when any host responds, the time (or delay) is also reported.

In Figure 8.8, I purposely misconfigured the Host Selection to be invalid (the starting Host is greater than the ending Host number). As expected the dialog box with the error is reported. You can examine the code that displays this dialog box in the *pingScan* event handler.

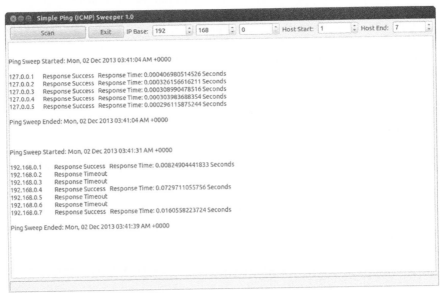

FIGURE 8.7

Ping Sweep execution.

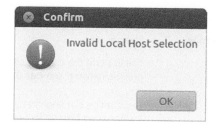

FIGURE 8.8

Error handling for misconfigured host range.

As you can see most of the work is related to setting up the GUI application, and creating the list of IP addresses to scan. Once that is completed, the code that leverages the ping.py module to perform the ping and retrieve the results is only one line of code. Send one and only one ping.

```
# Perform the Ping
delay = ping.do_one(ipAddress, timeout=2)
```

One of the things to keep in mind when performing a Ping Sweep to identify endpoints is to run the scan often as endpoints that are unavailable, are shutdown or have failed may not be available the first time you scan. I will provide you with a challenge problem in the summary questions to improve this application to cover this issue.

PORT SCANNING

Once I have identified endpoints within our network, the next step is to perform a port scan. What exactly is a port scan, or more specifically a TCP/IP port scan? Computers that support communication protocols utilize ports in order to make connections to other parties. In order to support different conversations with multiple parties, ports are used to distinguish various communications. For example, web servers can use the Hypertext Transfer Protocol (HTTP) to provide access to a web page which utilizes TCP port number 80 by default. The Simple Mail Transfer Protocol or SMTP uses port 25 to send or transmit mail messages. For each unique IP address, a protocol port number is identified by a 16-bit number, commonly known as the port number 0-65,535. The combination of a port number and IP address provides a complete address for communication. The parties that are communicating will each have an IP address and port number. Depending on the direction of the communication both a source and destination address (IP address and port combination) are required.

Ports are divided into three basic categories as in Table 8.1.

Table 8.1 Categories of Network Ports

Category	Port Range	Usage
Well-known ports	0-1023	These ports are used by system processes that provide network services that are widely used
Registered ports	1024-49,151	Registration is managed by the Internet Corporation for Assigned Names and Numbers (ICANN). Or, more specifically, by Internet Assigned Numbers Authority (IANA) which is now operated by ICANN. [ICANN]
Dynamic ports	49,152-65,535	The ports are typically ephemeral in nature (or short-lived). The ports are allocated automatically from a predefined range by the operating system as needed. On servers these ports are used to continue communication connections with clients that originally connected to well-known ports such as the File Transfer Protocol or FTP

Examples of well-known ports

Some well-known ports that you may be familiar with are given in Table 8.2 (note that this is just a sample of the list).

Examples of registered ports

A short example of registered ports that you may be familiar with are in Table 8.3 (Note that this is just a sample of the list.)

To develop the simplest Port Scanner in Python, I need to know just a few things:

(1) What IP address to target?
(2) What port range should I scan?
(3) Whether I should display all the results or should I only display the ports that were found to be open. In other words ports that I could successfully connect to.

Figure 8.9 depicts the GUI for our simple Port Scanner. The GUI allows the user to specify the IP address to scan along with the port range. The GUI also includes a checkbox that allows the user to specify whether all the results or only the successful results are displayed.

I have provided detailed documentation in line with the program so you can walk through the program reading the comments for clarity. Figure 8.10 depicts the launch of the startup Port Scanner GUI. As you can see in Figure 8.10, I launched the program from the command line with administrative privilege. This is necessary as administrator privilege is required to perform the port scan network operations.

Table 8.2 Examples of Well-known Ports

Service Name	Port Number	Transport Protocol	Description
echo	7	tcp	Echo
echo	7	udp	Echo
ftp	21	tcp	File Transfer [Control]
ftp	21	udp	File Transfer [Control]
ssh	22	tcp	The Secure Shell (SSH) Protocol
ssh	22	udp	The Secure Shell (SSH) Protocol
telnet	23	tcp	Telnet
telnet	23	udp	Telnet
smtp	25	tcp	Simple Mail Transfer
smtp	25	udp	Simple Mail Transfer
nameserver	42	tcp	Host Name Server
nameserver	42	udp	Host Name Server
http	80	tcp	World Wide Web HTTP
http	80	udp	World Wide Web HTTP
nntp	119	tcp	Network News Transfer Protocol
nntp	119	udp	Network News Transfer Protocol
ntp	123	tcp	Network Time Protocol
ntp	123	udp	Network Time Protocol
netbios-ns	137	tcp	NETBIOS Name Service
netbios-ns	137	udp	NETBIOS Name Service
snmp	161	tcp	SNMP
snmp	161	udp	SNMP

Table 8.3 Examples of Registered Ports

Service Name	Port Number	Transport Protocol	Description
nlogin	758	tcp	nlogin service
nlogin	758	udp	nlogin service
telnets	992	tcp	telnet protocol over TLS/SSL
telnets	992	udp	telnet protocol over TLS/SSL
pop3s	995	tcp	pop3 protocol over TLS/SSL (was spop3)
pop3s	995	udp	pop3 protocol over TLS/SSL (was spop3)

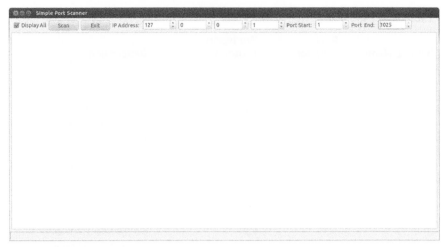

FIGURE 8.9

Port Scanner GUI.

```
chet@PythonForensics: ~/Desktop/Python Samples/Network Samples
chet@PythonForensics:~/Desktop/Python Samples/Network Samples$ sudo python portScanner.py
[sudo] password for chet:
```

FIGURE 8.10

Port Scanner program launch.

Before diving into the code take a look at the overall layout of the program. I recommend that you start by examining the "Setup the Application Windows" section a couple pages down in the code. Then, I would move back to the beginning of the code and examine the portScan event handler starting with "def portScan(event)":

As you can see most of the work is related to setting up the GUI application and setting up the list of host ports to scan. Once that is done, the code that actually scans each port and checks the result is only a few lines as shown here.

```
# open a socket
reqSocket = socket(AF_INET, SOCK_STREAM)

# Try Connecting to the specified IP, Port

response = reqSocket.connect_ex((baseIP, port))
```

```
#
# Python Port Scanner
#

import wxversion
wxversion.select("2.8")

import wx              # Import the GUI module wx
import sys             # Import the standard library module sys
import ping            # Import the ICMP Ping Module
from socket import *   # Import the standard library module socket

from time import gmtime, strftime # import time functions

#
# Event Handler for the portScan Button Press
#

def portScan(event):

    # First, I need to check that the starting port is <= ending port value

    if portEnd.GetValue() < portStart.GetValue():

        # This is an improper setting
        # Notify the user and return

        dlg = wx.MessageDialog(mainWin,"Invalid Host Port Selection",
        "Confirm", wx.OK | wx.ICON_EXCLAMATION)

        result = dlg.ShowModal()
        dlg.Destroy()
        return

    # Update the Status Bar

    mainWin.StatusBar.SetStatusText('Executing Port Scan .... Please
    Wait')

    # Record the Start Time

    utcStart = gmtime()
    utc = strftime("%a, %d %b %Y %X +0000", utcStart)
    results.AppendText("\n\nPort Scan Started: "+ utc+ "\n\n")

    # Build the base IP Address String
    # Extract data from the ip Range and host name user selections
    # Build a Python List of IP Addresses to Sweep
```

```
baseIP = str(ipaRange.GetValue())+
        '.'+str(ipbRange.GetValue())+
        '.'+str(ipcRange.GetValue())+
        '.'+str(ipdRange.GetValue())

# For the IP Addresses Specified, Scan the Ports Specified

for port in range(portStart.GetValue(), portEnd.GetValue()+1):

    try:

        # Report the IP Address to the Window Status Bar
        mainWin.StatusBar.SetStatusText('Scanning: '+ baseIP+'
        Port: '+str(port))

        # open a socket
        reqSocket = socket(AF_INET, SOCK_STREAM)

        # Try Connecting to the specified IP, Port

        response = reqSocket.connect_ex((baseIP, port))

        # if we receive a proper response from the port
        # then display the results received

        if(response == 0) :
            # Display the ipAddress and Port
            results.AppendText(baseIP+'\t'+str(port)+'\t')
            results.AppendText('Open')
            results.AppendText("\n")
        else:

            # if the result failed, only display the result
            # when the user has selected the "Display All" check box
            if displayAll.GetValue() == True:
                results.AppendText(baseIP+'\t'+str(port)+'\t')
                results.AppendText('Closed')
                results.AppendText("\n")

        # Close the socket
        reqSocket.close()

    except socket.error, e:
        # for socket Errors Report the offending IP
        results.AppendText(baseIP+'\t'+str(port)+'\t')
        results.AppendText('Failed: ')
        results.AppendText(e.message)
        results.AppendText("\n")
```

```
# Record and display the ending time of the sweep
utcEnd = gmtime()
utc = strftime("%a, %d %b %Y %X +0000", utcEnd)
results.AppendText("\nPort Scan Ended: "+ utc + "\n\n)"

# Clear the Status Bar
mainWin.StatusBar.SetStatusText('')
```

```
# End Scan Event Handler ============================
```

```
#
# Program Exit Event Handler
#

def programExit(event):
    sys.exit()
```

```
# End Program Exit Event Handler ==================
```

```
#
# Setup the Application Windows ==================
#

app = wx.App()
```

```
# define window
mainWin = wx.Frame(None, title="Simple Port Scanner", size
=(1200,600))
```

```
#define the action panel

panelAction = wx.Panel(mainWin)
```

```
#define action buttons
# I'm creating two buttons, one for Scan and one for Exit
# Notice that each button contains the name of the function that will
# handle the button press event. Port Scan and ProgramExit respectively

displayAll = wx.CheckBox(panelAction, -1, 'Display All', (10, 10))
displayAll.SetValue(True)
```

```
scanButton = wx.Button(panelAction, label='Scan')
scanButton.Bind(wx.EVT_BUTTON, portScan)
```

```
exitButton = wx.Button(panelAction, label='Exit')
exitButton.Bind(wx.EVT_BUTTON, programExit)
```

```
# define a Text Area where I can display results

results = wx.TextCtrl(panelAction, style = wx.TE_MULTILINE | wx.
HSCROLL)

# Base Network for Class C IP Addresses has 3 components
# For class C addresses, the first 3 octets define the network i.e 127.0.0
# the last 8 bits define the host i.e. 0-255

# Thus I setup 3 spin controls one for each of the 4 network octets
# I also, set the default value to 127.0.0.0 for convenience

ipaRange = wx.SpinCtrl(panelAction, -1, ")
ipaRange.SetRange(0, 255)
ipaRange.SetValue(127)

ipbRange = wx.SpinCtrl(panelAction, -1, ")
ipbRange.SetRange(0, 255)
ipbRange.SetValue(0)

ipcRange = wx.SpinCtrl(panelAction, -1, ")
ipcRange.SetRange(0, 255)
ipcRange.SetValue(0)

ipdRange = wx.SpinCtrl(panelAction, -1, ")
ipdRange.SetRange(0, 255)
ipdRange.SetValue(1)

# Add a label for clarity

ipLabel = wx.StaticText(panelAction, label="IP Address: ")

# Next, I want to provide the user with the ability to set the port range
# they wish to scan. Maximum is 20 - 1025

portStart = wx.SpinCtrl(panelAction, -1, ")
portStart.SetRange(1, 1025)
portStart.SetValue(1)

portEnd = wx.SpinCtrl(panelAction, -1, ")
portEnd.SetRange(1, 1025)
portEnd.SetValue(5)

PortStartLabel = wx.StaticText(panelAction, label="Port Start: ")
PortEndLabel = wx.StaticText(panelAction, label="Port End: ")

# Now I create BoxSizer to automatically align the different components
neatly
```

```
# First, I create a horizontal Box
# I'm adding the buttons, ip Range and Host Spin Controls

actionBox = wx.BoxSizer()

actionBox.Add(displayAll, proportion=0, flag=wx.LEFT|wx.CENTER,
border=5)
actionBox.Add(scanButton, proportion=0, flag=wx.LEFT, border=5)
actionBox.Add(exitButton, proportion=0, flag=wx.LEFT, border=5)

actionBox.Add(ipLabel, proportion=0, flag=wx.LEFT|wx.CENTER,
border=5)

actionBox.Add(ipaRange, proportion=0, flag=wx.LEFT, border=5)
actionBox.Add(ipbRange, proportion=0, flag=wx.LEFT, border=5)
actionBox.Add(ipcRange, proportion=0, flag=wx.LEFT, border=5)
actionBox.Add(ipdRange, proportion=0, flag=wx.LEFT, border=5)

actionBox.Add(PortStartLabel, proportion=0, flag=wx.LEFT|wx.CENTER,
border=5)
actionBox.Add(portStart, proportion=0, flag=wx.LEFT, border=5)

actionBox.Add(PortEndLabel, proportion=0, flag=wx.LEFT|wx.CENTER,
border=5)
actionBox.Add(portEnd, proportion=0, flag=wx.LEFT, border=5)

# Next I create a Vertical Box that I place the Horizontal Box components
# inside along with the results text area

vertBox = wx.BoxSizer(wx.VERTICAL)
vertBox.Add(actionBox, proportion=0, flag=wx.EXPAND | wx.ALL, border=5)
vertBox.Add(results, proportion=1, flag=wx.EXPAND | wx.LEFT | wx.
BOTTOM | wx.RIGHT, border=5)

# I'm adding a menu and status bar to the main window

mainWin.CreateStatusBar()

# Finally, I use the SetSizer function to automatically size the windows
# based on the definitions above

panelAction.SetSizer(vertBox)

# Display the main window

mainWin.Show()
```

```
# Enter the Applications Main Loop
# Awaiting User Actions

app.MainLoop
```

Now that you have reviewed the code, Figures 8.11 and 8.12 depict program execution. The only difference between the two figures is the setting of the Display All checkbox.

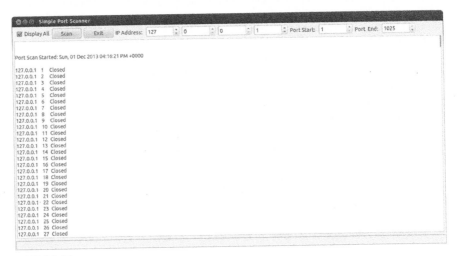

FIGURE 8.11

Port Scanner execution with Display All selected.

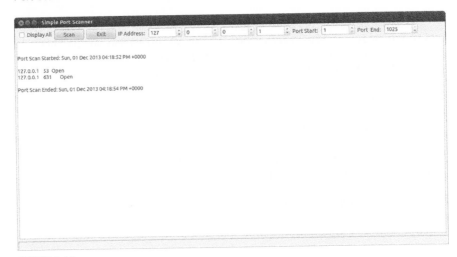

FIGURE 8.12

Port Scanner execution with Display NOT selected.

CHAPTER REVIEW

In this chapter, I first introduced the concept of digital investigation of a network. Then I walked through the fundamentals required to perform basic synchronous network socket operations within Python. I created three programs: (1) Server and (2) Client in order to demonstrate how connections are made. Next, I discussed the concept of a ping sweep and the value it can bring to network-based investigations. I then created a basic ping sweeper application. This application employed two third-party modules: wxPython and ping.py. wxPython was used to create a simple GUI application to control ping sweep operations. Finally, I developed a port scanning application again using a GUI, and created the application entirely in Python.

In Chapter 9 "Network Investigation Part II," I will expand the Port Scan application to provide examples of OS fingerprinting and provide an example of passive monitoring to identify host and port usage.

SUMMARY QUESTIONS

1. What are the investigative benefits that can be obtained when performing a ping sweep?
2. What are the investigative benefits that can be obtained when performing a port scan?
3. Modify the ping sweep application to save the results of the sweep in a Python list.
4. Modify the ping sweep application and add additional scanning options. For example:
   a. Program the scan to automatically and repeatedly run at predefined intervals to identify a broader range of endpoints. Keep track of the IPs identified in the list (or you might choose a set for this operation, why would a Python set be beneficial?).
   b. Create a stealth mode that randomly pings the hosts within the specified address range over a multiday time period.
5. Modify the port scan application to expand the range of allowed ports.
6. Integrate the port scan and ping sweep applications in such a way that port scans will be executed automatically against hosts responding to a ping and ignore nonresponding hosts.

Additional Resources

Internet Corporation for Assigned Numbers and Names, http://www.icann.org/.
The Hunt for Red October, http://www.tomclancy.com/book_display.php?isbn13= 9780425240335.
Python Ping Module, https://pypi.Python.org/pypi/ping.
wxPython GUI environment, www.wxPython.org.

Network Forensics: Part II

9

CHAPTER CONTENTS

INTRODUCTION

As we discovered in Chapter 8, Python has a rich set of Standard Library capabilities to perform network interface, discovery, and analysis. The Ping Sweep and Port Scan applications are quite straightforward once you become familiar with the underlying libraries and modules. However, interactive scanning and probing has several important limitations:

1. In order for the sweeps and scans to be effective, the targets (hosts, routers, switches printers, servers) need to be powered on and functional in order to interact with them.
2. The environment that you are working in must be tolerant to these types of "noisy" scanning activity. Actually, most intrusion prevention systems (IPS) are precisely looking for this type of activity and will categorize them as attacks and respond accordingly, unless they are configured to ignore them. This is more difficult to accomplish than you might think, and most cyber-security folks are not inclined to make configuration changes to their IPS.
3. Port scans are only effective when services owning these ports respond to the probes, as we would expect. Malicious services that we may be searching for do not necessarily play nice and would not respond to these novice inquiries.
4. Many of the malicious services utilize the User Datagram Protocol (UDP) when communicating with their handlers and can operate silently when being probed by vulnerability assessment technologies.
5. Finally, the operators of critical infrastructure environments are unlikely to allow active scanning and probing of those networks, because in many cases the probing activity may disrupt operations and crash systems. If this were to happen in a supervisory control and data acquisition environment, these disruptions or system crashes could shut the lights off for thousands of customers or worse.

PACKET SNIFFING

Network (or packet) sniffing is another method that can be used, and when used properly can provide insight. Network sniffing, again if done well, can provide three critical benefits over port scanning:

1. The sniffer is completely silent and will not place a single packet on the network ensuring zero impact on network operations.
2. The sniffer is an observer that can run for hours, days, weeks, months, or even continuously collecting information that will more completely describe activities of local hosts, servers, network devices, or even rogue devices that were previously undetected.
3. Finally, it can capture activities that are stealthy and only occur periodically or sporadically.

In the primitive form, a packet sniffer (also referred to a network sniffer) captures all of the packets of data that pass through a given network interface. In order to capture these packets, your network interface must be in *Promiscuous Mode* and the interface needs to be connected to a port that has visibility to all of the packets. For example, if you are interested in a specific subnet, you would connect the sniffer to a switch or hub on that subnet. Most modern switches today support port mirroring via a Switched Port ANalyzer (SPAN) or Remote Switched Port ANalyzer as shown in Figures 9.1 and 9.2. These ports are typically connected to IPS, network monitoring devices or performance measurement devices that can detect network loading.

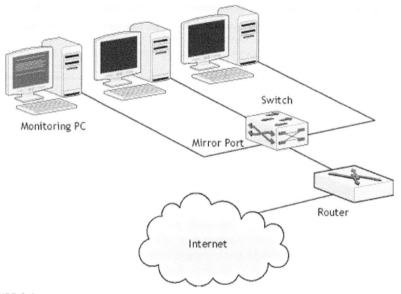

FIGURE 9.1

SPAN port diagram.

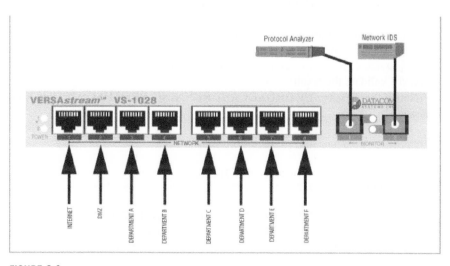

FIGURE 9.2

SPAN port connections.

SPAN ports are most commonly attributed to Cisco (where they were originally referred to as port mirroring). Modern switches can be configured to mirror specific network ports to a common interface used for network monitoring and interface with a variety of security appliances.

RAW SOCKETS IN PYTHON

In order to perform packet sniffing in Python, we need the following:

1. We must be using a network interface card (NIC) that has the ability to operate in Promiscuous Mode.
2. On most modern operating systems—i.e., Windows, Linux, and Mac OS X—you must also have administrator privilege.
3. Once we have accomplished $1 + 2$, we can create a raw socket.

What is Promiscuous Mode or Monitor Mode?

When a capable NIC is placed in Promiscuous Mode, it allows the NIC to intercept and read each arriving network packet in its entirety. If the NIC is not in Promiscuous Mode, it will only receive packets that are specifically addressed to the NIC. Promiscuous Mode must be supported by the NIC and by the operating system and any associated driver. Not all NICs support Promiscuous Mode, however it is pretty easy to determine if you have a NIC and OS capable of Promiscuous Mode.

Setting Promiscuous Mode Ubuntu 12.04 LTS Example

On Linux you can place your NIC into Promiscuous Mode by using *ifconfig* command. (Note administrative rights are required.)

Command to enable Promiscuous Mode:

```
chet@PythonForensics:~$ sudo ifconfig eth0 promisc
```

Next I validate the result:

(Notice the message UP BROADCAST RUNNING **PROMISC** MULTICAST message.)

```
chet@PythonForensics:~$ sudo ifconfig

eth0 Link encap:Ethernet HWaddr 00:1e:8c:b7:6d:64
inet addr:192.168.0.25 Bcast:192.168.0.255 Mask:255.255.255.0
        inet6 addr: fe80::21e:8cff:feb7:6d64/64 Scope:Link
        UP BROADCAST RUNNING PROMISC MULTICAST MTU:1500 Metric:1
        RX packets:43284 errors:0 dropped:0 overruns:0 frame:0
        TX packets:11338 errors:0 dropped:0 overruns:0 carrier:0
        collisions:0 txqueuelen:1000
        RX bytes:17659022 (17.6 MB) TX bytes:1824060 (1.8 MB)
```

Next I have turned off Promiscuous Mode and validate the result: You notice that the message now states: UP BROADCAST RUNNING MULTICAST without the PROMISC

```
chet@PythonForensics:~$ sudo ifconfig eth0 -promisc

chet@PythonForensics:~$ sudo ifconfig eth0

eth0 Link encap:Ethernet HWaddr 00:1e:8c:b7:6d:64

inet addr:192.168.0.25 Bcast:192.168.0.255 Mask:255.255.255.0
          inet6 addr: fe80::21e:8cff:feb7:6d64/64 Scope:Link
          UP BROADCAST RUNNING MULTICAST MTU:1500 Metric:1
          RX packets:43381 errors:0 dropped:0 overruns:0 frame:0
          TX packets:11350 errors:0 dropped:0 overruns:0 carrier:0
          collisions:0 txqueuelen:1000
          RX bytes:17668285 (17.6 MB) TX bytes:1827000 (1.8 MB)
```

Once you have determined that you have a NIC capable of entering Promiscuous Mode, we are ready to work with raw sockets in Python.

Raw sockets in Python under Linux

Special Note: I will be using a Linux environment throughout the rest of this chapter. Since the code for handling raw sockets differs between operating systems, the code that interfaces with the raw socket will need to be modified to support Windows.

Creating a raw socket is quite straightforward in Python, as the script below demonstrates. The script accomplishes the following:

(1) Enable Promiscuous Mode on the NIC
(2) Create a raw socket
(3) Capture the next *TCP packet* passing by the NIC
(4) Print the contents of the packet
(5) Disable Promiscuous Mode on the NIC
(6) Close the raw socket

```
# Note: Script must be run with admin privledge

# import the socket and os libraries
import socket
import os

# issue the command to place the adapter in promiscious mode
ret = os.system("ifconfig eth0 promisc)"

# if the command was successful continue
```

```
if ret == 0:

    # Create a Raw Socket in Linux
    # AF_INET specifies ipv4 packets
    # SOCK_RAW specifies a raw protocol at the network layer
    # IPPROTO_TCP specifies the protocol to capture

    mySocket = socket.socket(socket.AF_INET, socket.SOCK_RAW,
    socket.IPPROTO_TCP)

    # Receive the next packet up to 255 bytes
    # Note this is a synchronous call and will wait until
    # a packet is received

    recvBuffer, addr = mySocket.recvfrom(255)

    # Print out the contents of the buffer

    print recvBuffer
    ret = os.system("ifconfig eth0 -promisc)"

else:
    # if the system command fails print out a message
    print 'Promiscious Mode not Set'
```

The script will create output as shown in Figure 9.3. As you can see the output of the packet contents appears quite cryptic.

Unpacking buffers

Extracting information from a buffer like this one may seem quite tedious, as we must parse the pertinent information from the buffer. In order to deal with buffered data like this one with a defined structured, Python provides the function unpack (). Many examples and applications of unpack are available on the web that parse various well-known data structures, however the explanation of how the functions work are typically left to the reader's imagination, or at least requires further research.

For illustration, you will find examples on the web like this one to extract information from an IPv4 header.

```
ipHeader = packet[0:20]
buffer = unpack('!BBHHHBBH4 s4 s', ipHeader)
```

E\000\0004   ÿ ̈e\000 ̈ ACK 2Å \000\000 SOH \000\000 SOH ACK SÇP CSI 2Ènμ RI ̧ PAD DLE SOH \000 ̵þ(\000\000 SOH SOH BS
\000[&δ\000[&é

FIGURE 9.3

Raw TCP/IP packet contents.

As with all chapters in this book, I want to make sure that you deeply understand how functions work, so that you can apply them to the challenge at hand, as well as to other problems in the future. The `unpack()` function takes two parameters, the first is a string that defines the format of the data held in the buffer and second is the buffer that needs to be parsed. The function returns a tuple which can be processed just like a `list`.

In order to figure this out, we must first study the structure of an IPv4 packet header as shown in Figure 9.4 and compare that with the format string "`!BBHHHBBH4 s4 s.`"

Each of the characters of the format string have a specific meaning which governs the processing of the `unpack()` function. If you get the format string wrong, then you will get garbage back, or if the buffer you pass as the second variable does not conform to the exact format you specify, the results will be incorrect.

Let us examine the meaning of each of the characters in the format string "`!BBHHHBBH4 s4 s.`" Note: other format specifications exist and are documented within the Standard Library documentation [UNPACK]:

Format	Python Type	Bytes
!	Big Endian	
B	Integer	1
H	Integer	2
s	String	n

IPv4 Header Format

Offsets	Bytes	0										1								2								3			
Octet	Bit	0	1	2	3	4	5	6	7	8	9	10	11	12	13	14	15	16	17	18	19	20	21	22	23	24	25	26	27	28	29	30	31
0	0	Version				IHL				DSCP						ECN		Total Length															
4	32	Identification																Flags			Fragment Offset												
8	64	Time To Live								Protocol								Header Checksum															
12	96	Source IP Address																															
16	128	Destination IP Address																															
20	160	Options (if IHL > 5)																															

FIGURE 9.4

Typical IPv4 packet header.

The first character in the format string represents the byte order of the data, for network packets this is in big endian format. This is represented as the exclamation point that is the first character in the format specification. You could also use the ">" greater than sign which also means big endian, but the explanation point is there for those of us who can never remember the typical byte order of network data. Actually, it is good to use the exclamation point because this immediately identifies the format string as relating to a network packet.

The table below provides a mapping of each of the format characters related to the IPv4 header.

```
"!BBHHHBBH4 s4 s"
```

Format	Size (Bytes)	Mapping to IPv4	Definition
B	1	Version and IHL	4-bit version field (this will be 4, for IPv4) 4-bit Internet Header Length representing the number of 32 bit words contained in the header
B	1	DSCP and ECN	7-bit Differentiated Services Code Point 1-bit Congestion Notification
H	2	Total length	16 bits defines the entire packet size
H	2	Identification	16 bits identifier for a group of IP fragments
H	2	Flags and fragment offset	3-bit fragmentation flag 13-bit fragment offset value
B	1	Time to live (TTL)	8-bit TTL value to prevent packet looping
B	1	Protocol	8-bit value identifying the protocol used in the data portion of the packet
H	2	Header Checksum value	16-bit checksum value for error detection
4 s	4	Source IP address	4-byte source IP address
4 s	4	Destination IP address	4-byte destination IP address

Now that you understand the meaning of the format string and the basic unpack() function. The following code will unpack an IPv4 header and then extract each of the fields into variables for processing. I also included the code here to convert the source and destination IP addresses into the human readable forms using the built-in socket method.

```
# unpack an IPv4 packet

# note the packet variable is a buffer returned from
```

```
# a socket.recvfrom() method that was illustrated in Figure 9.3.

ipHeaderTuple = unpack('!BBHHHBBH4s4s', packet)

# Field Contents

verLen       = ipHeaderTuple[0]    # Field 0: Version and Length
dscpECN      = ipHeaderTuple[1]    # Field 1: DSCP and ECN
packetLength = ipHeaderTuple[2]    # Field 2: Packet Length
packetID     = ipHeaderTuple[3]    # Field 3: Identification
flagFrag     = ipHeaderTuple[4]    # Field 4: Flags/Frag Offset
timeToLive   = ipHeaderTuple[5]    # Field 5: Time to Live (TTL)
protocol     = ipHeaderTuple[6]    # Field 6: Protocol Number
checkSum     = ipHeaderTuple[7]    # Field 7: Header Checksum
sourceIP     = ipHeaderTuple[8]    # Field 8: Source IP
destIP       = ipHeaderTuple[9]    # Field 9: Destination IP

# Convert the sourceIP and destIP into a
# standard dotted-quad string representation
# for example '192.168.0.5'

sourceAddress = socket.inet_ntoa(sourceIP);
destAddress   = socket.inet_ntoa(destIP);

# Extract the version and header size, this will give
# us the offset to the data portion of the packet

version     = verLen >> 4 # get upper nibble version
length      = verLen & 0x0F # get lower nibble header length
ipHdrLength = length * 4 # calculate the hdr size in bytes
fragOffset  = flagFrag & 0x1FFF # get lower 13 bits...
fragment    = fragOffset * 8 # calculate start of fragment
```

Next, we would use the same process to extract fields from the data portion of the packet, which in this case is the TCP header. You can determine the type of the data portion of the packet by examining the *protocol* field. Figure 9.5 depicts a typical TCP header and the format string "!HHLLBBHHH" along with the unpack() function, this can be used to extract the individual fields of the TCP header.

```
# By using the results of the IPv4 header unpacking, we can
# strip the TCP Header from the original packet

# Note the ipHdrLength is the offset from the beginning of
# the buffer. The standard length of a TCP packet is 20
# bytes. For our purposes these 20 bytes contain the
# the pertinent information we are looking for

stripTCPHeader = packet[ipHdrLength:ipHdrLength+20]
```

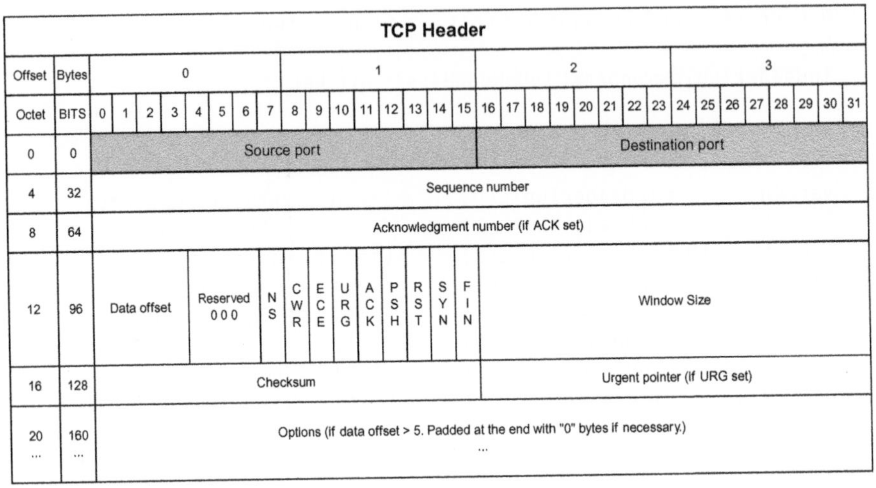

			TCP Header			

FIGURE 9.5

Typical TCP packet header.

```
# unpack returns a tuple, for illustration I will extract
# each individual values using the unpack() function

tcpHeaderBuffer = unpack('!HHLLBBHHH', stripTCPHeader)

sourcePort                = tcpHeaderBuffer[0]
destinationPort           = tcpHeaderBuffer[1]
sequenceNumber            = tcpHeaderBuffer[2]
acknowledgement           = tcpHeaderBuffer[3]
dataOffsetandReserve      = tcpHeaderBuffer[4]
tcpHeaderLength           = (dataOffsetandReserve >> 4) * 4
flags                     = tcpHeaderBuffer[5]
FIN                       = flags & 0x01
SYN                       = (flags >> 1) & 0x01
RST                       = (flags >> 2) & 0x01
PSH                       = (flags >> 3) & 0x01
ACK                       = (flags >> 4) & 0x01
URG                       = (flags >> 5) & 0x01
ECE                       = (flags >> 6) & 0x01
CWR                       = (flags >> 7) & 0x01
windowSize                = tcpHeaderBuffer[6]
tcpChecksum               = tcpHeaderBuffer[7]
urgentPointer             = tcpHeaderBuffer[8]
```

Now that we have the basics under our belt, let us look at:

1. How to place our NIC into Promiscuous Mode
2. How to create a raw socket in Linux
3. How to unpack the packet to obtain the individual fields

We are ready to build an application that can capture network packets and extract the information that will allow us to monitor traffic.

PYTHON SILENT NETWORK MAPPING TOOL (PSNMT)

Now that we have the basics for sniffing a network packet, I need to parse the data and extract the information I need. For this example, I am not interested in collecting packets and simply printing the results, rather I want to achieve the following objectives:

(1) Collect IP addresses that are active on the network I am monitoring. (I plan to leave the monitor in place for a long period of time to capture network devices that only turn on periodically or sporadically.)
(2) Collect IP addresses of remote computers that are interacting with my local network. These could be web, mail, or a plethora of Cloud services.
(3) Collect service ports being used by local and/or remote computers. Specifically, I am interested in "Well Defined Ports": 0-1023 or "Registered Ports": 1024-49151.
(4) Next I wish to report only unique entries. In other words, if the local host 192.168.0.5 is discovered and is found to be using host port 80, I only want to see that unique entry once, not each time it is discovered.
(5) Finally, to limit the scope of the program, I want to collect only TCP or UDP packets within an IPv4 environment. The program can be easily expanded to handle other protocols and IPv6 in the future.

In order to meet the requirements stated above I only need to extract the following fields from the headers:

(1) Protocol
(2) Source IP address
(3) Destination IP address
(4) Source port
(5) Destination port

Examining Figures 9.4 and 9.5, the Protocol field, along with the Source and Destination IP addresses exist in the IPv4 header, while the Source and Destination ports are in the TCP header. This means I will have to parse out both headers to obtain the needed information. I have also included Figure 9.6 which depicts the UDP header, which I also use to handle UDP packet extraction.

There are several technical issues that need to be addressed along with the high level requirements:

(1) What type of data element should I use to store the information collected?
    a. I am going to use a simple list to hold the data collected from the packets and append data to the lists for each packet received.

```
ipObservations=[]
```

		UDP Header																																	
Offsets	Bytes				0							1								2							3										
Octet	BITS	0	1	2	3	4	5	6	7	8	9	10	11	12	13	14	15	16	17	18	19	20	21	22	23	24	25	26	27	28	29	30	31
0	0	Source port															Destination port															
4	32	Length															Checksum															

FIGURE 9.6

Typical UDP packet header.

(2) Since the `socket.recvfrom()` method is synchronous, how will I signal when to stop collection, and how will I limit the time of the collection activities?

  a. I am going to use the Python Standard Library *signal* module and integrate this into the collection loop. I set this up by first creating a class myTimeout that will be raised by a handler when a specified time has expired. I then integrate the myTimeout exception handler into the try/except handler of the receive packet loop.

```
class myTimeout(Exception):
    pass

def handler(signum, frame):
    print 'timeout received', signum
    raise myTimeout()

# Set the signal handler
signal.signal(signal.SIGALRM, handler)

# set the signal to expire in n seconds
signal.alarm(n)
...
...
try:

    while True:
        recvBuffer, addr=mySocket.recvfrom(65535)

        src,dst=decoder.PacketExtractor(recvBuffer,\ False)
        sourceIPObservations.append(src)
        destinationIPObservations.append(dst)

except myTimeout:
    pass
```

(3) How will I create only unique entries?

    a. The code above will record every pair of source IP/Port and destination IP/Port, with a result being an unsorted list and will contain duplicate entries. To solve this problem, once the collection is complete, I will use a little knowledge of Python data types to help here. Once collection is completed (for the entire time frame), I first convert the `list` into a `set`, this will immediately collapse any duplicates (as this is a fundamental property of sets). Then I will convert the set back to a list and then sort the list.

```
uniqueSrc = set(map(tuple, ipObservations))
finalList =  list(uniqueSrc)
finalList.sort()
```

(4) How should I output the results?

    a. In order to provide a workable list, the program will generate a comma-separated value (CSV) file that can then be further processed or examined in a worksheet.

PSNMT SOURCE CODE

The source code is broken into the following five source files. Each of the files contains detailed comments describing all aspects of the program. Figure 9.7 depicts the WingIDE environment for this application.

Source	Purpose
psnmt.py	Main program setup and loop
decoder.py	Decoder for raw packets
_commandparser.py	Parser for the user command line
_csvHandler.py	Handler for creating/writing csv file output
_classLogging.py	Class for handling forensic logging

psnmt.py source code

```
#
# Python Passive Network Monitor and Mapping Tool
#

# Import Standard Library Modules
import socket          # network interface library used for raw sockets
import signal          # generation of interrupt signals i.e. timeout
import os              # operating system functions i.e. file I/o
import sys             # system level functions i.e. exit()
```

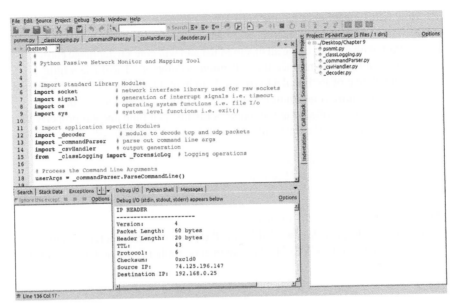

FIGURE 9.7

WingIDE environment for the PSNMT application.

```python
# Import application specific Modules
import decoder            # module to decode tcp and udp packets
import _commandParser     # parse out command line args
import _csvHandler        # output generation
from _classLogging import _ForensicLog # Logging operations

# Process the Command Line Arguments
userArgs = _commandParser.ParseCommandLine()

# create a log object
logPath = os.path.join(userArgs.outPath, "ForensicLog.txt")
oLog = _ForensicLog(logPath)

oLog.writeLog("INFO", "PS-NMT Started")

csvPath = os.path.join(userArgs.outPath, "ps-nmtResults.csv")
oCSV = _csvHandler._CSVWriter(csvPath)

# Setup the protocol to capture

if userArgs.TCP:
    PROTOCOL = socket.IPPROTO_TCP
elif userArgs.UDP:
    PROTOCOL = socket.IPPROTO_UDP
```

```python
else:
    print 'Capture protocol not selected'
    sys.exit()

# Setup whether output should be verbose

if userArgs.verbose:
    VERBOSE = True
else:
    VERBOSE = False

# Calculate capture duration
captureDuration = userArgs.minutes * 60

# Create timeout class to handle capture duration

class myTimeout(Exception):
    pass

# Create a signal handler that raises a timeout event
# when the capture duration is reached

def handler(signum, frame):
    print 'timeout received', signum
    raise myTimeout()

# Enable Promiscious Mode on the NIC

ret = os.system("ifconfig eth0 promisc")

if ret == 0:

    oLog.writeLog("INFO", 'Promiscious Mode Enabled')
    # create an INET, raw socket
    # AF_INET specifies        ipv4
    # SOCK_RAW specifies       a raw protocol at the network layer
    # IPPROTO_TCP or UDP       Specifies the protocol to capture
    try:
        mySocket = socket.socket(socket.AF_INET, socket.SOCK_RAW,
        PROTOCOL)
        oLog.writeLog("INFO", 'Raw Socket Open')
    except:
        # if socket open fails
        oLog.writeLog("ERROR", 'Raw Socket Open Failed')
        del oLog
        if VERBOSE:
            print 'Error Opening Raw Socket'
        sys.exit()
```

```
# Set the signal handler to the duraton specified by the user

signal.signal(signal.SIGALRM, handler)
signal.alarm(captureDuration)

# create a list to hold the results from the packet capture
# I'm only interested in Protocol Source IP, Source Port, Destination
IP, Destination Port

ipObservations =[]

# Begin receiving packets until duration is received
# the inner while loop will execute until the timeout

try:

    while True:

            # attempt recieve (this call will wait)
            recvBuffer, addr =mySocket.recvfrom(255)

            # decode the received packet
            content =decoder.PacketExtractor(recvBuffer, VERBOSE)

            # append the results to our list
            ipObservations.append(content)

            # write details to the forensic log file
            oLog.writeLog('INFO', \
                        'RECV: '+content[0]+\
                        'SRC  : '+content[1]+\
                        'DST  : '+content[3])

    except myTimeout:
        pass

# Once time has expired disable Promiscous Mode
ret =os.system("ifconfig eth0 -promisc")
oLog.writeLog("INFO", 'Promiscious Mode Diabled')

# Close the Raw Socket
mySocket.close()
oLog.writeLog("INFO", 'Raw Socket Closed')

# Create unique sorted list

uniqueSrc =set(map(tuple, ipObservations))
finalList =list(uniqueSrc)
finalList.sort()
```

```
            # Write each unique sorted packet to the csv file
            for packet in finalList:
                oCSV.writeCSVRow(packet)

            oLog.writeLog('INFO', 'Program End')

            # Close the Log and CSV objects
            del oLog
            del oCSV

    else:
        print 'Promiscious Mode not Set'
```

decoder.py source code

```
# Packet Extractor / Decoder Module
#

import socket, sys
from struct import *

# Constants
PROTOCOL_TCP=6
PROTOCOL_UDP=17

# PacketExtractor
#
# Purpose: Extracts fields from the IP, TCP and UDP Header
#
# Input: packet: buffer from socket.recvfrom() method
#        displaySwitch: True: Display the details, False omits
# Output: result list containing
#                   protocol, srcIP, srcPort, dstIP, dstPort
#
def PacketExtractor(packet, displaySwitch):

    #Strip off the first 20 characters for the ip header
    stripPacket=packet[0:20]

    #now unpack them
    ipHeaderTuple=unpack('!BBHHHBBH4s4s', stripPacket)

    # unpack returns a tuple, for illustration I will extract
    # each individual values
                                        # Field Contents
    verLen      =ipHeaderTuple[0]       # Field 0: Version and Length
    dscpECN     =ipHeaderTuple[1]       # Field 1: DSCP and ECN
```

```
packetLength = ipHeaderTuple[2]        # Field 2: Packet Length
packetID    = ipHeaderTuple[3]         # Field 3: Identification
flagFrag    = ipHeaderTuple[4]         # Field 4: Flags and Fragment
                                       Offset
timeToLive  = ipHeaderTuple[5]         # Field 5: Time to Live (TTL)
protocol    = ipHeaderTuple[6]         # Field 6: Protocol Number
checkSum    = ipHeaderTuple[7]         # Field 7: Header Checksum
sourceIP    = ipHeaderTuple[8]         # Field 8: Source IP
destIP      = ipHeaderTuple[9]         # Field 9: Destination IP

# Calculate / Convert extracted values

version     = verLen >> 4              # Upper Nibble is the version
                                       Number
length      = verLen & 0x0F            # Lower Nibble represents the
                                       size
ipHdrLength = length * 4               # Calculate the header length in
                                       bytes
```

covert the source and destination address to typical dotted notation strings

```
sourceAddress = socket.inet_ntoa(sourceIP);
destinationAddress = socket.inet_ntoa(destIP);

if displaySwitch:
    print '========================='
    print 'IP HEADER'
    print '_____'
    print 'Version:'        + str(version)
    print 'Packet Length:' + str(packetLength) + ' bytes'
    print 'Header Length:' + str(ipHdrLength)  + ' bytes'
    print 'TTL:'            + str(timeToLive)
    print 'Protocol:'       + str(protocol)
    print 'Checksum:'       + hex(checkSum)
    print 'Source IP:'      + str(sourceAddress)
    print 'Destination IP:' + str(destinationAddress)


# _____

if protocol == PROTOCOL_TCP:

    stripTCPHeader = packet[ipHdrLength:ipHdrLength+20]

    # unpack returns a tuple, for illustration I will extract
    # each individual values using the unpack() function

    tcpHeaderBuffer = unpack('!HHLLBBHHH', stripTCPHeader)
```

```
    sourcePort          = tcpHeaderBuffer[0]
    destinationPort     = tcpHeaderBuffer[1]
    sequenceNumber      = tcpHeaderBuffer[2]
    acknowledgement     = tcpHeaderBuffer[3]
    dataOffsetandReserve= tcpHeaderBuffer[4]
    tcpHeaderLength     = (dataOffsetandReserve >> 4) * 4
    tcpChecksum         = tcpHeaderBuffer[7]

if displaySwitch:
    print
    print 'TCP Header'
    print '_____'

    print 'Source Port:        '+str(sourcePort)
    print 'Destination Port : '+str(destinationPort)
    print 'Sequence Number :  '+str(sequenceNumber)
    print 'Acknowledgement :  '+str(acknowledgement)
    print 'TCP Header Length: '+str(tcpHeaderLength) +
                            ' bytes'
    print 'TCP Checksum: '+hex(tcpChecksum)
    print

return(['TCP', sourceAddress, sourcePort, destinationAddress,
destinationPort])

elif protocol == PROTOCOL_UDP:

    stripUDPHeader = packet[ipHdrLength:ipHdrLength+8]

    # unpack returns a tuple, for illustration I will extract
    # each individual values using the unpack() function

    udpHeaderBuffer = unpack('!HHHH' , stripUDPHeader)

    sourcePort      = udpHeaderBuffer[0]
    destinationPort = udpHeaderBuffer[1]
    udpLength       = udpHeaderBuffer[2]
    udpChecksum     = udpHeaderBuffer[3]

    if displaySwitch:
        print
        print 'UDP Header'
        print '_____'

    print 'Source Port:        '+str(sourcePort)
    print 'Destination Port : '+str(destinationPort)
    print 'UDP Length:         '+str(udpLength) +' bytes'
```

```
        print 'UDP Checksum: '+hex(udpChecksum)
        print

    return(['UDP', sourceAddress, sourcePort, destinationAddress,
    destinationPort])

else:
    # For expansion protocol support

    if displaySwitch:
        print 'Found Protocol : '+str(protocol)

return(['Unsupported',sourceAddress,0, \ destinationAddress,0])
```

commandParser.py

```python
#
# PSNMT Argument Parser
#

import argparse        # Python Standard Library - Parser for command-line
                       # options, arguments
import os              # Standard Library OS functions

# Name: ParseCommand() Function
#
# Desc: Process and Validate the command line arguments
#            use Python Standard Library module argparse
#
# Input: none
#
# Actions:
#            Uses the Standard Library argparse to process the command line
#
def ParseCommandLine():

    parser=argparse.ArgumentParser('PS-NMT')

    parser.add_argument('-v', '--verbose', help="Display    packet
    details", action='store_true')

    # setup a group where the selection is mutually exclusive and
    required.
    group=parser.add_mutually_exclusive_group(required=True)
    group.add_argument('--TCP', help='TCP    Packet    Capture',
    action='store_true')
```

```
        group.add_argument('--UDP',        help='UDP       Packet       Capture',
        action='store_true')
        parser.add_argument('-m','--minutes', help='Capture Duration in min-
        utes',type=int)
        parser.add_argument('-p',  '--outPath',  type=ValidateDirectory,
        required=True, help="Output Directory")

        theArgs=parser.parse_args()

        return theArgs

    # End Parse Command Line ============================

    def ValidateDirectory(theDir):

        # Validate the path is a directory
        if not os.path.isdir(theDir):
            raise argparse.ArgumentTypeError('Directory does not exist')

        # Validate the path is writable
        if os.access(theDir, os.W_OK):
            return theDir
        else:
            raise argparse.ArgumentTypeError('Directory is not writable')
    #End ValidateDirectory ====================================
```

classLogging.py source code

```
import logging
#
# Class: _ForensicLog
#
# Desc: Handles Forensic Logging Operations
#
# Methods constructor: Initializes the Logger
#          writeLog:    Writes a record to the log
#          destructor:  Writes message and shutsdown the logger

class _ForensicLog:

    def __init__(self, logName):
        try:
            # Turn on Logging
            logging.basicConfig(filename=logName,level=logging.
            DEBUG,format='%(asctime)s %(message)s')
        except:
            print "Forensic Log Initialization Failure... Aborting"
            exit(0)
```

```python
    def writeLog(self, logType, logMessage):
        if logType == "INFO":
            logging.info(logMessage)
        elif logType == "ERROR":
            logging.error(logMessage)
        elif logType == "WARNING":
            logging.warning(logMessage)
        else:
            logging.error(logMessage)
        return

    def __del__(self):
        logging.info("Logging Shutdown")
            logging.shutdown()
```

csvHandler.py source code

```python
import csv #Python Standard Library - for csv files

#
# Class: _CSVWriter
#
# Desc: Handles all methods related to comma separated value operations
#
# Methods constructor: Initializes the CSV File
#         writeCVSRow: Writes a single row to the csv file
#         writerClose: Closes the CSV File

class _CSVWriter:

    def __init__(self, fileName):
        try:
            # create a writer object and then write the header row
            self.csvFile = open(fileName, 'wb')
            self.writer = csv.writer(self.csvFile,      delimiter=',',
            quoting=csv.QUOTE_ALL)
            self.writer.writerow( ('Protocol','Source IP', 'Source Port',
            'Destination IP', 'Destination Port') )
        except:
            log.error('CSV File Failure')

    def writeCSVRow(self, row):

            self.writer.writerow( (row[0], row[1], str(row[2]), row
            [3], str(row[4])) )

    def __del__(self):
        self.csvFile.close()
```

PROGRAM EXECUTION AND OUTPUT

As you can see, the `psnmt` Python application is constructed as a command line application. This makes sense for this type of application because it is likely to be executed as a *cron* job (scheduled to run at certain times for example).

The command line has the following parameters:

Parameter	Purpose and Usage
-v	Verbose: Writes intermediate results to standard output when specified
-m	Minutes: Duration in minutes to perform collection activities
–TCP | –UDP	Protocol: Defines the application protocol to capture
-p	Produces: Defines the output directory for the forensic log and csv file

Example command line:

```
sudo Python psnmt -v -TCP -m 60 -p /home/chet/Desktop
```

Note: sudo (is used to force the execution of the command with administrative rights, which is required). This command will capture TCP packets for 60 min, produce verbose output and create a log and csv file on the user's desktop.

Figures 9.8 and 9.9 show sample executions for both TCP and UDP captures. These runs created both csv and forensic log files and entries.

```
chet@PythonForensics: ~/Desktop/Chapter 9
chet@PythonForensics:~/Desktop/Chapter 9$ sudo python ps-nmt.py -v -m 2 --TCP -p /home/chet/Desktop/Chapter\ 9
IP HEADER
------------------------
Version:        4
Packet Length:  60 bytes
Header Length:  20 bytes
TTL:            43
Protocol:       6
Checksum:       0x5227
Source IP:      74.125.196.147
Destination IP: 192.168.0.25

TCP Header
--------------------
Source Port:       443
Destination Port : 56652
Sequence Number :  621577023
Acknowledgement :  2310411757
TCP Header Length: 40 bytes
TCP Checksum:      0x6d8c

IP HEADER
------------------------
Version:        4
Packet Length:  60 bytes
Header Length:  20 bytes
TTL:            43
Protocol:       6
Checksum:       0xf9f3
Source IP:      74.125.196.147
Destination IP: 192.168.0.25

TCP Header
--------------------
Source Port:       443
Destination Port : 56653
Sequence Number :  1824497575
Acknowledgement :  1049873182
TCP Header Length: 40 bytes
TCP Checksum:      0x6d67
```

FIGURE 9.8

psnmt TCP sample run.

```
⊗ ⊝ ⊕   chet@PythonForensics: ~/Desktop/Chapter 9

chet@PythonForensics:~/Desktop/Chapter 9$ sudo python psnmt.py -v -m 2 --UDP -p '/home/chet/Desktop/Chapter 9'
IP HEADER
-----------------------
Version:        4
Packet Length:   61 bytes
Header Length:   20 bytes
TTL:            64
Protocol:       17
Checksum:       0x98fe
Source IP:      127.0.0.1
Destination IP: 127.0.0.1

UDP Header
------------------
Source Port:      52309
Destination Port : 53
UDP Length:       41 bytes
UDP Checksum:     0xfe3c

IP HEADER
-----------------------
Version:        4
Packet Length:   121 bytes
Header Length:   20 bytes
TTL:            58
Protocol:       17
Checksum:       0x86f7
Source IP:      66.153.128.98
Destination IP: 192.168.0.25

UDP Header
------------------
Source Port:      53
Destination Port : 23992
UDP Length:       101 bytes
UDP Checksum:     0x474f

IP HEADER
```

FIGURE 9.9

psnmt UDP sample run.

Forensic log
TCP capture example

```
2014-01-19 11:29:51,050 PS-NMT Started
2014-01-19 11:29:51,057 Promiscious Mode Enabled
2014-01-19 11:29:51,057 Raw Socket Open
2014-01-19 11:29:55,525 RECV: TCP SRC : 173.194.45.79 DST : 192.168.0.25
2014-01-19 11:29:55,526 RECV: TCP SRC : 173.194.45.79 DST : 192.168.0.25
2014-01-19 11:29:56,236 RECV: TCP SRC : 74.125.196.147 DST : 192.168.0.25
2014-01-19 11:29:56,270 RECV: TCP SRC : 74.125.196.147 DST : 192.168.0.25
2014-01-19 11:29:56,270 RECV: TCP SRC : 74.125.196.147 DST : 192.168.0.25
2014-01-19 11:29:56,271 RECV: TCP SRC : 74.125.196.147 DST : 192.168.0.25
2014-01-19 11:29:56,527 RECV: TCP SRC : 74.125.196.147 DST : 192.168.0.25
2014-01-19 11:29:56,543 RECV: TCP SRC : 74.125.196.147 DST : 192.168.0.25
2014-01-19 11:29:56,544 RECV: TCP SRC : 74.125.196.147 DST : 192.168.0.25
2014-01-19 11:29:56,546 RECV: TCP SRC : 74.125.196.147 DST : 192.168.0.25
2014-01-19 11:30:37,437 RECV: TCP SRC : 66.153.250.240 DST : 192.168.0.25
2014-01-19 11:30:37,449 RECV: TCP SRC : 66.153.250.240 DST : 192.168.0.25
2014-01-19 11:30:54,546 RECV: TCP SRC : 173.194.45.79 DST : 192.168.0.25
2014-01-19 11:30:55,454 RECV: TCP SRC : 74.125.196.147 DST : 192.168.0.25
2014-01-19 11:31:35,487 RECV: TCP SRC : 66.153.250.240 DST : 192.168.0.25
2014-01-19 11:31:51,063 Promiscious Mode Diabled
```

```
2014-01-19 11:31:51,064 Raw Socket Closed
2014-01-19 11:31:51,064 Program End
2014-01-19 11:31:51,064 Logging Shutdown
```

UDP capture example

```
2014-01-19 13:27:09,366 PS-NMT Started
2014-01-19 13:27:09,371 Promiscious Mode Enabled
2014-01-19 13:27:09,372 Raw Socket Open
2014-01-19 13:27:09,528 Logging Shutdown
2014-01-19 13:36:33,472 PS-NMT Started
2014-01-19 13:36:33,477 Promiscious Mode Enabled
2014-01-19 13:36:33,477 Raw Socket Open
2014-01-19 13:36:45,234 Logging Shutdown
2014-01-19 13:37:51,748 PS-NMT Started
2014-01-19 13:37:51,754 Promiscious Mode Enabled
2014-01-19 13:37:51,754 Raw Socket Open
2014-01-19 13:37:59,534 RECV: UDP SRC : 127.0.0.1 DST : 127.0.0.1
2014-01-19 13:37:59,546 RECV: UDP SRC : 66.153.128.98 DST : 192.168.0.25
2014-01-19 13:37:59,546 RECV: UDP SRC : 127.0.0.1 DST : 127.0.0.1
2014-01-19 13:37:59,549 RECV: UDP SRC : 66.153.162.98 DST : 192.168.0.25
2014-01-19 13:38:09,724 RECV: UDP SRC : 127.0.0.1 DST : 127.0.0.1
2014-01-19 13:38:09,879 RECV: UDP SRC : 66.153.128.98 DST : 192.168.0.25
2014-01-19 13:38:09,880 RECV: UDP SRC : 127.0.0.1 DST : 127.0.0.1
2014-01-19 13:38:10,387 RECV: UDP SRC : 127.0.0.1 DST : 127.0.0.1
2014-01-19 13:38:10,551 RECV: UDP SRC : 66.153.128.98 DST : 192.168.0.25
2014-01-19 13:38:10,551 RECV: UDP SRC : 127.0.0.1 DST : 127.0.0.1
2014-01-19 13:38:45,114 RECV: UDP SRC : 66.153.128.98 DST : 192.168.0.25
2014-01-19 13:38:46,112 RECV: UDP SRC : 66.153.128.98 DST : 192.168.0.25
2014-01-19 13:39:45,410 RECV: UDP SRC : 66.153.128.98 DST : 192.168.0.25
2014-01-19 13:39:51,760 Promiscious Mode Diabled
2014-01-19 13:39:51,761 Raw Socket Closed
2014-01-19 13:39:51,761 Program End
2014-01-19 13:39:51,761 Logging Shutdown
```

CSV file output example

Figures 9.10 and 9.11 depict a sample output of the CSV file created by PSNMT.

	A	B	C	D	E
1	Protocol	Source IP	Source Port	Destination IP	Destination Port
2	TCP	127.0.0.1	36480	127.0.0.1	54792
3	TCP	127.0.0.1	54792	127.0.0.1	36480
4	TCP	66.153.25(	443	192.168.0.25	35027
5	TCP	74.125.19(	443	192.168.0.25	56580
6	TCP	74.125.19(	443	192.168.0.25	56581

FIGURE 9.10

Sample TCP output file shown in Excel.

	A	B	C	D	E
1	Protocol	Source IP	Source Port	Destination IP	Destination Port
2	UDP	127.0.0.1	53	127.0.0.1	35633
3	UDP	127.0.0.1	53	127.0.0.1	51420
4	UDP	127.0.0.1	53	127.0.0.1	52309
5	UDP	127.0.0.1	35633	127.0.0.1	53
6	UDP	127.0.0.1	51420	127.0.0.1	53
7	UDP	127.0.0.1	52309	127.0.0.1	53
8	UDP	66.153.12{	53	192.168.0.25	11303
9	UDP	66.153.12{	53	192.168.0.25	23992
10	UDP	66.153.12{	53	192.168.0.25	35021
11	UDP	66.153.12{	53	192.168.0.25	43421
12	UDP	66.153.12{	53	192.168.0.25	56857
13	UDP	66.153.12{	53	192.168.0.25	58487
14	UDP	66.153.16{	53	192.168.0.25	23992

FIGURE 9.11

Sample UDP output file shown in Excel.

CHAPTER REVIEW

In this chapter, I introduced the raw sockets and how they can be utilized to capture network packets. In order to do so, I explained the Promiscuous Mode of modern network adapters and demonstrated how to configure a NIC for this operation. I also discussed the importance of network sniffing in order to more thoroughly map and monitor network activities. I used the unpack() function to extract each field from the IPv4, TCP and UDP packets and described in detail, how to apply this to buffered data. Finally, I created an application that collects and records either TCP or UDP traffic isolating unique Source IP, Source Port, Destination IP, and Destination Port combinations. This Python application can be controlled through command line arguments in order to easily integrate with *cron* jobs or other scheduling mechanisms. As part of the command line, I used a signaling mechanism to stop packet collection after a specified time period has expired.

SUMMARY QUESTION/CHALLENGE

I decided to pose only one question in this chapter, more of a challenge problem actually that will take the PSNMT application to the next level:

1. In order to make this current application more useful, the translation of port numbers into well-known services is necessary in order to determine the likely use or uses of each IP address that we extracted from the captured packets. Using the reserved and well-known port usage maps provided and defined by the Internet Engineering Task Force [IETF], (or by reading /etc/services) expand the

PSNMT application to isolate each local IP address and list the services that they are likely running on each. When possible, attempt to broadly classify the operating system behind each IP address through the examination of port usage (at least classify each IP as Windows, Linux, or other).

Additional Resources

http://docs.Python.org/2/library/struct.html?highlight = unpack#struct.unpack.
http://www.ietf.org/assignments/service-names-port-numbers/service-names-port-numbers.
    txt.

Multiprocessing for Forensics

CHAPTER CONTENTS

INTRODUCTION

As the footprint of digital evidence and digital crime widens, our ability to perform examinations in a timely fashion is clearly strained. According to DFI News "The backlog of caseloads from law enforcement agencies has grown from weeks to months worldwide. Digital forensic specialists cannot be trained fast enough and the number of specialists required to analyze the mountains of digital evidence in common crimes is simply beyond budget constraints" (DFI, 2013). Many digital investigation tools today are single threaded, meaning that the software can only execute one command at a time. These tools were invariably originally developed before multi-core processors were commonplace. In this chapter, I introduce the multiprocessing capabilities of Python that relate to some common forensic challenges. In Chapter 11, I will transfer these applications to the cloud and demonstrate how to increase performance by expanding access to additional cores and allowing forensic operations to be performed on a cloud platform.

WHAT IS MULTIPROCESSING?

Simply stated multiprocessing is the simultaneous execution of a program on two or more central processing units (CPUs) or cores. In order to provide significant performance improvements, the developer of forensic applications must define areas of the code that have the following characteristics:

(1) The code is processor-intensive.
(2) It is possible to break the code apart into separate processing threads that can execute in parallel.
(3) The processing between threads can be load-balanced. In other words, the goal is to distribute processing such that each of the threads complete at approximately the same time.

As you may already surmise, the problem with general purpose forensic tools is this: if they were not engineered to meet the objectives above from the start, adapting them to modern multi-core architectures may prove to be difficult. In addition, licensing of such technologies to run simultaneously on multi-cores or in the cloud may be cost-prohibitive. Finally, many of the most commonly used forensic tools operate within the Windows environment which is not ideally suited to run simultaneously on thousands of cores.

PYTHON MULTIPROCESSING SUPPORT

The Python Standard Library includes the package "multiprocessing" (Python multiprocessing module). Using the Python Standard Library for multiprocessing is a great place to begin multiprocessing and will ensure compatibility across a wide range of computing platforms, including the cloud. We utilize the multiprocessing package in typical fashion starting by importing the package multiprocessing. After import of the package, I execute the help(multiprocessing) function to reveal the details. I have eliminated some of the extraneous data produced by help, and I have highlighted the functions and classes that I will be utilizing to develop a couple of multiprocessing examples.

```
import multiprocessing

help(multiprocessing)

# NOTE this is only a partial excerpt from the output
# of the Help command

Help on package multiprocessing:

NAME
    multiprocessing
```

PACKAGE CONTENTS
    connection
    dummy (package)
    forking
    heap
    managers
    pool
    process
    queues
    reduction
    sharedctypes
    synchronize
    util

CLASSES
    class **Process**(__builtin__.object)
     | Process objects represent activity that is run in a separate
        process
     |
     | The class is analagous to 'threading.Thread'
     |
     | Methods defined here:
     |
     | __init__(self, group=None, target=None, name=None, args=(),
        kwargs={})
     |
     | __repr__(self)
     |
     | is_alive(self)
     | Return whether process is alive
     |
     | join(self, timeout=None)
     | Wait until child process terminates
     |
     | run(self)
     | Method to be run in sub-process; can be overridden in
            sub-class
     |
     | **start(self)**
     | **Start child process**
     |
     | terminate(self)
     | Terminate process; sends SIGTERM signal or uses
            TerminateProcess()
     |
FUNCTIONS
    Array(typecode_or_type, size_or_initializer, **kwds)
        Returns a synchronized shared array

```
BoundedSemaphore(value=1)
    Returns a bounded semaphore object

Condition(lock=None)
    Returns a condition object

Event()
    Returns an event object

JoinableQueue(maxsize=0)
    Returns a queue object

Lock()
    Returns a non-recursive lock object

Manager()
    Returns a manager associated with a running server process

    The managers methods such as 'Lock()', 'Condition()' and 'Queue()'
    can be used to create shared objects.

Pipe(duplex=True)
    Returns two connection object connected by a pipe

Pool(processes=None, initializer=None, initargs=(),
    maxtasksperchild=None) Returns a process pool object

Queue(maxsize=0)
    Returns a queue object

RLock()
    Returns a recursive lock object

RawArray(typecode_or_type, size_or_initializer)
    Returns a shared array

RawValue(typecode_or_type, *args)
    Returns a shared object

Semaphore(value=1)
    Returns a semaphore object

Value(typecode_or_type, *args, **kwds)
    Returns a synchronized shared object

active_children()
    Return list of process objects corresponding to live child
    processes
```

```
allow_connection_pickling()
    Install support for sending connections and sockets between
    processes

cpu_count()
    Returns the number of CPUs in the system

current_process()
    Return process object representing the current process

freeze_support()
    Check whether this is a fake forked process in a frozen
    executable. If so then run code specified by commandline
    and exit.

VERSION
    0.70a1
AUTHOR
    R. Oudkerk (r.m.oudkerk@gmail.com)
```

One of the first functions within the multiprocessing package you will be interested in is cpu_count(). Before you can distribute processing among multiple cores, you need to know how many cores you have access to.

```
import multiprocessing

multiprocessing.cpu_count()

4
```

As you can see on my Windows laptop, I have four CPU cores to work with; it would be a shame if my Python code only ran on one of those cores. Without applying the multiprocessing package and designing multi-core processing methods into my algorithm, my Python code would run on exactly one core.

Let us move on to our first example of applying multiprocessing within a Python program that has some forensic implication and relevance.

SIMPLEST MULTIPROCESSING EXAMPLE

In this first example I chose to develop the simplest multiprocessing example I could think of that would maximize the use of the four cores I have on my laptop. The program has a single function named SearchFile(), the function takes two parameters: (1) a filename and (2) the string that I wish to search for in that file. I am using a simple text file as my search target that contains a dictionary of words. The file is 170 MB in size which even on modern systems should create some I/O latency. I provide two examples, first a program that does not employ multiprocessing and simply makes four successive calls to the SearchFile function. The second example creates four processes and distributes the processing evenly between the four cores.

Single core file search solution

```
# Simple Files Search Single Core Processing

import time

def SearchFile(theFile, theString):
    try:
        fp = open(theFile,'r')
        buffer = fp.read()
        fp.close()
        if theString in buffer:
            print 'File: ', theFile, 'String: ',\
                    theString, '\t', 'Found'
        else:
            print 'File: ', theFile, 'String: ', \
                    theString, '\t', 'Not Found'
    except:
        print 'File processing error'

startTime = time.time()

SearchFile('c:\\TESTDIR\\Dictionary.txt', 'thought')
SearchFile('c:\\TESTDIR\\Dictionary.txt', 'exile')
SearchFile('c:\\TESTDIR\\Dictionary.txt', 'xavier')
SearchFile('c:\\TESTDIR\\Dictionary.txt', '$Slllb!')

elapsedTime = time.time() - startTime
print 'Duration: ', elapsedTime

# Program Output

File: c:\TESTDIR\Dictionary.txt String: thought      Found
File: c:\TESTDIR\Dictionary.txt String: exile      Found
File: c:\TESTDIR\Dictionary.txt String: xavier      Found
File: c:\TESTDIR\Dictionary.txt String: $Slllb!   Not Found
Duration: 4.3140001297 Seconds
```

Multiprocessing file search solution

The multiprocessing solution is depicted below and as you can see the performance is substantially better even considering the file I/O aspects of opening, reading, and closing the associated file each time.

```python
# Simple Files Search MultiProcessing

from multiprocessing import Process
import time

def SearchFile(theFile, theString):
    try:
        fp = open(theFile,'r')
        buffer = fp.read()
        fp.close()
        if theString in buffer:
            print 'File: ', theFile, 'String: ', theString,
            '\t', 'Found'
        else:
            print 'File: ', theFile, 'String: ', theString,
            '\t', 'Not Found'
    except:
        print 'File processing error'

#
# Create Main Function
#

if __name__ == '__main__':

    startTime = time.time()

    p1 = Process(target=SearchFile,
        \args=('c:\\TESTDIR\\Dictionary.txt', 'thought') )
    p1.start()

    p2 = Process(target=SearchFile, \
        args=('c:\\TESTDIR\\Dictionary.txt', 'exile') )
    p2.start()

    p3 = Process(target=SearchFile, \
        args=('c:\\TESTDIR\\Dictionary.txt', 'xavier') )
    p3.start()

    p4 = Process(target=SearchFile, \
        args=('c:\\TESTDIR\\Dictionary.txt', '$Slllb') )
    p4.start()

    # Next we use the join to wait for all processes to complete

    p1.join()
    p2.join()
```

```
        p3.join()
        p4.join()

        elapsedTime = time.time() - startTime
        print 'Duration: ', elapsedTime

# Program Output

File: c:\TESTDIR\Dictionary.txt String:      thought      Found
File: c:\TESTDIR\Dictionary.txt String:      exile      Found
File: c:\TESTDIR\Dictionary.txt String:      xavier      Found
File: c:\TESTDIR\Dictionary.txt String:      $Slllb      Not Found
Duration: 1.80399990082
```

MULTIPROCESSING FILE HASH

Certainly one of the most frequently used forensic tools is the one-way cryptographic
hash. As you already know Python includes a hashing library as part of the Standard
Library. As an experiment, I am going to perform a SHA512 Hash of four separate
instances of the same file using a nonmultiprocessing method. I will set up a timer as
well to calculate the elapsed time to perform the single-threaded approach.

Single core solution

```
# Single Threaded File Hasher

    import hashlib
    import os
    import sys
    import time

    # Create a constant for the local directory
    HASHDIR = 'c:\\HASHTEST\\'
    # Create an empty list to hold the resulting hash results
    results = []

try:
    # Obtain the list of files in the HASHDIR
    listOfFiles = os.listdir(HASHDIR)

    # Mark the starting time of the main loop
    startTime = time.time()

    for eachFile in listOfFiles:

        # Attempt File Open
        fp = open(HASHDIR+eachFile, 'rb')
```

```
                # Then Read the contents into a buffer
                fileContents = fp.read()

                # Close the File
                fp.close()

                # Create a hasher object of type sha256
                hasher = hashlib.sha256()

                # Hash the contents of the buffer
                hasher.update(fileContents)

                # Store the results in the results list
                results.append([eachFile, hasher.hexdigest()])

                # delete the hasher object
                del hasher

        # Once all the files have been hashed calculate
        # the elapsed time

        elapsedTime = time.time() - startTime

    except:

        # If any exceptions occur notify the user and exit

        print('File Processing Error')
        sys.exit(0)

# Print out the results
# Elapsed Time in Seconds and the Filename / Hash Results

print('Elapsed Time: ', elapsedTime)
for eachItem in results:
    print eachItem

# Program Output
# Note: Each File Processed is identical
# With a Size: 249 MB

Elapsed Time: 27.8510000705719 Seconds
['image0.raw',
'41ad70ff71407eae7466eef403cb20100771ca7499cbf1504f8ed67e6d869e5b']
['image1.raw',
'41ad70ff71407eae7466eef403cb20100771ca7499cbf1504f8ed67e6d869e5b']
['image2.raw',
'41ad70ff71407eae7466eef403cb20100771ca7499cbf1504f8ed67e6d869e5b']
['image3.raw',
'41ad70ff71407eae7466eef403cb20100771ca7499cbf1504f8ed67e6d869e5b']
```

Multi-core solution A

Much of the art associated with multiprocessing is decomposing a problem into slices that can run simultaneously across multiple cores. Once each of the individual slices have completed, the results from each slice are merged into a final result. The biggest mistake that is typically made is the lack of careful consideration of these two points. Purchasing systems with multi-cores and then just running any solution on that multi-core system does not necessarily buy you much over a single core solution.

Using our single solution as a baseline, I will create a multi-core solution that leverages the four cores available on my laptop. For this first example, I will instantiate the object Process, one for each core. When creating each Process object, I only need to provide two parameters: (1) the `target =` which in this case is the name of the function that will be called when the `object.start()` method is called. (2) the `args =` which is the argument tuple to be passed to the function. In this example, only one argument is passed, namely, the name of the file to hash. Once I have instantiated an object, I execute the `object.start()` method to kick off each process. Finally, I utilize the `object.join()` method for each object; this causes execution to be halted in the `main()` process until the processes have completed. You can include a parameter with `object.join()` which is a timeout value for the process. For example `object.join(20)` would allow the process 20 s to complete.

```
# Multiprocessing File Hasher A

import hashlib
import os
import sys
import time
import multiprocessing

# Create a constant for the local directory
HASHDIR = 'c:\\HASHTEST\\'

#
# hashFile Function, designed for multiprocessing
#
# Input: Full Pathname of the file to hash
#
#

def hashFile(fileName):

    try:

        fp = open(fileName, 'rb')

        # Then Read the contents into a buffer
        fileContents = fp.read()
```

```
            # Close the File
            fp.close()

            # Create a hasher object of type sha256
            hasher = hashlib.sha256()

            # Hash the contents of the buffer
            hasher.update(fileContents)

            print(fileName, hasher.hexdigest())

            # delete the hasher object
            del hasher

    except:
            # If any exceptions occur notify the user and exit
            print('File Processing Error')
            sys.exit(0)

    return True

#
# Create Main Function
#

if __name__ == '__main__':

    # Obtain the list of files in the HASHDIR
    listOfFiles = os.listdir(HASHDIR)

    # Mark the starting time of the main loop
    startTime = time.time()

    # create 4 sub-processes to do the work
    # one of each core in this test

    # Each Process  contains:
    #               Target function hashFile() it this example
    #               Filename:  picked from the list generated
    #                          by os.listdir()
    #                          once again an instance of the
    #                          249 MB file is used
    #
    # Next we start each of the processes

    coreOne = multiprocessing.Process(target=hashFile,
                        args=(HASHDIR+listOfFiles[0],))
```

```
        coreOne.start()

        coreTwo = multiprocessing.Process(target=hashFile,
                                args=(HASHDIR+listOfFiles[1],) )
        coreTwo.start()

        coreThree = multiprocessing.Process(target=hashFile,
                                args=(HASHDIR+listOfFiles[2],) )
        coreThree.start()

        coreFour = multiprocessing.Process(target=hashFile,
                                args=(HASHDIR+listOfFiles[3],) )
        coreFour.start()
```

In this example, I was leveraging the knowledge of the hardware I was running the application on in order to maximize the distribution of processing. The Python multiprocessing library will automatically handle the distribution of the processes as cores become available. Also, since I could determine the number of cores available by using (multiprocessing.cpu_count()). I could have used that information to manually distribute the processing as well.

```
        # Next we use join to wait for all processes to complete

        coreOne.join()
        coreTwo.join()
        coreThree.join()
        coreFour.join()

        # Once all the processes have completed and files have been
        # hashed and results printed
        # I calculate the elapsed time

        elapsedTime = time.time() - startTime

        print('Elapsed Time: ', elapsedTime)

# Program Output
# Note: Each File Processed is identical
# With a Size: 249 MB

c:\\HASHTEST\\image2.raw 41ad70ff71407eae7466eef403cb20100771ca-
7499cbf1504f8ed67e6d869e5b
c:\\HASHTEST\\image1.raw 41ad70ff71407eae7466eef403cb20100771ca-
7499cbf1504f8ed67e6d869e5b
c:\\HASHTEST\\image3.raw 41ad70ff71407eae7466eef403cb20100771ca-
7499cbf1504f8ed67e6d869e5b
c:\\HASHTEST\\image0.raw 41ad70ff71407eae7466eef403cb20100771ca-
7499cbf1504f8ed67e6d869e5b
Elapsed Time: 8.40999984741211 Seconds
```

As you can see by distributing the processing across the four cores produced the desired results by significantly improving the performance of the hashing operations.

Multi-core solution B

Here is another option for distributing processing among multiple cores that yields a small performance improvement over the multi-core solution A, and additionally provides a much cleaner implementation when you are calling the same functions with different parameters. This is a likely scenario if you consider that in your design for forensic applications. Additionally, this solution only requires the use of a single class: pool that can handle the entire multi-core processing operations in a single line of code. I have highlighted the simplified implementation below.

```
# Multiprocessing File Hasher B

import hashlib
import os
import sys
import time
import multiprocessing

# Create a constant for the local directory
HASHDIR = 'c:\\HASHTEST\\'

#
# hashFile Function, designed for multiprocessing
#
# Input: Full Pathname of the file to hash
#
#

def hashFile(fileName):

    try:

        fp = open(fileName, 'rb')

        # Then Read the contents into a buffer
        fileContents = fp.read()

        # Close the File
        fp.close()

        # Create a hasher object of type sha256
        hasher = hashlib.sha256()

        # Hash the contents of the buffer
        hasher.update(fileContents)
```

```
        print(fileName, hasher.hexdigest())

        # delete the hasher object
        del hasher

    except:
        # If any exceptions occur notify the user and exit
        print('File Processing Error')
        sys.exit(0)

    return True

#
# Create Main Function
#

if __name__ == '__main__':

    # Obtain the list of files in the HASHDIR
    listOfFiles = os.listdir(HASHDIR)

    # Mark the starting time of the main loop
    startTime = time.time()

    # Create a process Pool with 4 processes mapping to
    # the 4 cores on my laptop

    corePool = multiprocessing.Pool(processes=4)

    # Map the corePool to the hashFile function
    results = corePool.map(hashFile, (HASHDIR+listOfFiles[0],\
                                      HASHDIR+listOfFiles[1],\
                                      HASHDIR+listOfFiles[2],\
                                      HASHDIR+listOfFiles[3],))


    # Once all the files have been hashed and results printed
    # I calculate the elapsed time

    elapsedTime = time.time() - startTime

    print('Elapsed Time: ', elapsedTime, 'Seconds')

# Program Output
# Note: Each File Processed is identical
# With a Size: 249 MB

Elapsed Time: , 8.138000085830688, Seconds
```

```
c:\\HASHTEST\\image0.raw, 41ad70ff71407eae7466eef403cb20100771ca-
7499cbf1504f8ed67e6d869e5b
c:\\HASHTEST\\image2.raw, 41ad70ff71407eae7466eef403cb20100771ca-
7499cbf1504f8ed67e6d869e5b
c:\\HASHTEST\\image1.raw, 41ad70ff71407eae7466eef403cb20100771ca-
7499cbf1504f8ed67e6d869e5b
c:\\HASHTEST\\image3.raw, 41ad70ff71407eae7466eef403cb20100771ca-
7499cbf1504f8ed67e6d869e5b
```

Reviewing the results of the three implementations we find the following:

Implementation	Processing time	MB (s)	Notes
Single core solution	27.851	35.76	Typical implementation today processing each file in sequence
Multi-core solution A	8.409	118.44	Use of `Process` Class along with `start` and `join` methods
Multi-core solution B	8.138	122.39	Use of `Pool` Class simplifying implementation for common function processing yielding slightly better performance

MULTIPROCESSING HASH TABLE GENERATION

Rainbow Tables have been around for quite some time, providing a way to convert known hash values into possible password equivalents. In other words, they provide a way to lookup a hash value and associate that hash with a string that would generate that hash. Since hash algorithms are one-way, for all practical purposes two strings of characters will not generate the same hash value. They are highly collision-resistant. Rainbow Tables are utilized to crack passwords to operating systems, protected documents, and network user logins.

In recent years, the process of salting hashes has made Rainbow Tables less effective as new tables would have to be generated as salt values are modified. These tables work because each password is hashed using the same process. In other words, two identical passwords would have the exact same hash value.

Today, this is prevented by randomizing hashed passwords, such that if two users use the same password, the hash values would be different. This is typically accomplished by appending a random string called a *salt* to a password prior to hashing.

Password = "letMeIn"

Salt = '&*6542Jk'

Combined Data to be Hashed: "&*6542JkletMeIn"

The salt does not need to be kept confidential as the purpose is to thwart the application of a rainbow or lookup table.

This means we need a fast way to generate more dynamic lookup tables. This is where multiprocessing can assist. Python actually has unique language mechanisms that support the generation of permutations and combinations built directly into the language that assists the developer. I will be using the itertools Standard Library (Python intertools module) to create the set of brute force passwords that I am looking for. The itertools module implements a number of iteration-like building blocks using a high-performance yet memory-optimized toolkit. Instead of having to develop permutation, combinations or product-based algebras, the library provides this for you.

First, I will create a simple Rainbow Table generator using a single core solution.

Single core password generator code

```
# Single Core Password Table Generator

# import standard libraries

import hashlib            # Hashing the results
import time               # Timing the operation
import itertools          # Creating controled combinations

#
# Create a list of lower case, upper case, numbers
# and special characters to include in the password table
#

lowerCase = ['a', 'b', 'c', 'd', 'e', 'f', 'g', 'h']
upperCase = ['G', 'H', 'I', 'J', 'K', 'L']
numbers = ['0', '1', '2', '3']
special = ['!', '@', '#', '$']

# combine to create a final list
allCharacters = []
allCharacters = lowerCase + upperCase + numbers + special

# Define Directory Path for the password file

DIR = 'C:\\PW\\'

# Define a hypothetical SALT value
SALT = "&45Bvx9"

# Define the allowable range of password length
PW_LOW = 2
PW_HIGH = 6

# Mark the start time
startTime = time.time()
```

```
# Create an empty list to hold the final passwords
pwList = []

# create a loop to include all passwords
# within the allowable range

for r in range(PW_LOW, PW_HIGH):
    #Apply the standard library interator
    #The product interator will generate the cartesian product
    # for allCharacters repeating for the range of
    # PW_LOW to PW_HIGH
    for s in itertools.product(allCharacters, repeat=r):
        # append each generated password to the
        # final list
        pwList.append(''.join(s))

# For each password in the list generate
# generate a file containing the
# hash, password pairs
# one per line

try:
    # Open the output file
    fp = open(DIR+'all', 'w')

    # process each generated password

    for pw in pwList:
        # Perform hashing of the password
        md5Hash = hashlib.md5()
        md5Hash.update(SALT+pw)
        md5Digest = md5Hash.hexdigest()
        # Write the hash, password pair to the file
        fp.write(md5Digest +'' + pw +'\n')
        del md5Hash
except:
    print 'File Processing Error'
    fp.close()

# Now create a dictionary to hold the
# Hash, password pairs for easy lookup

pwDict = {}

try:
    # Open each of the output file
    fp = open(DIR+'all', 'r')
    # Process each line in the file which
```

```
          # contains key, value pairs
          for line in fp:
              # extract the key value pairs
              # and update the dictionary
              pairs = line.split()
              pwDict.update({pairs[0] : pairs[1]})
          fp.close()
      except:
          print 'File Handling Error'
          fp.close()

      # When complete calculate the elapsed time

      elapsedTime = time.time() - startTime
      print 'Elapsed Time: ', elapsedTime
      print 'Passwords Generated: ', len(pwDict)
      print

      # print out a few of the dictionary entries
      # as an example

      cnt = 0
      for key,value in (pwDict.items()):
          print key, value
          cnt += 1
          if cnt > 10:
              break;

      print

      # Demonstrate the use of the Dictionary to Lookup a password using a
      known hash
      # Lookup a Hash Value

      pw = pwDict.get('c6f1d6b1d33bcc787c2385c19c29c208')
      print 'Hash Value Tested = c6f1d6b1d33bcc787c2385c19c29c208'
      print 'Associated Password= '+ pw

      # Program Output

      Elapsed Time: 89.117000103
      Passwords Generated: 5399020

      3e47ac3f51daffdbe46ab671c76b44fb  K23IH
      a5a3614f49da18486c900bd04675d7bc  $@fL1
      372da5744b1ab1f99376f8d726cd2b7c  hGfdd
      aa0865a47331df5de01296bbaaf4996a  21ILG
```

```
c6f1d6b1d33bcc787c2385c19c29c208  #I#$$
c3c4246114ee80e9c454603645c9a416  #$b$g
6ca0e4d8f183c6c8b0a032b09861c95a  L1H21
fd86ec2191f415cdb6c305da5e59eb7a  HJg@h
335ef773e663807eb21d100e06b8c53e  a$HbH
d1bae7cd5ae09903886d413884e22628  ba21H
a2a53248ed641bbd22af9bf36b422321  GHcda
```

```
Hash Value Tested = 2bca9b23eb8419728fdeca3345b344fc
Associated Password= #I#$$
```

As you can see the code is quite succinct and straightforward, it leverages the itertools and hashing library to generate a brute force list. The result is a reference-able list of over 5.3 million salted passwords in under 90 seconds.

Multi-core password generator

Now that I have created a successful model for generating password combinations and created a dictionary with the resulting key/value pairs, I want to once again apply multiprocessing in order to generate a scalable solution. As you can see from the single core solution, it required just under 90 seconds to generate a little more than 5.3 million pairs. As we expand the number of characters to include in our generation and expand the size of allowable passwords beyond 5, the number of combinations grows exponentially. As I mentioned earlier, setting up an approach that lends itself to multiprocessing is the key. Now let us examine how well this actually scales by reviewing the multi-core solution.

Multi-core password generator code

```
# Multi-Core Password Table Generator

    # import standard libraries

    import hashlib          # Hashing the results
    import time             # Timing the operation
    import itertools        # Creating controled combinations
    import multiprocessing  # Multiprocessing Library

    #
    # Create a list of lower case, upper case, numbers
    # and special characters to include in the password table
    #

    lowerCase = ['a', 'b', 'c', 'd', 'e', 'f', 'g', 'h']
    upperCase = ['G', 'H', 'I', 'J', 'K', 'L']
    numbers = ['0', '1', '2', '3']
    special = ['!', '@', '#', '$']
```

```
# combine to create a final list
allCharacters = []
allCharacters = lowerCase + upperCase + numbers + special

# Define Directory Path for the password files
DIR = 'C:\\PW\\'

# Define a hypothetical SALT value
SALT = "&45Bvx9"

# Define the allowable range of password length

PW_LOW  = 2
PW_HIGH = 6

def pwGenerator(size):

    pwList = []

    # create a loop to include all passwords
    # with a length of 3-5 characters

    for r in range(size, size+1):
        #Apply the standard library interator
        for s in itertools.product(allCharacters, repeat=r):
            # append each generated password to the
            # final list
            pwList.append('.join(s))

    # For each password in the list generate
    # an associated md5 hash and utilize the
    # hash as the key

    try:
        # Open the output file
        fp = open(DIR+str(size), 'w')

        # process each generated password

        for pw in pwList:
            # Perform hashing of the password
            md5Hash = hashlib.md5()
            md5Hash.update(SALT+pw)
            md5Digest = md5Hash.hexdigest()
            # Write the hash, password pair to the file
            fp.write(md5Digest +''+ pw +'\n')
            del md5Hash
```

```
        except:
            print 'File Processing Error'

        finally:
            fp.close()

#
# Create Main Function
#

if __name__ == '__main__':

    # Mark the starting time of the main loop
    startTime = time.time()

    #create a process Pool with 4 processes
    corePool = multiprocessing.Pool(processes=4)

    #map corePool to the Pool processes
    results = corePool.map(pwGenerator, (2, 3, 4, 5))

    # Create a dictionary for easy lookups
    pwDict = {}

    # For each file

    for i in range(PW_LOW, PW_HIGH):
        try:
            # Open each of the output files
            fp = open(DIR+str(i), 'r')
            # Process each line in the file which
            # contains key, value pairs
            for line in fp:
                # extract the key value pairs
                # and update the dictionary
                pairs = line.split()
                pwDict.update({pairs[0] : pairs[1]})
            fp.close()
        except:
            print 'File Handling Error'
            fp.close()

    # Once all the files have been hashed
    # I calculate the elapsed time

    elapsedTime = time.time() - startTime
    print'Elapsed Time: ', elapsedTime, 'Seconds'
```

```
# print out a few of the dictionary entries
# as an example
print 'Passwords Generated: ', len(pwDict)
print
cnt = 0
for key,value in (pwDict.items()):
    print key, value
    cnt += 1
    if cnt > 10:
        break;

print

# Demonstrate the use of the Dictionary to Lookup
# a password using a known hash value

pw = pwDict.get('c6f1d6b1d33bcc787c2385c19c29c208')
print 'Hash Value Tested = \ 2bca9b23eb8419728fdeca3345b344fc'

print 'Associated Password= '+ pw

# Program Output

Elapsed Time: 50.504999876 Seconds
Passwords Generated: 5399020

3e47ac3f51daffdbe46ab671c76b44fb K23IH
a5a3614f49da18486c900bd04675d7bc $@fL1
372da5744b1ab1f99376f8d726cd2b7c hGfdd
aa0865a47331df5de01296bbaaf4996a 21ILG
c6f1d6b1d33bcc787c2385c19c29c208 #I#$$
c3c4246114ee80e9c454603645c9a416 #$b$g
6ca0e4d8f183c6c8b0a032b09861c95a L1H21
fd86ec2191f415cdb6c305da5e59eb7a HJg@h
335ef773e663807eb21d100e06b8c53e a$HbH
d1bae7cd5ae09903886d413884e22628 ba21H
a2a53248ed641bbd22af9bf36b422321 GHcda

Hash Value Tested = 2bca9b23eb8419728fdeca3345b344fc
Associated Password= #I#$$
```

As expected, the multi-core approach improves the performance and the solution is still straightforward and easily readable.

Reviewing the results of the single and multi-core implementations of the Rainbow Tables we find the following.

Implementation Rainbow generator	Processing time (s)	Passwords per second	Notes
Single core solution	89.11	~60 K	Typical implementation today processing using a single core
Multi-core solution	50.50	~106 K	Use of `Pool` Class simplifying implementation

In addition to the performance results, the output of the generated key value pairs (MD5 hash and associated password are written to a file) and can be used later as part of a larger repository. Since the outputs are simple text files as shown in Figure 10.1 they are easily readable.

```
SALTED Password MD5 HASH           Associated Password
17ae80e34251ad4e2a61bc81d28b5a09 aa
9e6e21b8664f1590323ecaae3447ebae ab
e708b3b343cfbc6b0104c60597fff773 ac
dcea12b90e71b523db8929cf6d86e39d ad
70a3c3c78c79437dfc626ff12605ccb3 ae
41afc8d925b0b94996035b4ef25346ec af
14b45c3a22caf6c2d5ed2e3daae152ee ag
3c4493267b90a86303c1d30784b8f33b ah
5cbba376bbb10688ece346cbfa9b8c28 aG
ffad7a79a9b2c646ef440d1447e18ebe aH
...

...
eba8905561738d699d47bd6f62e3341c eeg2
13605b276258b214fdafccac0835fc67 eeg3
0e3a4e8aded5858c94997d9f593c4fa3 eeg!
a6ab3da0c0cc7dc22d2a4cfe629ba0f2 eeg@
8f005cf0ea4b2bf064da85e1b2405c00 eeg#
60c797433e1f1ff9175a93373cf1a6ff eeg$
e847612d8cab3184caa4d120c212afec eeha
75cc13015bd40e2a6da4609458bfbe01 eehb
```

FIGURE 10.1

Plaintext Rainbow Table output abridged.

CHAPTER REVIEW

In this chapter, I began the process of addressing multi-core processing using Python by leveraging the cores already available on your laptop or desktop system. I introduce a couple of different approaches to multiprocessing and provide an overview of the Python Standard Library `multiprocessing`. I also examined two common digital investigation mainstay functions that can benefit from multiprocessing: (1) File Hashing and (2) Rainbow Table generation.

In Chapter 11, I will demonstrate how you can take this approach into the cloud and leverage cloud services that could offer 10, 50, 100, or even a 1000 cores to expand the horizon of multiprocessing from the desktop to the cloud.

SUMMARY QUESTION/CHALLENGE

1. What other digital investigation or forensic applications do you believe could benefit from multiprocessing?
2. What are some of the key elements when designing multiprocessing solutions?
3. What is the best defense today against Rainbow Table-based password attacks?
4. The Rainbow Table example is limited by resources and will fail when the program runs out of memory. How would you modify the program such that it could continue to generate password/hash combinations in the face of memory limitations?

Additional Resources

http://www.net-security.org/article.php?id=1932&p=1.
http://docs.python.org/2/library/itertools.html#module-itertools.
http://docs.python.org/3.4/library/multiprocessing.html#module-multiprocessing.

Rainbow in the Cloud

11

CHAPTER CONTENTS

INTRODUCTION

One of the significant advantages of building applications in Python is the ability to deploy applications on virtually any platform, including of course the cloud (see Figure 11.1). This not only means that you can execute Python on cloud servers, but you can launch them from any device you have handy, desktop, laptop, tablet, or smartphone.

PUTTING THE CLOUD TO WORK

In Chapter 10, I created a simple application that searches a dictionary for certain words. I created a single core application and then one that leverages multiple cores.

As you can see in Figure 11.2, I have executed the two programs that perform the simple dictionary search program. I executed them from my iPad with the application running in the cloud. This code is unchanged from the version created in Chapter 10:

    sp.py is the single processing version
    mp.py is the multiprocessing version

In Figure 11.3, I execute both the Simple Single Core and Multi-Core application from my desktop browser. As you can see the Multi-Core runs a bit faster even though I am only running the multiprocessing application on two-core cloud computers at Python Anywhere.

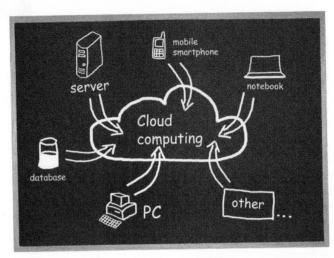

FIGURE 11.1

Typical cloud configuration.

Note that in these examples I have not changed a line of code to execute the Python code in the cloud. Since the code is executed by a standard Python interpreter and I have used Python Standard Libraries the code just runs. If you utilize third-party libraries then you will have to get those added to the cloud-based Python installations (this is not impossible to do), but it is much easier if we stick with the Standard Library. I am using the cloud service Python Anywhere or www.pythonanywhere.com as shown in Figure 11.4. Python Anywhere is a terrific place to start experimenting with Python applications in the cloud. Signup is free for a minimal account, giving you access to a couple of cores and storage for your programs. I have a $12/month plan and this gives me 500 GB of storage and 20,000 CPU seconds allowed per day. The seconds are seconds of CPU time—so any time that any processor spends working on your code, internally it is measured in nanoseconds. Most online cloud services reference the Amazon definition of the CPU second which is: "the equivalent CPU capacity of a 1.0–1.2 GHz 2007 Opteron or 2007 Xeon 64 bit processors."

CLOUD OPTIONS

Many cloud options exist that allow access to as few as 2 and as many as 1000 cores on which to execute. Table 11.1 provides an overview of just a few that you could investigate further (note, some are ready to run Python code, others require you to set up your own Python environment). In addition, some have a custom application interface or application interface (API) that you must use for multiprocessing, while others use a native approach.

FIGURE 11.2

Cloud execution from iPad.

FIGURE 11.3

Desktop execution of the simple and multiprocessing Python applications executing in the cloud.

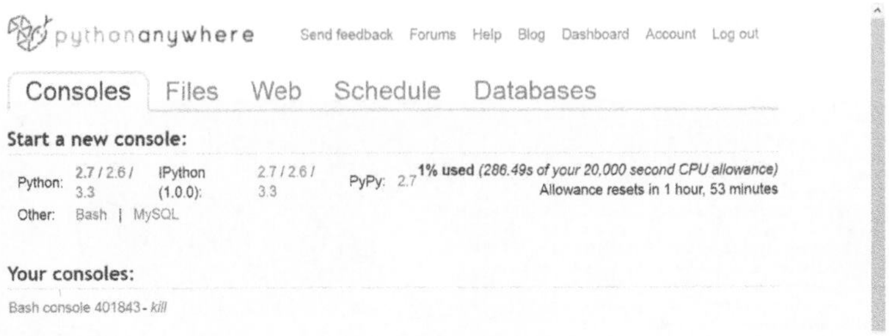

FIGURE 11.4

Python Anywhere Home Page.

Table 11.1 A Few Python Cloud Options

Cloud Service	URL	Notes
[PythonAnywhere]	pythonanywhere.com	Runs native Python code for version 2.6, 2.7, 3.3 Figure 11.5
[PiCloud]	picloud.com	Runs native Python code, but requires the import of their cloud module for multiprocessing. See Figures 11.6 and 11.7
[Digital Ocean]	digitalocean.com	Requires you to install a Python package for the environment and your application. See Figures 11.8 and 11.9
Others	Amazon, Google, ATT, IBM, Rackspace just to mention a few	As you expand your applications these services offer a variety of solutions

CREATING RAINBOWS IN THE CLOUD

There are considerable trade-offs and options available for creating high performance Python-based investigation platforms. One of the interesting applications that is suited nicely for cloud execution is the generation of Rainbow Tables discussed and experimented with in Chapter 10. Moving both the single and multiprocessing versions of this application to the cloud requires some considerations. First, I have decided to use Python Anywhere to demonstrate this capability. As I mentioned earlier, it is a great way to get started in the cloud, because the environment executes native Python applications for version 2.6, 2.7, and 3.3. Since I have made sure to only use Standard Library modules and core language elements, portability to the

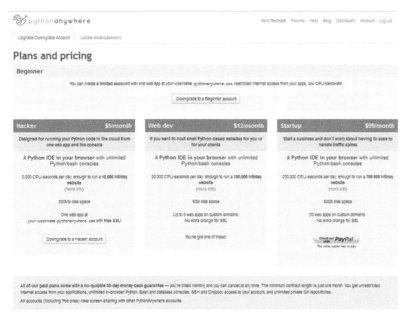

FIGURE 11.5

Python Anywhere Plans.

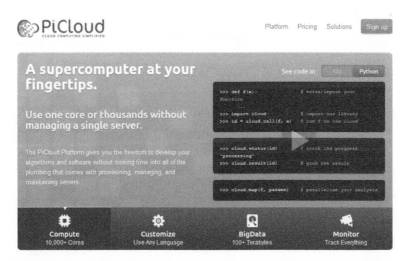

FIGURE 11.6

PiCloud Home Page.

Public Cloud

Signing up gives you instant access to our public cloud solution. Your workloads run on our cloud, which means you get on-demand access to as many cores as you need. If you're looking to use PiCloud with private infrastructure, see our private cloud offering.

Computation

You pay only for what you use. There is no minimum fee. We charge you for the number of core hours your functions consume. Each of your functions can be run on any of the cores we offer. Please note, that while our pricing is expressed in hours for clarity, your actual charge will be prorated by the millisecond.

Core Type	Compute Units [1]	Memory	Disk	Max Multicore [2]	Price/Hour
c1 (default)	1	300 MB	15 GB	1	$0.05
c2	2.5	800 MB	30 GB	8	$0.13
f2	5.5 w/ HT	3.7 GB	100 GB	16	$0.22
m1	3.25	8 GB	140 GB	8	$0.30
s1 [3]	0.5 to 2	300 MB	4 GB	1	$0.04

[1] A **compute unit as** defined by Amazon provides "the equivalent CPU capacity of a 1.0-1.2 GHz 2007 Opteron or 2007 Xeon processor." All of our cores have 64-bit architectures.

FIGURE 11.7

PiCloud Plans.

FIGURE 11.8

Digital Ocean Home Page.

Monthly	Hourly	Memory	CPU	Storage	Transfer	Get Started
$160	$0.238	16GB	8 Cores	160GB SSD	6TB	Sign Up
$320	$0.476	32GB	12 Cores	320GB SSD	7TB	Sign Up
$480	$0.705	48GB	16 Cores	480GB SSD	8TB	Sign Up
$640	$0.941	64GB	20 Cores	640GB SSD	9TB	Sign Up
$960	$1.411	96GB	24 Cores	960GB SSD	10TB	Sign Up

FIGURE 11.9

Digital Ocean Plans.

Python Anywhere cloud is pretty simple. However, I am going to make a couple of significant changes to the experimental code that I developed in Chapter 10:

(1) Minimize the memory usage within the programs by eliminating the use of the lists and dictionaries.
(2) Simplify the characters used to keep the resulting password generation reasonable
(3) Expand the generated password lengths to 4- to 8-character passwords

The resulting code listings for both the single and multiprocessing versions are shown here:

Single Core Rainbow

```
# Single Core Password Table Generator

# import standard libraries

import hashlib            # Hashing the results
import time               # Timing the operation
import sys
import os
import itertools          # Creating controled combinations


#
# Create a list of characters to include in the
# password generation
#

chars = ['a', 'b', 'c', 'd', 'e', 'f', 'g', 'h']

# Define a hypothetical SALT value
SALT="&45Bvx9"
# Define the allowable range of password length
PW_LOW=4
PW_HIGH=8

print 'Processing Single Core'
print os.getcwd()
print 'Password Character Set: ', chars
print 'Password Lenghts: ', str(PW_LOW), ' - ', str(PW_HIGH)

# Mark the start time
startTime=time.time()

# Open a File for writing the results

try:
```

```
            # Open the output file
            fp=open('PW-ALL', 'w')
        except:
            print 'File Processing Error'
            sys.exit(0)

    # create a loop to include all passwords
    # within the allowable range

    pwCount=0

    for r in range(PW_LOW, PW_HIGH+1):

        #Apply the standard library interator
        for s in itertools.product(chars, repeat=r):

            # Hash each new password as they are
            # generated

            pw=''.join(s)
            try:
                md5Hash=hashlib.md5()
                md5Hash.update(SALT+pw)
                md5Digest=md5Hash.hexdigest()

                # Write the hash, password pair to the file
                fp.write(md5Digest+' '+pw+'\n')
                pwCount+= 1
                del md5Hash
            except:
                print 'File Processing Error'

    # Close the output file when complete
    fp.close()

    # When complete calculate the elapsed time
    elapsedTime=time.time() - startTime
    print 'Single Core Rainbow Complete'
    print 'Elapsed Time: ', elapsedTime
    print 'Passwords Generated: ', pwCount
    print
```

Multi-Core Rainbow

```
# Multi-Core Password Table Generator

    # import standard libraries

    import hashlib               # Hashing the results
```

```
import time            # Timing the operation
import os
import itertools       # Creating controled combinations
import multiprocessing # Multiprocessing Library

#
# Create a list of characters to include in the
# password generation
#

chars=['a', 'b', 'c', 'd', 'e', 'f', 'g', 'h']

# Define a hypothetical SALT value
SALT="&45Bvx9"

# Define the allowable range of password length

PW_LOW=4
PW_HIGH=8


def pwGenerator(size):

    pwCount=0
    # create a loop to include all passwords
    # within range specified

    try:

        # Open a File for writing the results
        fp=open('PW-'+str(size), 'w')

        for r in range(size, size+1):

            #Apply the standard library interator

            for s in itertools.product(chars, repeat=r):
                # Process each password as they are
                # generated
                pw=''.join(s)

                # Perform hashing of the password
                md5Hash=hashlib.md5()
                md5Hash.update(SALT+pw)
                md5Digest=md5Hash.hexdigest()

                # Write the hash, password pair to the file
                fp.write(md5Digest+' '+pw+'\n')
                pwCount+= 1
```

```
                    del md5Hash

        except:
            print 'File/Hash Processing Error'
        finally:
                fp.close()
                print str(size),' Passwords Processed =', pwCount

#
# Create Main Function
#

if __name__ == '__main__':

    print 'Processing Multi-Core'
    print os.getcwd()
    print 'Password string: ', chars
    print 'Password Lengths: ', str(PW_LOW),' - ', str(PW_HIGH)

    # Mark the starting time of the main loop
    startTime=time.time()

    #create a process Pool with 5 processes
    corePool=multiprocessing.Pool(processes=5)

    #map corePool to the Pool processes
    results=corePool.map(pwGenerator, (4, 5, 6, 7, 8))

    elapsedTime=time.time() - startTime

    # When complete calculate the elapsed time

    elapsedTime=time.time() - startTime
    print 'Multi-Core Rainbow Complete'
    print 'Elapsed Time: ', elapsedTime
    print 'Passwords Generated: ', pwCount
    print
```

You can see the results of executing both the single core and multi-core solutions on the Python Anywhere Cloud, respectively, in Figures 11.10 and 11.11. I have also included the execution from my Linux box in Figure 11.12. The actual performance will vary of course based on many factors. Since my Linux box is dedicated and is running a quad-core processor at 3.0 GHz it outperforms the cloud service. The single core and multi-core results demonstrate a proportional result with the multi-core solution outperforming the single core solution as expected (see Table 11.2).

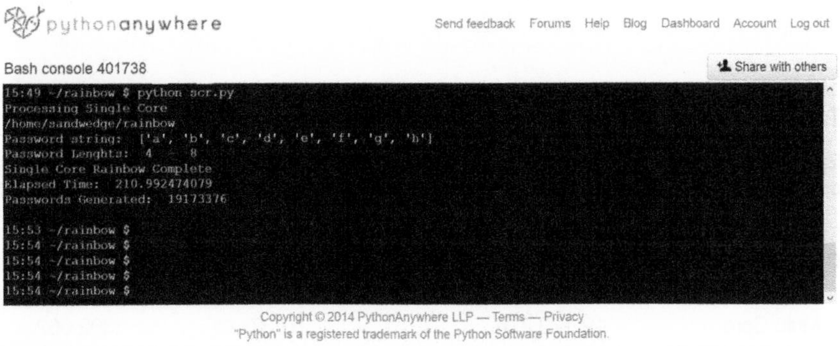

FIGURE 11.10

Python Anywhere Single Core Execution Results.

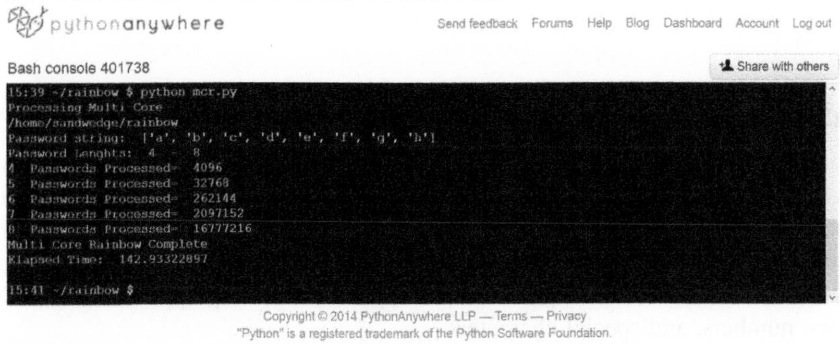

FIGURE 11.11

Python Anywhere Multi-Core Execution Results.

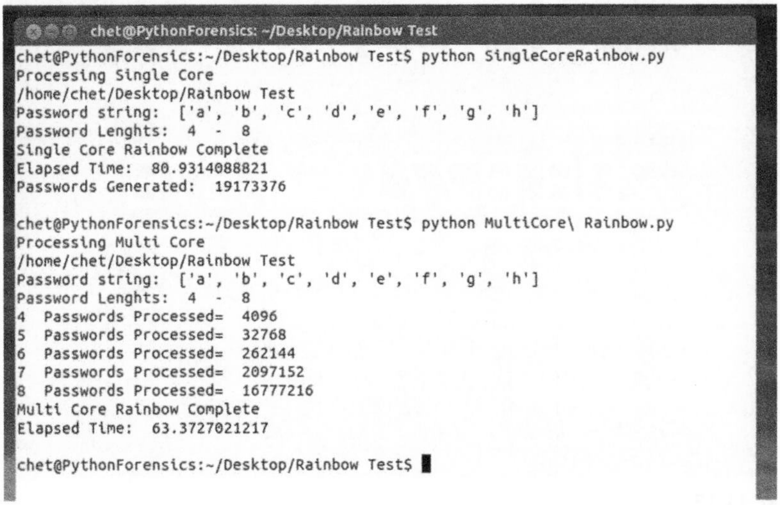

FIGURE 11.12

Standalone Linux Single/Multi-Core Execution Results.

Table 11.2 Summary of Execution Results

Execution configuration	Passwords generated and processed	Time to process(s)	Passwords per second
Standalone Quad Core Linux			
Single Core	19,173,376	80.93	236,913
Multi-Core	19,173,376	63.37	302,562
Python Anywhere			
Single Core	19,173,376	210.99	90,873
Multi-Core	19,173,376	142.93	134,145

PASSWORD GENERATION CALCULATIONS

One question you might be asking at this point is how many unique combinations of passwords are there? In order to be reasonable, let us start with the number of possible 8-character passwords by just using lowercase letters. The answer is shown in Figure 11.13 calculated by elPassword [elPassword]. In Figure 11.14, elPassword calculates the number of unique 8-character passwords using upper and lowercase letters, numbers, and special characters.

FIGURE 11.13

elPassword 8-character combinations of lowercase letters.

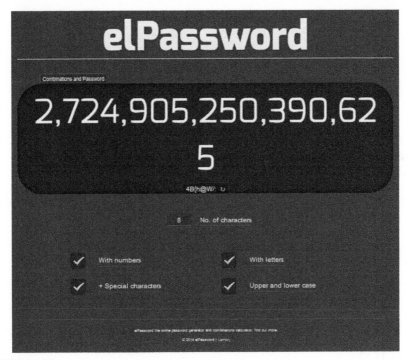

elPassword 8-character full ASCII character set.

Using the online resource from LastBit, [LastBit] along with our best performance of 302,000 passwords per second, we can calculate the length of time required for a brute force attack. In Figure 11.15–11.18, I performed four separate runs. The first two using all lowercase characters with 1 and 100 computers, and the last two using the full ASCII set with 100 and 10,000 computers, respectively. Try them out for yourself.

Password length:	8	
Speed:	302000	passwords per second
Number of computers:	1	
☑ chars in lower case	☐ common punctuation	
☐ chars in upper case	☐ full ASCII	
☐ digits		
	Calculate!	
Brute Force Attack will take up to **9 days**		

FIGURE 11.15

Last Bit calculation lowercase using 1 computer.

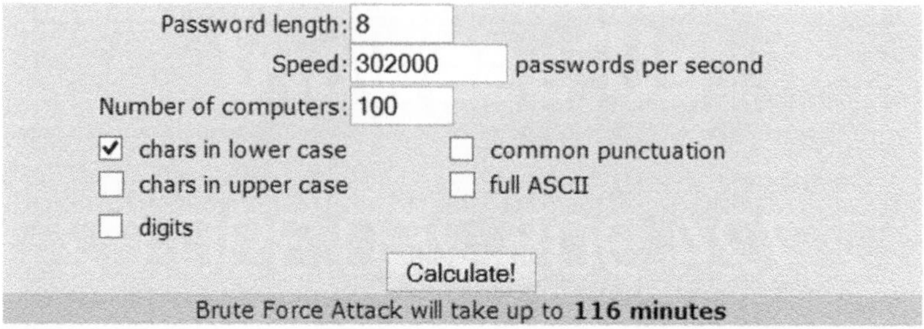

Password length: 8
Speed: 302000 passwords per second
Number of computers: 100
☑ chars in lower case ☐ common punctuation
☐ chars in upper case ☐ full ASCII
☐ digits
Calculate!
Brute Force Attack will take up to **116 minutes**

FIGURE 11.16

Last Bit calculation lowercase using 100 computers.

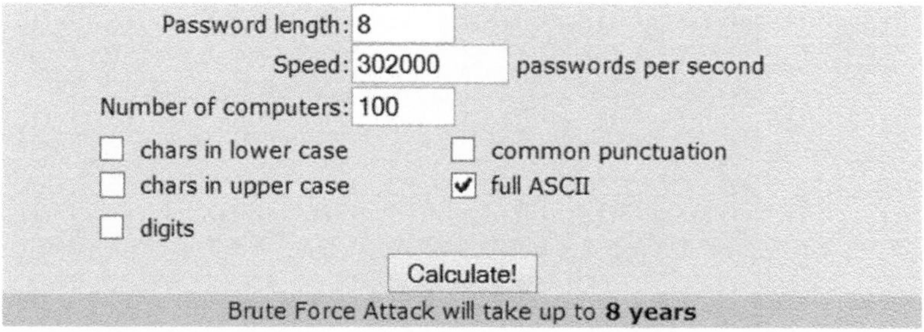

Password length: 8
Speed: 302000 passwords per second
Number of computers: 100
☐ chars in lower case ☐ common punctuation
☐ chars in upper case ☑ full ASCII
☐ digits
Calculate!
Brute Force Attack will take up to **8 years**

FIGURE 11.17

Last Bit calculation ASCII set using 100 computers.

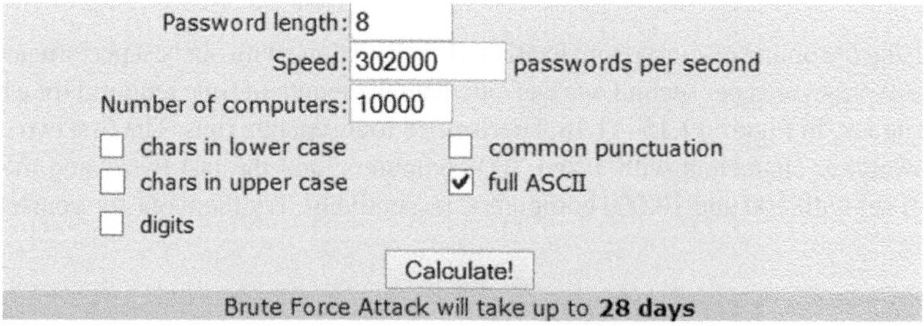

Password length: 8
Speed: 302000 passwords per second
Number of computers: 10000
☐ chars in lower case ☐ common punctuation
☐ chars in upper case ☑ full ASCII
☐ digits
Calculate!
Brute Force Attack will take up to **28 days**

FIGURE 11.18

Last Bit calculation ASCII set using 10,000 computers.

CHAPTER REVIEW

In this chapter I introduced Python Anywhere, a cloud service that runs native Python code in the cloud. I demonstrated how simple it is to run native Python code in the cloud from multiple platforms. I then modified the Rainbow Table password generator to minimize memory usage, reduced the characters, and expanded the generation to include password lengths of 4- to 8-character solutions. I then examined the performance of each result to determine how long it would take both on a higher performance Linux platform and in the cloud. I took those results and extrapolated them in order to determine the time and computers needed to reasonably crack 8-character passwords.

SUMMARY QUESTION/CHALLENGE

1. What other applications would be useful to execute within cloud environments that would benefit the forensic and investigation community?
2. As of this writing, Intel and AMD are experimenting with single processor core counts of 16, 32, 64, and 96 cores. If we extrapolate just a few years in the future it would not be unreasonable to expect the achievement of 1000-core CPUs. How will this change our ability to generate and hash passwords, crack encryption, or search data?
3. Develop and test your own multi-core solution on your desktop environment. Design them such that they can be easily deployed to a cloud platform like Python Anywhere. Establish a free account on Python Anywhere and experiment with your single and multi-core solutions.

Additional Resources

http://www.pythonanywhere.com.
http://www.picloud.com.
http://www.digitalocean.com.
http://projects.lambry.com/elpassword/.
http://lastbit.com/pswcalc.asp.

Looking Ahead

CHAPTER CONTENTS

INTRODUCTION

The world of digital investigation and computer forensics is approaching 25 years in age. I had the privilege of working with Ron Stevens from the New York State Police who was one of the early pioneers and one of the first troopers in the country to successfully collect evidence from computers and use that evidence to convict those involved in criminal activity. "As one of the first law enforcement agencies to respond to the threats posed by the techno-criminal, the New York State Police launched the Computer Crime Unit in 1992" (Stevens, 2001).

I also had the privilege of serving as the primary investigator on the first digital forensic research effort sponsored by the Air Force Research Laboratory in 1998. The effort was conceived by two pioneers in the field working at the U.S. Air Force Research Lab, Joe Giordano and John Feldman. The effort was entitled: Forensic Information Warfare Requirements and resulted in a comprehensive report that outlined a set of requirements for the field moving forward. (FIW Report, 1999)

However, it would be a mistake to think of digital investigation, cybercrime investigation, or computer forensics as a mature science or discipline today. The following is an excerpt from a presentation I gave at the First Digital Forensic Research Workshop in 2001 (DFRWS, 2001).

Digital Evidence Fundamentals

- Digital evidence is vast, complicated, and can be easily manipulated, concealed, destroyed, or never found
- Connecting the dots can be an arduous process, fraught with uncertainty and in many cases is inconclusive
- The distributive nature of cyber-crime and cyber-terrorism makes tracing the perpetrators, the victims, and the technology used to execute the attack or crime difficult

– Our results will likely be challenged, thrown out, ignored, misunderstood, and constantly questioned

Cyber-forensic technologies must be:

– Reliable
– Accurate
– Nonreputable
– Easy to use
– Foolproof
– Secure
– Flexible
– Heterogeneous
– Distributed
– Automatic
– Free, or at least cheap

Fundamental questions—Cyber-forensic technologies

– Who collected the digital evidence?
– With what tool or technology?
– By what standard or practice is this based?
– Who audits and validates the practices?
– How are the identities of the digital detectives bound to the digital evidence?
– How was the evidence handled once identified?
– How is the evidence validated, and by whom?
– For how long is it valid?
– How is it stored and secured?
– How is the integrity of digital evidence assured?
– What technology was used to assure it?
– Why do I trust the tool or technology?
  – Who developed it?
  – Where and under what conditions was it developed?
  – What underlying software and hardware does the technology rely on?
  – Who validated or accredited the technology and the process?
  – Which version(s) are accredited?
  – Who trained and accredited the users
– Is the evidence distinctive?
– Is the evidence privileged?
– Is the evidence corroborated?
  – When was the file created, modified, or destroyed?
  – When was the transaction executed?
  – When was a message transmitted or received?
  – When was the virus or worm launched?
  – When was the cyber-attack initiated?
  – How long after the reconnaissance stage was completed did the attack commence?
  – In what time-zone?

- At what point was the system log still valid?
- Did the suspect have the opportunity to commit the crime?

Fundamental questions

- Where is the suspect in cyber-space?
- How can I trace his or her steps?
  - Technically
  - Legally
- Where are they likely to strike next?
- Are they working with accomplices or insiders?
- What capabilities do they posses?
  - Bandwidth
  - Computing power
  - Savvy
  - Resources
- Have we seen them before?
  - Are they more sophisticated now vs. a year ago?
- Who are their accomplices?

Summary

- We must focus our attention on identifying and addressing the key fundamental elements of digital forensics and digital evidence
- We must work together to build technologies that address the issues surrounding these fundamental elements
- We need to perform research where the goal is to use the science of forensics to help answer the harder questions surrounding cyber-criminals and terrorists
  - Their location, sophistication, likely next targets
  - What do we need to do to stop them?
  - How do we improve our defenses against them?

The scary part about this short trip down memory lane is that I could give this presentation today, and it would still be for the most part relevant. The big question is where we go from here and how will Python Forensics play a role?

WHERE DO WE GO FROM HERE?

This book has identified key areas where research and development of new solutions are possible when combining core challenge problems with the Python language. It could certainly be argued that other languages could produce viable solutions to these challenges. However, the questions are:

- Would these alternative solutions be open source and free?
- Would they be cross platform ready (Windows, Mac, Linux, Mobile, and in the Cloud)?

– Would they be accessible and readable by anyone?

– Would they have the global worldwide support?

– Do they support a collaborative environment that would provide an on-ramp for computer scientists, social scientists, law enforcement professionals, or students new to the field?

The next big steps from my view are as follows:

(1) Creation of a true collaborative environment where people can share information (challenge problems, ideas, and solutions).

(2) Obtain nonintimidating support as technology is advanced in support of new investigative challenges.

(3) Development of a repository of programs and scripts that could be downloaded, applied to real word problems, expanded, and improved.

(4) Integration with on-demand training courses to dive deeply into core areas of Python and forensics.

(5) A validation/certification process that would allow third-party organizations (such as NIST) to validate Python supplied solutions for use by law enforcement. Once validated they could be safely utilized on real cases. Once the process has been created much of the validation work could be automated through the use of standardized forensic test images to accelerate the validation process.

(6) Vendors could supply application interfaces that open the possibility to integrate new Python-based solutions into existing forensic technologies. This would actually improve the capabilities of vendor solutions, allow them to address new issues in a more timely fashion, and make their products more valuable in the marketplace.

(7) The creation of a cloud-based experimental platform that has thousands (or even hundreds of thousands) of processor cores, petabytes of storage, and terabytes of memory that could be applied and harnessed to solve computationally difficult problems. In addition, this environment would be open to academia and students in order to rapidly advance classroom problems. Collaboration across universities, colleges, practitioners, vendors, and researchers to solve truly hard problems. The environment could provide a competition surface for new innovations, and teams could compete on the national and international stage. Benchmarks for specific solution types could be created in order to understand the performance characteristics of various solutions.

(8) Key challenge problems for consideration:

Throughout this book, I provided Python-based examples for several key areas. These examples provide the basics, however, much more work is needed. I have identified some of the key challenges that require additional work and focus.

a. *Advanced searching and indexing*: search and indexing are certainly core elements during any investigation. However, improving the speed, accuracy, and relevance of search and index results is necessary. Investigators need solutions that can provide the following in a timely fashion:

    i. Search and index results that deliver information that is relevant to their case. This rich search/index capability must uncover information that is not obvious or is missed by present-day technologies. For example, search results that include time and spatial connections into clear view.

    ii. Search and index results that connect information from multiple cases together, identifying connections between accomplices, Internet, phone, time, location, and behavioral analysis that were previously unconnected.

b. *Metadata extraction*: Images and multimedia content contain a plethora of metadata, including but not limited to time, date, the device they were created on, location information, subject content, and much more. The extraction, connection, and reasoning about this information is today left to the investigator. New innovations bring the promise of rapidly extracting and connecting this information to provide a broader more comprehensive view of the crime scene.

c. *Event synchronization*: According to Statistic Brain (2014) in 2013 there were an average of 58 million tweets per day from over 645 million registered Twitter users. In addition, (Statistic Brain, 2014) 5.9 Billion Google searches per day and over 2 trillion searches for the year 2013 were recorded. This is only a fraction of the total Internet events that occur each day and each year. Our ability to synchronize and reason about events whether from the Internet, a corporate network or even an individual desktop may seem beyond comprehension. We need to develop new innovations that can make sense, isolate, and provide conclusive proof about such actions and events.

d. *Natural language*: The Internet has certainly broken down boundaries and provided interaction and communication instantly across the globe. As I just scratched the surface of Natural Language Processing (NLP) in Chapter 7, you can see the potential power of being able to process language. The application for NLP for the extraction of meaning, determining authorship, deciphering intent are all within our grasp. Expanding these technologies to process a wide range of languages, improving deductive reasoning, extracting persons, places and things, and assessing likely past, present or future actions are possible.

e. *Advancement in Python.* The printed examples and source code provided in this book were developed for Python 2.7.x in order to ensure the broadest compatibility across computing platforms. However, all the examples will also be available online for download with solutions for 2.7.x and 3.3.x.

    Python and third-party Python libraries continue to expand at the speed of the Internet. Some even claim Python will be the last programming language you will ever have to learn. I think this is a bit overstated however, some of the attributes of the language will be fundamental to future languages. At the time of this writing February 9, 2014 to be exact, Python Version 3.4 was released. According to the Python Programming Language Official Web (www.python.org), the major language improvements included:

1. a "pathlib" module providing object-oriented file system paths
2. a standardized "enum" module
3. a build enhancement that will help generate introspection information for built-ins
4. improved semantics for object finalization
5. adding single-dispatch generic functions to the standard library
6. a new C API for implementing custom memory allocators
7. changing file descriptors to not be inherited by default in subprocesses
8. a new "statistics" module
9. standardizing module metadata for Python's module import system
10. a bundled installer for the *pip* package manager
11. a new "tracemalloc" module for tracing Python memory allocations
12. a new hash algorithm for Python strings and binary data
13. a new and improved protocol for pickled objects
14. a new "asyncio" module, a new framework for asynchronous I/O

As you can see the language evolution continues at a brisk pace along with the development of new and improved third-party Python libraries that help accelerate forensic and digital investigation tools. There are so many third-party libraries and tools, I decided to list just my top 10.

1. Pillow. A new library that builds off of the more traditional Python Image Library for those that process and examine digital images.
2. wxPython. For those of you that need to build cross platform graphical user interfaces this is my preferred toolkit.
3. Requests. One of the best http interface libraries.
4. Scrapy. If your forensics investigations require you to perform web scraping, this library will help you build new and innovative approaches.
5. Twisted. For those needing to develop asynchronous network applications.
6. Scapy. For those who perform packet sniffing and analysis, scapy provides a host of features that can speed your development.
7. NLTK. Natural Language Toolkit—This toolkit is vast and for those investigating text and language constructs, it is a must.
8. IPython. When experimenting with new language elements, libraries, or modules this advanced Python Shell will assist you in every aspect of your work or struggles.
9. WingIDE. This is not a library, but this Integrated Development Environment gets my vote for the best IDE. The Professional version provides even the most savvy researcher with the tools they need.
10. Googlemaps. Many forensic applications collect geographically tagged information, this package allows you to easily integrate with the Google mapping system.

f. *Multiprocessing*: In order to effectively attack any of these areas, our ability to access the power of the latest processors and cloud-based solutions is essential (Figure 12.1). "The International Technology Roadmap for Semiconductors 2011," a roadmap forecasting semiconductor development drawn up by experts from semiconductor companies worldwide, forecasts that by 2015 there will be an electronics product with nearly 450 processing cores, rising to nearly 1500 cores by 2020 (Heath).

What is available today from the two major processor manufactures, Intel® and AMD® are depicted in Figures 12.2 and 12.3. For under $1000 you can own these processors and for under $3000 you can build a system with two processors yielding 20-32 cores, 64 GB of memory and a couple of terabytes of storage. This is certainly a step toward multicore and multiprocessing solutions, and when coupled with well-designed multicore

FIGURE 12.1

Multiprocessing in the Cloud.

FIGURE 12.2

AMD 6300 Series 16 Core Processor.

FIGURE 12.3

Intel Xeon E7 Series 10 Core 20 Thread Processor.

Python applications could take a giant step toward advancing the state-of-the-art. Once we see these production solutions produce 64, 128, 256, and 1024 cores on a single processor, the world will change once again.

CONCLUSION

Applying the Python language to digital investigation and forensic applications has great promise. What is needed is a collaborative community that includes: practitioners, researchers, developers, professors, students, investigators, examiners, detectives, attorneys, prosecutors, judges, vendors, governments, and research institutes. In addition, a cloud-based computing platform with thousands of cores, petabytes of storage, and terabytes of memory is necessary.

I challenge you to participate. If everyone reading this book would submit one idea, challenge problem or solution that would be a tremendous start. Visit Python-Forensics.Org to get started. ... I would love to hear from you!

Additional Resources

Fighting Cyber Crime hearing before the subcommittee on Crime of the Committee on the Judiciary, http://commdocs.house.gov/committees/judiciary/hju72616.000/hju72616_0f.htm; 2001.

Forensic Information Warfare Requirements Study F30602-98-C-0243. Final technical report, February 2, 1999, Prepared by WetStone Technologies, Inc.

A road map for digital forensic research, Utica, New York, http://www.dfrws.org/2001/dfrws-rm-final.pdf; August 7–8, 2001.

January 1, 2014, http://www.statisticbrain.com/twitter-statistics/.

Cracking the 1,000-core processor power challenge. Nick Heath, http://www.zdnet.com/cracking-the-1000-core-processor-power-challenge-7000015554/.

Index

Note: Page numbers followed by *b* indicate boxes, *f* indicate figures and *t* indicate tables.

Printed and bound by CPI Group (UK) Ltd, Croydon, CR0 4YY

03/10/2024

01040327-0016